A STUDY GUIDE
TO STEINBECK

(Part II)

edited by

Tetsumaro Hayashi
Ball State University

The Scarecrow Press, Inc.
Metuchen, N.J., & London
1979

Library of Congress Cataloging in Publication Data (Revised)

Hayashi, Tetsumaro.
    Study guide to Steinbeck (Part II).

    Includes bibliographies and index.
    I.   Steinbeck, John, 1902-1968--Study--Outlines,
syllabi. I. Title.
PS3537. T3234Z7142   813'. 5'2   74-735
ISBN 0-8108-1220-7

Dedicated to
DIDIER AND LOTTE GRAEFFE
in Honor of Their Active Retirement
from the University of Florida
as a Token of Gratitude and Affection

CONTENTS

ACKNOWLEDGMENTS

As I prepared for the manuscript of A Study Guide to Steinbeck (Part II), a sequel to my 1974 book, A Study Guide to Steinbeck: A Handbook to His Major Works, I accumulated a debt of gratitude. There are many individuals to thank, but I hope to acknowledge especially the following who have truly made the publication of this book possible:

First, The Scarecrow Press, which recognized the educational value of this project from its inception and encouraged me to complete it. Second, Dr. Reloy Garcia, Professor of English at Creighton University, a well-known scholar who generously endorsed the book with his Introduction. Third, Dr. Richard F. Peterson, one of the distinguished contributors to this book, who offered me his pertinent advice and generous assistance in completing the manuscript in the final stage. Lastly, all the contributors, with whom I had the privilege of working in this project, who proved to be not only first-rate scholars but dedicated and cooperative educators who sincerely shared with me their faith in the value of this teaching-oriented book.

It is to these educators, scholars, and friends that I should like to express my profound gratitude.

Tetsumaro Hayashi
Muncie, Indiana
June 19, 1978

SPECIAL ACKNOWLEDGMENTS

Quotations from John Steinbeck's writings in this book are made by generous permission of the Steinbeck Literary Estate through Mrs. Shirley Fisher, McIntosh and Otis, Inc., 475 Fifth Avenue, New York, N.Y., 10017.

I am grateful to the Viking/Penguin Press, Inc., 625 Madison Avenue, New York, New York 10022, for granting us permission to quote Steinbeck in this book. My special thanks are due to Mr. Thomas H. Guinzburg, President, and Miss Sylvia Goldman, Permissions Department, of the Viking/Penguin Press, Inc.

Tetsumaro Hayashi

PREFACE

In 1972 I conceived the idea of editing a book on John
Steinbeck which would serve students, teachers, and reference
librarians as a teaching-oriented research guide; most of the
previous book-length studies of Steinbeck had been published
either exclusively for scholars or for the general public. I
had the good fortune to have Professor Warren French as my
mentor on this project, which was initially called Teaching
Steinbeck. He was the first distinguished scholar of American literature to endorse it and he offered generous and expert advice to me during the time I was editing the book.
Teaching Steinbeck ultimately became A Study Guide to Steinbeck: A Handbook to His Major Works (Scarecrow Press,
1974). Although the book was received warmly by reference
librarians and teachers, some critics commented on the absence of a chapter on East of Eden and on several other
Steinbeck novels. In response to that positive criticism and
because of the increasing popularity of such works as East of
Eden, The Moon Is Down, A Russian Journal, and even Cup
of Gold, I decided to edit A Study Guide to Steinbeck (Part
II) as a sequel to my 1974 book.

The idea that the part is related to the whole is especially true in Steinbeck studies. Without a full appreciation
of Steinbeck's total literary canon, it is impossible to assess
properly his impressive literary achievement. Furthermore,
it is often a great challenge to encounter Steinbeck's comparatively unexplored literary masterpieces. For A Study
Guide to Steinbeck (Part II) I selected works of Steinbeck's
which either were not treated or were insufficiently discussed
in my 1974 book, and which are often being taught and studied
today in colleges and universities. With equally serious concern, I selected as contributors only those dedicated teacher-
scholars who are seriously interested in the mission of teaching Steinbeck's literature. Mr. Roy S. Simmonds of England,
a government official, is the only exception; however, he has
been teaching Steinbeck in a broader sense of the term

1

through his numerous contributions to the Steinbeck Quarterly
and other scholarly and professional journals.

Though the ultimate purpose of A Study Guide to Steinbeck (Part II) is to enlighten both college students and classroom teachers on Steinbeck's works not treated in my 1974
book, particularly those which remain popular and even controversial today, my contributors and I have made special
efforts to be helpful to non-English-majoring students who
study Steinbeck's literature in humanities courses or in basic
English composition courses. The book, therefore, is not
for erudite and advanced scholars already conversant with
the background of Steinbeck's literature.

When A Study Guide to Steinbeck's "The Long Valley"
(Ann Arbor, Michigan: Pierian Press, 1976) was published,
Professor Reloy Garcia of Creighton University, a distinguished scholar, endorsed the book with this notable statement: "No scholar should ever denigrate the teaching aspect
of his profession. Teaching is the soul of research, and research not worth taking into the class is not worth taking out
of the study." It was indeed in this spirit that I edited A
Study Guide to Steinbeck (Part II). Steinbeck is a very teach-
able author simply because his literature is worth teaching
and studying; he enlightens us and our world today just as
much or even more than he did in 1939 when he wrote The
Grapes of Wrath, for he remains a prophet whose vision en-
ables us to see the world a little more clearly. His literature mirrors the world with notable universal themes and
characters that transcend time and locality.

As Horace declares in his Ars Poetica, "Omni tulit
punctum qui miscuit utile dulce." John Steinbeck never
failed to offer two of the most important elements in literature: the pleasing quality (style, humor, pathos, compassion,
setting, characters, and language) and the instructive quality
(his preoccupation with good and evil, non-teleology and teleology, his holistic view, and his group-man concept, his interest in myth, philosophy, marine biology, and psychology).
A fascinating and experimental artist, Steinbeck daringly
tried one genre after another: novel, short story, play, essay, diary, war correspondence. He used a variety of
sources to enrich his own: classical mythology, Arthurian
legend, Medieval, Renaissance, Continental, British, American, and Oriental literature and philosophy. As a result, he
created a gallery of characters, many of whom are truly
memorable.

I invite you to read Steinbeck, to study and teach his literature, and to use this guide as a springboard to discover a new dimension in Steinbeck studies.

Tetsumaro Hayashi

March 22, 1978

INTRODUCTION

Several years ago I had the pleasure of writing an essay on John Steinbeck's The Winter of Our Discontent for inclusion in A Study Guide to Steinbeck: A Handbook to His Major Works, the parent volume to this collection. In preparation for this brief introduction I re-read that book, in the process immodestly reviewing my own theme. Reality is a harsh mistress, and I would write that essay differently today. In the intervening years I have come to appreciate Steinbeck even more than when the first Study Guide was in preparation, and I was younger then and in a hurry. The book I then so impetuously criticized as somewhat thin, now strikes me as a deeply penetrating study of the American condition. I did not even realize, at the time, that we had a condition. His work thus rewards a returning reader, is seemingly amplified by our own enriched experience.

This point may well be worth making in light of the mild controversy that followed the exclusion of the works in this volume from the parent collection four years ago. Disappointed critics championed their own favorite works in a discussion about what constitutes a "major" Steinbeck work. It was this disagreement that led Dr. Hayashi to prepare a sequel to the 1974 edition. Rather than arguing the merits of every individual work, he included them all and thus eliminated the problem, a solution he is to be congratulated for.

When the first volume appeared we were in the middle of an even larger controversy concerning the relationship of scholarship to teaching. Many teachers felt, and still feel, that research is somehow prepared at the expense of sound teaching, as if research were an obscene little secret, or a family sin. Others felt, and still feel, that advocates of "pure" teaching do so merely to cover their own inability to publish. It is increasingly difficult to find responsible people who will advocate either extreme publicly (and thus be honest about their hypocrisy), but it would be naive not to

4

admit that many very bright people privately hold foolish and
even stupid views on occasion. Personally, I think that both
of these positions are indeed both foolish and stupid, but
they will not go away simply because we say so or want
them to. If they go away at all it will be because of the efforts of people like the contributors to this collection and its
predecessor, who do not feel that teaching and research are
in any fundamental sense at odds. They work quietly but
persistently to strike a balance between teaching and research,
to write something in the privacy of the study that will acti-
vate or enlighten a classroom.

Good intentions are redeemed only by good accomplish-
ments, as is the case with this collection. The articles
here are of uniformly high quality, the conclusions and observations striking and well supported, the essays well written and interesting.

In format this book is much like the early Guide,
each of the essays having a background section, a plot synopsis, a critical explication, a research paper section and
a bibliography. The single major difference between the
two books in format is that this collection allows five scholars to prepare two essays each, and thus allows the reader
to evaluate and appreciate the contributors on two occasions,
confronting different critical problems. This is an interesting experiment which I would like to see again. It works,
of course, only when the essays and their authors accomplish their individual objectives--to enlighten the pieces--and
their collective objective--to enlighten the whole of Steinbeck.
Twenty people have been brought together in these two team
projects by a common affection for the work of John Steinbeck. I support such efforts as strongly as I can, particularly when the burden is so light and the company so familiar and articulate.

Reloy Garcia
Professor of English
Creighton University

Chapter 1

A GUIDE TO STEINBECK STUDIES:
QUESTIONS AND ANSWERS

by Tetsumaro Hayashi

Although the Steinbeck Society of America has existed
for over thirteen years and the Steinbeck Quarterly has been
published by the Society for over eleven years, many scholars, students, and reference librarians have only recently
discovered our existence. As they do, they sometimes ask
us why we have not publicized the Society and the journal
more widely. We have, in fact, tried hard to inform the
public of the Society, its publications, and it services for
quite some time.

Many readers learned of the Society and its publications through Steinbeck: The Man and His Work, edited by
Richard Astro and Tetsumaro Hayashi (Corvallis: Oregon
State University Press, 1971), in which my invitation to join
the Steinbeck Society is printed. In fact, I have in a way
regretted making this promotional statement in a scholarly
book, for many of the things I said there are no longer completely accurate or up-to-date. As the Society grows, its
constitution and regulations change, as with any organization; therefore, I have spelled out the dimensions, aims,
and responsibilities of our organization and its publications
in this guide.

One of the chief services the Society has rendered
has been informational. Many reference librarians, scholars, high school teachers, student-teachers, and college professors have asked me a variety of reference questions. I
have done my best to answer many of them, and when I
could not, I have referred them to Steinbeck collectors, bib-
liographers, biographers, and other specialists in various
fields.

The reference questions have been enormously varied,

but there have been repeated demands for answers to certain
standard questions. In this guide I have attempted to collect
the most frequently asked questions and to answer them as
concisely as possible. In this way I have augmented my own
reference service to our members and gone beyond the human limitations placed on me by duties as a college professor, as well as an editor, director, public lecturer, and
academic advisor. If this article assists interested scholars
and beginning students with answers to some of the most frequently raised questions pertaining to Steinbeck studies, I
shall be gratified.

A.   STEINBECK QUARTERLY

1.   IS THERE ANY JOURNAL DEVOTED TO CRITICISM OF
     JOHN STEINBECK?

        Yes, the Steinbeck Quarterly has been published since
1969 by the John Steinbeck Society of America under the
sponsorship of Ball State University. If you wish to sub-
scribe to the journal, you must first become a member of
the Steinbeck Society of America (English Department, Ball
State University, Muncie, Indiana 47306, U. S. A.). The
membership fee is $10. 00, payable in January every year.
        The journal publishes critical essays on Steinbeck and
occasionally bibliographical articles. The "Miscellanies" section edited by Donald L. Siefker includes all kinds of reports
about seminars, conferences, works in progress, new edi-
tions, translations, doctoral dissertations, play productions,
etc. The annual index usually appears in the winter-spring
issues and the summer-fall issues are usually combined.
        As a member in good standing, you will receive both
the Steinbeck Quarterly and the Steinbeck Monograph Series;
you are encouraged to submit articles on original topics within 15 typed pages. (See regulations for the submission which
are stated in the Steinbeck Quarterly.) You will be invited
to attend the annual Steinbeck Society Meeting held annually
during the Modern Language Association Convention. (See
the announcement in the Steinbeck Quarterly and PMLA about
the annual meeting.)

2.   IF A PARTICULAR ISSUE OF THE STEINBECK QUAR-
     TERLY OR THE STEINBECK MONOGRAPH SERIES HAP-
     PENS TO BE OUT OF PRINT, WHERE CAN I BUY A
     REPRINT COPY OR A MICROFILM?

Write to: The Kraus Reprint Company
           Route 100
           Millwood, New York   10546

or to: Xerox University Microfilms
        300 North Zeeb Road
        Ann Arbor, Michigan   48106.

3. HOW SHOULD I SUBMIT AN UNSOLICITED ARTICLE
    ON STEINBECK TO THE STEINBECK QUARTERLY?

    Read the regulations in the latest Steinbeck Quarterly
in your university or public library, and follow A Manual of
Style (latest edition) bibliographically.

4. WHO WOULD EVALUATE MY UNSOLICITED ARTICLE
    FOR POSSIBLE PUBLICATION AFTER SUBMISSION TO
    THE STEINBECK QUARTERLY?

    Usually two specialist readers, who are appointed by
the editor-in-chief, will evaluate your article and report to
the editor-in-chief whether or not it is publishable and if so,
under what conditions. If necessary, a third reader will be
appointed.

5. WHAT IS MEANT BY A CONDITIONAL ACCEPTANCE?

    If your required revisions meet the readers' approval,
your article will be published; if not, it will be finally rejected.

6. WHAT KIND OF ARTICLES DO YOU PREFER TO PUB-
    LISH IN THE STEINBECK QUARTERLY?

    Review the latest Steinbeck Quarterly, in which only
those articles which we regard as a contribution to Steinbeck
scholarship are published. Your article should be of similar
quality.

7. WHICH DO YOU PUBLISH MORE: ASSIGNED ARTICLES
    OR UNSOLICITED ARTICLES?

    Both. It depends upon the special needs of a particu-
lar issue, too.

8. IS THERE A COLUMN CALLED "WORKS IN PROGRESS"
    IN THE STEINBECK QUARTERLY? WHERE MAY I

SEND REPORTS ON STEINBECK BOOKS OR SEMINARS
OR CONFERENCES?

No, but the "Miscellanies" section of the Steinbeck
Quarterly often lists works in progress. Send reports to:
Professor Donald L. Siefker, Managing Editor
Steinbeck Quarterly
Bracken Library
Ball State University
Muncie, Indiana   47306
U. S. A.
(Be sure to be specific about your report: what, when,
where, who, etc.)

9.   WHERE ARE THE ARTICLES PUBLISHED IN THE
     STEINBECK QUARTERLY INDEXED?

They are annually indexed by Donald L. Siefker in
the winter-spring issue of the Steinbeck Quarterly.

10.   DO I HAVE TO BUY AN ANNUAL INDEX SEPARATELY?

If you are a member, no.   It is usually included in
the winter-spring issue of the Steinbeck Quarterly.

11.   DO YOU PLAN TO PUBLISH A CUMULATIVE INDEX?

We plan to do so once in ten years.   See the Steinbeck Quarterly 11 (Spring 1978), which includes The Cumulative Index to the Steinbeck Quarterly, 1-10 (1968-1977).

12.   TELL ME SOMETHING ABOUT THE RICHARD W.
      BURKHARDT PRIZE FOR THE BEST STEINBECK
      ARTICLE OF THE YEAR AND THE ROBERT L.
      CARMIN PRIZE FOR THE BEST STEINBECK REVIEW
      OF THE YEAR (STEINBECK QUARTERLY).

In 1975 the editor and all the contributors* to A Study
Guide to Steinbeck's "The Long Valley," edited by Tetsumaro
Hayashi (Ann Arbor, Michigan: Pierian Press, 1976),
donated the income from the manuscript for this book to the
Ball State University Foundation in order to establish the
Best Essay Fund.   With this fund the Steinbeck Society has

───────────────
*The contributors' names are listed in SQ, 9 (Summer-Fall
1976), 81.

honored the winners for the Best Article/Best Review of the
Year with the Burkhardt Prize and the Carmin Prize since
1976. The dual purpose of this fund is to honor the nomi-
nees and to express our appreciation to our sponsors: Dr.
Richard W. Burkhardt and Dr. Robert L. Carmin of Ball
State University, who have made a number of Steinbeck projects possible.

13. WHAT ARE THE MAJOR FUNCTIONS OF THE EDITOR-
    IAL BOARD OF THE STEINBECK QUARTERLY?

     They evaluate all incoming articles--both assigned
and unsolicited--and recommend to the Editor-in-Chief whether
or not the materials are publishable and under what conditions. Mostly established scholars, they serve as judges
and advisors to the Editor-in-Chief. Unless the members
of the Board disagree, the Editor-in-Chief usually remains
noncommittal in the final decision on the acceptance/rejection
of solicited articles. The Board is composed of scholars
from six universities in the U. S. A. and one in Canada.

              B.   STEINBECK MONOGRAPH SERIES

14. IS THERE A MONOGRAPH SERIES DEVOTED TO
    CRITICISM OF JOHN STEINBECK?

     Since 1971 the Steinbeck Society of America has pub-
lished the Steinbeck Monograph Series annually. It was initi-
ated by Tetsumaro Hayashi, General Editor/Project Director,
in 1970. Ball State University has sponsored the publication
of the Steinbeck Monograph Series since 1971. When you
become a member of the Society, you receive a new release
once a year. A non-member may purchase the monographs,
usually at $4. 00-$5. 00 each. The price may vary according to
the size of each issue, however.

15. WHERE CAN I BUY A REPRINT COPY OF A MONO-
    GRAPH?

     See A. 2.

16. MAY I SEND UNSOLICITED MATERIAL TO THE
    STEINBECK MONOGRAPH SERIES?

     No. But you can send an unsolicited article not ex-
ceeding 15 typed pages to the Steinbeck Quarterly.

C. THE STEINBECK SOCIETY OF AMERICA

17. IS THERE A PROFESSIONAL AND LEARNED SOCIETY
DEVOTED TO CRITICISM OF JOHN STEINBECK?

Yes. Founded in 1966 by Tetsumaro Hayashi and
Preston Beyer, and sponsored by Ball State University,
Muncie, Indiana since 1968, the Steinbeck Society, under the
presidency of Tetsumaro Hayashi, aims to accomplish the
following:
1. to promote Steinbeck studies;
2. to publish the Steinbeck Quarterly (winter-spring
and summer-fall issues) and the Steinbeck Monograph Series (one issue per year);
3. to exchange information among members on such
scholarly activities as Steinbeck conferences,
seminars, lectures, works in progress, etc.;
4. to report on the latest research trends and publications; and
5. to sponsor or co-sponsor Steinbeck conferences
whenever possible.

18. TELL ME SOMETHING ABOUT THE MLA STEINBECK
SOCIETY MEETING WHICH HAS BEEN ANNUALLY
HELD SINCE 1972.

The Steinbeck Society Meeting is held annually during
the MLA Convention to promote Steinbeck scholarship, to
exchange information about recent Steinbeck criticism, to
recruit new members of the Steinbeck Society, to publicize
the leadership, service, and activity of the Steinbeck Society,
and to strengthen solidarity among members.

19. ARE THE STEINBECK CONFERENCE PAPERS PUB-
LISHED?

Yes:
(1) Steinbeck Conference, University of Connecticut,
directed by John Seelye, 1969.
These papers by Pascal Covici, Jr., Peter
Lisca, and James R. Reed were included in
John Steinbeck: The Grapes of Wrath; Text and
Criticism, edited by Peter Lisca.
Write to: The Viking Press
625 Madison Avenue
New York, New York 10022
U.S.A.

(2) Steinbeck Conference, Oregon State University,
     directed by Richard Astro in 1970.
     Steinbeck: The Man and His Work, edited by
     Richard Astro and Tetsumaro Hayashi (1971).
     Write to: Oregon State University Press
                 Corvallis, Oregon 97331
                 U. S. A.
(3) "Steinbeck Conference and Film Festival," San
     Jose State University, directed by Martha H.
     Cox in 1971.
     Steinbeck Quarterly, 4 (Summer 1971), edited
     by T. Hayashi, R. Astro and M. H. Cox.
                 Steinbeck Quarterly
                 English Department
                 Ball State University
                 Muncie, Indiana 47306
                 U. S. A.   (out of print)
     Contact: The Kraus Reprint Company
                 Route 100
                 Millwood, New York 10546
                 U. S. A.
(4) First Steinbeck Society Meeting (MLA, New York
     City, 1972).
     The University of Windsor Review (Special
     Steinbeck Issue), 8 (Spring 1973), edited by
     John Ditsky.
     Write to: Editor
                 The University of Windsor Review
                 Windsor 11, Ontario
                 Canada.
(5) Second Steinbeck Society Meeting (MLA, Chicago,
     1973).
     Steinbeck Quarterly 7 (Summer-Fall 1974),
     edited by T. Hayashi.
(6) "Steinbeck and the Sea" Conference, Oregon State
     University Marine Science Center, directed by
     R. Astro and J. Hedgpeth (1974).
     Steinbeck and the Sea, edited by Richard Astro
     and Joel Hedgpeth (1975)
     Write to: Sea Grant Communications
                 Oregon State University
                 Corvallis, Oregon 97331
                 U. S. A.
(7) Third Steinbeck Society Meeting (MLA, New York,
     1974)
     Steinbeck Quarterly 9 (Winter 1976), edited by
     T. Hayashi.

(8)   Fourth Steinbeck Society Meeting (MLA, San
      Francisco, 1975).
      Steinbeck Quarterly, 10 (Winter 1977), edited
      by T. Hayashi.
(9)   The Bicentennial Steinbeck Seminar held at Taylor
      University, Upland, Indiana, on May 1, 1976 and
      The Dedication of the Steinbeck Collection held at
      the Alexander M. Bracken Library, Ball State
      University on March 26, 1976.
      Steinbeck's Prophetic Vision of America, eds.
      Tetsumaro Hayashi and Kenneth D. Swan (Stein-
      beck Society, Ball State University, 1976).
(10) The First International Steinbeck Congress held
      at Kyushu University, Fukuoka, Japan on August
      19-20, 1976.
      John Steinbeck: East and West, eds.
      Tetsumaro Hayashi, Yasuo Hashiguchi, and
      Richard Peterson (Steinbeck Society, 1978).

20.   WHICH COUNTRIES ARE MOST ACTIVE IN STEINBECK
      STUDIES?

           U. S. A. , Japan, and Canada.

21.   WHAT IS THE MEMBERSHIP STATUS OF THE STEIN-
      BECK SOCIETY?

           It has been steadily rising, but not enough to match
      inflation.   The Steinbeck Society must increase its paid mem-
      berships to keep up with the rising cost of publications and
      operations.   As of 1978 we have over 400 paid members in
      the U. S. A. and abroad.

22.   HAS THERE EVER BEEN AN INTERNATIONAL STEIN-
      BECK CONGRESS?

           The first one was held at Kyushu University, Japan
      on August 19-20, 1976.   It was jointly sponsored by the
      Kyushu American Literature Society, Japan and the Steinbeck
      Society of America.   See the program in the Steinbeck Quart-
      erly, 9 (Spring 1976), 60-61.

23.   MAY A NON-MEMBER OF THE STEINBECK SOCIETY
      SUBMIT AN UNSOLICITED ARTICLE ON STEINBECK
      FOR POSSIBLE PUBLICATION?

           Yes, but your membership status is required for
      final acceptance for publication.

24. COULD I, A NON-MEMBER, ATTEND THE ANNUAL
    MLA STEINBECK SOCIETY MEETING?

        Yes, if you plan to join the Society.

            D. RESEARCH AND TEACHING

25. WHERE IS THE BEST SOURCE OF BIOGRAPHICAL
    DATA ON JOHN STEINBECK AVAILABLE?

    Elaine Steinbeck and Robert Wallsten's Steinbeck: A
Life in Letters (New York: Viking Press, 1975), Richard
Astro's biographical article in John Steinbeck: A Dictionary
of His Fictional Characters, ed. by Tetsumaro Hayashi
(Metuchen, N. J. : Scarecrow Press, 1976), and the Steinbeck
issue of San Jose Studies, 1 (November 1975) should be
consulted. Jackson Benson will be publishing his authorized
biography of John Steinbeck in the near future.

26. ARE THERE ANY BIBLIOGRAPHIES ON JOHN STEIN-
    BECK?

        The best primary bibliography is Adrian H. Goldstone
and John R. Payne's John Steinbeck: A Bibliographical Catalogue of the Adrian H. Goldstone Collection (Austin: Humanities Research Center, University of Texas, 1974). A handy
bibliography of secondary work, criticism and movies is
Tetsumaro Hayashi's A New Steinbeck Bibliography (1929-
1971) (Metuchen, N. J. : Scarecrow Press, 1973).
        To update the materials, however, you should con-
stantly consult such reference guides as the MLA Bibliography, and the indexes of such journals as American Literature, Journal of Modern Literature, Modern Fiction Studies,
Steinbeck Quarterly, and Twentieth-Century Literature.

27. WHICH LIBRARIES IN THE UNITED STATES HAVE
    OUTSTANDING STEINBECK COLLECTIONS?

        The Steinbeck Research Center of San Jose State Univer-
sity, San Jose, California; the University of Texas Library,
Austin, Texas; the Bancroft Library of the University of Cali-
fornia at Berkeley, California; the Bracken Library, Ball State
University, Muncie, Indiana; the University of Virginia Library,
Charlottesville, Virginia; the Stanford University Library, Palo
Alto, California; and the Salinas Public Library, Salinas, Cali-
fornia are reported to have outstanding Steinbeck collections.

28. I AM A FOREIGN SCHOLAR OF AMERICAN LITERA-
     TURE. WHICH UNIVERSITY SHOULD I VISIT AND
     UNDER WHICH SCHOLAR SHOULD I STUDY JOHN
     STEINBECK IN THE UNITED STATES (OR CANADA)?

     See No. 27 and choose the best university library.
If you wish to work under an eminent Steinbeck scholar, I
would like to recommend especially the following scholars:
Professors Richard Astro (Northeastern University), Martha
H. Cox (San Jose State University, California), Robert
DeMott (Ohio University), John Ditsky (University of Windsor,
Canada), Warren French (Indiana University-Purdue Univer-
sity at Indianapolis), Reloy Garcia (Creighton University,
Nebraska), Peter Lisca (University of Florida).

29. WHAT AREAS SHOULD I EXPLORE IN STEINBECK'S
     LITERATURE?

     The following topics are still to be explored: Stein-
beck's sources; the unpublished materials including the manu-
scripts, letters, postcards, and others; the re-evaluation of
East of Eden; a textual study of Steinbeck's works; his publications abroad; his lesser-known works such as The Wayward Bus, The Winter of Our Discontent, Cup of Gold, The
Moon Is Down, Viva Zapata!; comparative studies; and Steinbeck's language. There are many other topics which should
be explored. Check No. 26 of this guide and use some of
the recommended bibliographies to find out what has been
done. See also "Advice to a Graduate Student" series in
SQ, 6 (Spring 1973), 45-52.

30. TO WHICH JOURNALS CAN I SEND AN UNSOLICITED
     ARTICLE ON JOHN STEINBECK FOR POSSIBLE PUB-
     LICATION?

     Besides the Steinbeck Quarterly, the following journals,
among many others, have published essays on Steinbeck:
American Literature, PMLA, Modern Fiction Studies, Twentieth-Century Literature, and Western American Literature.

31. IS THERE A RESEARCH FELLOWSHIP SUPPORTED BY
     THE STEINBECK SOCIETY OF AMERICA?

     No. The Steinbeck Society of America is not a grant
foundation. Various foundations are listed in The Foundation
Directory, ed. by Marianne O. Lewis, published by the
Foundation Center, 888 Seventh Avenue, New York, New
York 10019.

32. WHY IS STEINBECK'S INTERNATIONAL REPUTATION
    RISING?

    The following reasons can be mentioned:
    1. Steinbeck's acceptance of the Nobel Prize in 1962;
    2. Re-evaluation taking place since 1968;
    3. The Steinbeck Society's work to promote Steinbeck
       studies since 1966; and
    4. The general public's awareness of his achieve-
       ments.

33. TO WHOM SHOULD I WRITE TO OBTAIN PERMISSIONS
    TO QUOTE STEINBECK'S WRITINGS IN MY BOOK?

    Write to: Mrs. Shirley Fisher, McIntosh and Otis,
               Inc.
               475 Fifth Avenue
               New York, New York   10017
               U. S. A.
    and to: The Viking Press (c/o Permissions Depart-
               ment)
               625 Madison Avenue
               New York, New York   10022
               U. S. A.

34. WHAT IS BALL STATE UNIVERSITY'S ROLE IN THE
    STEINBECK SOCIETY?

    Ball State University has been sponsoring almost all
Steinbeck Society projects including the publication of the
Steinbeck Quarterly and the Steinbeck Monograph Series, and
the operational costs such as secretarial, mailing, and reference service expenses.   Without Ball State University's
generous financial and administrative sponsorship, none of
the Steinbeck Society projects could continue.

35. HOW MANY DOCTORAL DISSERTATIONS ON JOHN
    STEINBECK HAVE BEEN COMPLETED IN THE U. S. A. ?
    HOW MANY OF THEM HAVE BEEN PUBLISHED AS
    BOOKS?

    Nearly forty have been completed as of 1978.   Only
two doctoral dissertations have ever been published: those
of Peter Lisca (1958) and Lester J. Marks (1969).   Seven-
teen (17) were completed in the 24-year span of 1946-1969
and eighteen (18) were completed in the next six years (1970-
1975).

36. WHICH WORKS OF STEINBECK DO HIGH SCHOOL
     TEACHERS USE MOST?

     Such works as The Pearl, America and Americans,
The Red Pony, Cannery Row, The Grapes of Wrath, and Of
Mice and Men.

ACKNOWLEDGMENTS

     I should like to express my special thanks to the
following scholars for their generous and pertinent advice on
this article: Professors Richard Astro (Northeastern University), Robert DeMott (Ohio University), John Ditsky (University of Windsor, Canada), Reloy Garcia (Creighton University), and Donald L. Siefker (Ball State University).

Chapter 2

STEINBECK'S CUP OF GOLD (1929)

by Martha Heasley Cox

I. BACKGROUND

Steinbeck's first published novel, Cup of Gold: A Life
of Henry Morgan, Buccaneer, with Occasional Reference to
History, appeared in August, 1929, under the Robert M.
McBride imprint. The novel was a greatly expanded and
often revised version of a short story written several years
before, entitled "A Lady in Infra-Red: Being the Sad Story
of Piracy Unrequited." The typescript carbon of that story,
held in the Stanford University Library, is undated, but
Steinbeck includes "a story of Henry Morgan" among a list
of stories he says he had completed in a letter to a Stanford
classmate Carl Wilhelmson, written in 1925,[1] the same year
Steinbeck left Stanford without a degree and went to New
York City for a year. Steinbeck worked his way on a freighter to New York and back again, visiting Panama, the Cup of
Gold of his novel, on the way. On his return to California
he lived for two years in the Lake Tahoe area, supporting
himself with odd jobs and serving as caretaker during the
winter months at Fallen Leaf Lodge, where he wrote and re-
wrote his first novel.

By his twenty-sixth birthday, Steinbeck had completed
Cup of Gold, but was unhappy with the result. On February
25, 1928, he wrote his Stanford roommate, Carlton Sheffield:

> I finished my novel and let it stand for a while,
> then read it over. And it was no good. The dis-
> appointment of that was bound to have some devas-
> tating, though probably momentary effect. You see,
> I thought it was going to be good. Even to the
> last page, I thought it was going to be good. And
> it is not. [2]

Two paragraphs later he returns to the subject obviously uppermost in his mind: "Isn't it a shame, Duke, that
a thing which has as many indubitably fine things in it as
my Cup of Gold, should be, as a whole, utterly worthless?
It is a sorrowful matter to me." After three more paragraphs, thoughts of his novel intervene again:

> I am finishing the Henry ms out of duty, but I
> have no hope of it anymore. I shall probably pack
> it in Limbo balls and place it among the lost hopes
> in the chest of the years. Goodbye, Henry. I
> thought you were heroic but you are only, as was
> said of you, a babbler of words and rather clumsy
> about it.

Almost a year later, in January, 1929, Amasa
Miller, a Stanford friend who was beginning his law career
in New York City and attempting to place Steinbeck's manu-
scripts there, wired him that Cup of Gold had been accepted
for publication. A note on Steinbeck's return telegram says
that seven other publishers had read and rejected the novel
(SLL, 14). He was greatly disappointed, however, in
McBride's handling of Cup of Gold, and chagrined by the
cover with its garishly-colored flamboyant pirate, designed
by his New York friend Mahlen Blaine. Steinbeck expressed
his dissatisfaction in a letter to Miller in which he asked if
his contract required him to submit another manuscript to
McBride: "I think McBride handled the last one as badly as
it could have been handled. A timid half-hearted advertising
campaign which aimed at the wrong people by mis-describing
the book, slowness, bad taste in jacket and blurb" (SLL, 24).
In a subsequent letter, however, he inquired: "Did McBride
sell enough of the Cup to pay for its publication? I know
that during the holidays every book sold out completely and
I wonder whether that had any effect. I hope they at least
made a decent interest on their outlay" (SLL, 25). McBride
issued a single edition of 2,476 copies and remaindered 939
to a Harlem dealer. [3] The profit from the 1,537 copies sold
or used for publicity purposes was too little even to pay
Steinbeck's $250 advance.

By 1932, when Miller returned McBride's copyright
to Steinbeck, he replied: "For myself I would hate to see
the Cup reissued. I've outgrown it and it embarrasses me"
(SLL, 62). The book was reissued in 1936 and a number of
times subsequently. In 1937 Steinbeck referred to his first
novel as a possible film in a letter to his agents, McIntosh

and Otis: "If you get any request for stories for Hollywood
remember there is that old Cup which is the only thing I
have ever done that would make a good picture" (SLL, 145).
Though the film was never made, Samuel Bischoff did acquire
the screen rights in 1945 for an independent production. 5

The first edition of Cup of Gold is now the rarest of
Steinbeck's novels, one that not even he owned. He inscribed
the copy held at the Steinbeck Research Center at San Jose
State University: "I wish I had a copy of this edition. John
Steinbeck." Lawrence Clark Powell said in 1938 that he had
seen but one copy in dust jacket. 6 The jacket on the Steinbeck Research Center copy carries this blurb which Steinbeck
found so offensive:

> Sign on for a magnificent adventure! Follow him,
> the king of freebooters, the bad, sad, mad Henry
> Morgan, from the black Welsh glens, his birth-
> place, to the gold and blue Sea of the Caribs,
> where he breathed his last on green Jamaica which
> he ruled for rakehell Charles II. Follow his in-
> credible career, this pirate who was knighted by a
> king. Watch the seahawk sway the scum of the
> sea--the blustering Brotherhood of Tortuga, the
> cut-throats of Goaves, outcast Frenchmen, Nether-
> landers, Portuguese--ravening sea-wolves that
> cower under his icy glare. Stand by as he goads
> them to an impossible task, the capture of Panama,
> that great, lovely city, the richest in the New
> World, invulnerable through its mountains, jungles,
> marshes and mail-clad army--Panama, justly called
> the Cup of Gold. Shrink, as you must, when its
> glories are laid waste, when its golden streets run
> with blood. What was his motive--lust for more
> treasure? Watch him again when the Cup of Gold
> is in the hollow of his hand, and with it Ysobel,
> La Santa Roja, whose beauty was the dangerous
> beauty of lightning. And listen to him, Morgan of
> the secret dream, as he meets his match. This
> encounter between the Sea Satan and the Red Saint
> is enthralling. It reveals, with the wizardy [sic]
> of a Merlin, the whole drama of man's quest of
> his ideal mate.

II. PLOT SYNOPSIS

Fifteen-year-old Henry Morgan lives in Cambria in

the Welsh glens with his father Old Robert, his mother
Elizabeth, and his grandmother Gwenliana.   On a cold winter
night, Dafydd, their former farmhand who went away to sea
years ago, returns "rich--and cold," forced like the ancient
mariner to tell his tale before he returns once more to the
jungle in the West Indies whence he came.

When Henry tells his father that he too must leave
his valley now, Robert insists that he first visit Merlin on
his Crag-top, tell him his plans, and listen to his advice.
Merlin pleads for the wild black hills of Cambria, the hills
of a million mysteries where great Arthur lived.   Henry
assures him that he will return to the hills he too loves
when he is whole again.   Merlin replies:

> You are a little boy.   You want the moon to drink
> from as a golden cup; and so, it is very likely
> that you will become a great man--if only you re-
> main a little child.   All the world's great have
> been little boys who wanted the moon; running and
> climbing, they sometimes caught a firefly. [7]

On the way back, Henry goes to the hut where Elizabeth, a small girl with yellow hair, lives with her father, a
poor tenant.   Drawn yet repelled by Elizabeth, Henry whis-
tles, sees her at the window and runs.   When he reaches
home, his mother forbids him to leave Cambria; but his
father gives him five pounds and a letter to his uncle, Sir
Edward, who lives in Jamaica.   Gwenliana prophesies that
Henry will shed blood, sack cities, plunder, govern, and
marry "a white-souled maiden of mighty rank."   That night
Henry commits his "first cowardice," leaving for Cardiff
before morning to avoid saying goodbye to his mother and
father.

In Cardiff, a sailor bound for Barbados takes Henry
to his ship where he is permitted to work in the galley to
help pay for his passage.   Henry is sold at Barbados, however, for a five-year term as an indentured slave to James
Flower, an inefficient, kindly old planter.   He makes Henry
his companion and teaches him Latin, Greek, and Hebrew
as they read books in his library.   After two years Henry
becomes the overseer, then the master of the plantation,
merciless in his power.   At eighteen, grown and strong, he
has paid himself a secret horde of golden coins as "a sort
of commission" for his success.   He buys a ship to carry
produce to Jamaica, christens it Elizabeth, and goes to sea.

When he returns, he brings Paulette, a sensuous, passionate
beauty, as house servant and mistress.

On the fourth Christmas, Flowers gives Henry the
torn fragments of his indenture papers as a gift, announces
that Henry is no longer his servant but his son, offers him
half his plantation now and all on his death. Henry replies,
however, that he must go buccaneering and sails for Port
Royal, where his uncle, a strutting counterpart of Henry's
real father, is Lieutenant Governor. Sir Edward's daughter
Elizabeth, a "proudly pretty" girl, appears briefly between
practice sessions on her harp. Henry reveals his buccaneering plans and asks for financial help. Sir Edward refuses
and warns Henry that he will have to punish him if he is
caught marauding. That night Henry meets the buccaneer
Griffo and buys a half-interest in his ship, but all of her
command.

They capture four vessels before they reach Tortuga,
where the mighty buccaneer Mansfeldt makes Morgan Vice-
Admiral of his fleet. When Mansfeldt is lost at sea, Morgan
becomes the paramount leader of the Spanish Main, sailing
the ocean for ten years, fighting, plundering, and burning.
Though he gains the adulation of his brotherhood, he is not
content, for he is lonely in his glory, despising the men who
fawn on him. He now hears the rumor of La Santa Roja,
the mysterious Red Saint of Panama, "the quest of every
man's heart" and "a new virgin for their worship." In need
of a friend to talk to and trust, Henry selects young Coeur
de Gris from among his followers and tells him of his long-
lost Elizabeth, now the daughter of an Earl in his embellished
story. But the Circe-like voice of the Red Saint coaxes,
mocks, jeers, and cozens Henry until he forgets the sea,
while the buccaneers, penniless in their long inactivity, lie
about the ships and curse their captain for a dreaming fool
as he struggles in the meshes of his fantasy.

Meanwhile, his uncle, suffering from mortal battle
wounds, tells his daughter that her cousin Henry should take
care of her, since he leaves her little money. Back in
Cambria, fifteen years after Henry's departure, Old Robert
visits Merlin, carrying the rumors about Henry's great deeds.
"So he has come to be the great man he thought he wanted to
be," Merlin muses. "If this is true, then he is not a man.
He is still a little boy and wants the moon" (108).

When Panamanians hear of Morgan's threatened inva-

sion, they hide their treasures and prepare to rebuff the
marauders, chiefly by gathering ten thousand wild bulls to
stampede upon the approaching horde.   Morgan, meanwhile,
sends messages over the Spanish Main, promising unlimited
plunder to every man who joins his conquest.   After Morgan
leads his forces toward Panama for nine exhausting days
with little food, he begins to wonder why he wished to conquer the city.   When Coeur de Gris tells him that he wants
the woman, not Panama, Morgan replies: "You cannot understand my yearning.   It is as though I strove for some un-
dreamed peace.   This woman is the harbor of all my quest-
ing.   I do not think of her as a female thing with arms and
breasts, but as a moment of peace after turmoil, a perfume
after rancid filth" (128).   Coeur de Gris assures him that
all men have the same desires, even the little epileptic
cockney following behind.

     As they approach the city, the Panamanian troops
ride headlong into a swamp, then loose the bulls to trample
the robbers.   Morgan's men fire into the herd and it stam-
pedes in terror and annihilates the Spanish ranks.   Now the
cup of gold lies helpless before Morgan.

     As the men rampage and loot and the city burns,
Morgan asks wearily for the Red Saint.   At dawn, she enters
the Hall of Audience as Henry awakes in the serpent chair;
she tells him that she is Ysobel, whom he has sought.
Shocked at her appearance--hair black as obsidian, opaque
eyes, a sharp, almost hawklike face--Henry remembers his
fair Elizabeth.   Drawn and yet repelled by Ysobel, he nevertheless announces: "You must marry me, Elizabeth--Ysobel.
I think I love you, Ysobel" (141).   She informs him that she
is satisfactorily married, but Morgan is undeterred by that
"dull circumstance."   Ysobel taunts him: "I am tired of
these words that never change.   Is there some book with
which aspiring lovers instruct themselves?" (143).   Henry
leaves the Palace and, in his frustration, kills the Cockney.
He returns for another encounter with Ysobel and she jousts
with him, stabbing him with a pen as she defends herself
against his advances.   When Coeur de Gris, who has been
with Ysobel on the previous night, appears and asks Henry
if she has capitulated, Henry kills him.   A messenger arrives with an offer of ransom from Ysobel's husband for her
return.

     Henry, "sick with a disease called mediocrity," now
desires nothing but peace and time to "ponder imponderables."

He receives the money for Ysobel's ransom and informs her
that henceforth he will be gallant for two reasons only--
money and advancement. Having decided that money is his
anchor, his security and comfort, he makes plans to keep
all the Panama plunder for himself. With the treasure
stored in one ship, he supplies kegs of rum for the men on
the beach, disables the other ships, and puts out to sea
alone with the riches.

When Morgan arrives at Port Royal, a great crowd
gives him a hero's welcome and takes him to the Governor,
who informs him that they are both ordered to England. Before they leave, Elizabeth flatters, cajoles, and finally tricks
Henry into marriage. In England, Morgan, too popular a
figure to punish, is knighted instead by Charles II, who ap-
points him Lieutenant-Governor of Jamaica with instructions
to stop all piracy.

Back in Port Royal, Henry sentences two of his old
pirate followers to be hanged. One gives him a talisman,
a rose pearl, as a gift for his wife, now a hectoring, brow-
beating, badgering scold. Soon the victim of an unexplained
disease, Henry is confronted on his deathbed by his faceless
sins until they cower and bow before an approaching form,
Elizabeth--little Elizabeth from Cambria with her glowing
hair. Elizabeth is replaced by a smoldering ember who
speaks to Morgan as both expire to the accompaniment of a
great Tone.

III. CRITICAL EXPLICATION

It is scarcely surprising that Steinbeck's readers,
including such Stanford friends as Webster (Toby) Street,
hardly knew what to make of such a strange amalgam.
Street remembers Steinbeck's sending him the typescript and
soliciting his opinion and advice. Though he has forgotten
his reply to Steinbeck, nearly fifty years later he recalls
vividly the experience and his reaction: though the pile of
typescript was thick and the task arduous, he read every
word; but he didn't care for the novel, particularly those
mystic Tones and overtones. [8] Steinbeck's correspondence
with another Stanford friend and fellow writer, Robert Cathcart, show that Street must have been candid in his reaction
even then, for Steinbeck wrote on March 13, 1928: "Toby
is finding a great many faults with my manuscript and they
are bad faults." He solicited Cathcart's criticism too,

promising, however, to follow none of his advice and setting
a rigid time schedule: "If you want to look at the cup of
gold, I have told Toby to give it to you, if you will read it
in one night. It is pretty rotten. I am realizing it more
and more." Cathcart was evidently not up to the one-night
assignment, or Street's and Steinbeck's endorsements were
not sufficiently enticing to spark his interest, for Steinbeck
wrote him again on April 14, more than a month later:

> Have you read the Cup of Gold and if you have,
> why in hell don't you return the mss to me. You
> know Bob I don't much give a damn what people
> think of that book. It is little more than an ex-
> periment and an exercise, but in its last form, I
> mean in the finished draft which is not completed,
> I do think you would like it. Furthermore I think
> the thing would make a play of some merit if you
> would like to trifle with it.

This time Cathcart read the novel and Steinbeck, true
to his promise, ignored Cathcart's criticism, considered it
worthless, in fact, except as an indication of his own failure.
The criticism's tenor is clear in Steinbeck's reply, which
also reveals both his early reaction to criticism and his
attitude toward plot structure:

> I can conceive no more unless or vain thing than
> that of an author defending his own work, for if
> his intent, all of his intent does not show in the
> work itself, then the work is faulty. And no
> amount of statement of what he intended will clear
> it. I could say to you that I do not believe in
> climaxes, that I went out of my way to avoid a
> climax, that I believe the great events of a man's
> life come about casually, but if the book has not
> told you that, then the book is not good nor well
> done. And so let that subject pass. Your criti-
> cism is worthless to me except in so far as it
> tells me that I failed to get over what I intended.

Professional critics were not much kinder in their
assessments of the published novel. Most of the few reviews
that appeared were brief, perfunctory announcements of the
book's publication and subject matter. Some who did more
did not please Steinbeck. One can almost hear the outrage
he felt when he wrote Miller: "Reviewers, after reading
that it was an adventure story said, quite truly, that it was

a hell of a bad adventure story.   It was worse than that.
It wasn't an adventure story at all" (SLL, 24).

Most later Steinbeck critics have found Cup of Gold
an interesting first novel, valuable for its insights into Steinbeck's early ideas and techniques, particularly for its introduction of themes and fictional devices that continued throughout the canon.   It will be my concern here to examine, as
space permits, the genesis and development of Cup of Gold;
the use of historical material; the autobiographical aspects;
the major influences and allusions; and some of the techniques, themes, characters, symbols, and stylistic devices
that originated in Cup of Gold and were to recur in Steinbeck's later work.

A look at Steinbeck's unpublished seed story, "The
Lady in Infra-Red: Being the Sad Story of Piracy Unrequited, "
is most instructive.   A remarkable performance, it should,
considering Steinbeck's later achievements, give hope to every
incipient writer and teacher of creative writing.   As a piece
of art, it ranks at least as far below Cup of Gold as that
work does below The Grapes of Wrath.   The twenty-three-
page carbon transcript in the Bender Library at Stanford
Library at Stanford University bears Steinbeck's penciled
note on page one: "This is considerably corrected and quite
a bit polished in the finished version. "   "Henry Morgan" is
typed at the top right corner of every page except the title
page and page four.

After a brief summary of Morgan's early career,
Steinbeck begins, by page two, to discuss Morgan's plans for
capturing Panama.   The rest of the story describes the gathering of the forces, the invasion, the looting and destruction
of the city, and Morgan's meeting and parting with the lady
in Infra Red.   Though the animals differ, Steinbeck's scenic
descriptions seem closer to those in Of Mice and Men than
to those in Cup of Gold: "The jungle came down to the river
and hung over it.   There were big brown pumas moving
about without the smallest shadow of a sound, striking like
fur covered steel traps.   On the water's edge you could see
colored snakes with shining figures on their backs. "   He
describes the "fearsome noises" along the river, "the screams
of the great cats, and the wailing of night birds and the
grinding of alligators. "   Morgan's crew for the Panama conquest consists of naked Indians, boat loads of Frenchmen,
barges of wild Englishmen, and big, lustful Caribs, "whose
lives were a continual play of passion. "   As in Cup of Gold,

they have little food for many days and the "cheeks of the
men went sinking in." Finally, "when their hearts were very
thin," they saw Panama. They fight the Spaniards, who lose
their nerve and run away to hide in the hills. While "wine
flowed and blood flowed," Henry Morgan went to the white
house of the Alcalde, ran his sword through the owner, and
set about collecting spoils. At dawn, Henry's "appetite for
gold was flagging," when suddenly he "jerked himself upright
and bellowed." To the dozen drunken pirates who respond,
he says: "All night long I have been gathering gold for all
of us, while you drowned yourselves with liquor and carried
on your courting. Now I want to play. Go over the women,
pick out the best and bring them here. No blacks now and
no hags. Jump!" His men return with "little bands of poor
disheveled wretches" and line them up in front of Henry. In
the line-up is one who is different: "Her black lace shawl
was unruffled. There was no spot or wrinkle on the flowing
skirt of white figured silk." When Henry reached for her
skirt to tear it off, she stabbed his wrist with a pin and "he
raised his eyes to the woman's face. It was then, rather
sharp, but very beautiful and not like the other women's
faces. The hair, black as crude oil and with the same rich
purple lights in it, was piled high on her head.... Her
brown eyes dug into the captain's brain, called him a dog."
In a moment the captain was in love. A queer plunging of
blood was in the breast of Henry Morgan. He looked out of
the window and gulped...."

Unfortunately for Steinbeck, Morgan, and the reader,
the captain has to call an interpreter in order to converse
with his new-found love. When he then asks, "Would Madame step into the side room to discuss matters?" her reply
in vicious Spanish overwhelms the translator, who nevertheless manages to impart: "Madame would not. Madame was
a decent married woman, and so she would have nothing at
all to do with a dirty pirate." Undaunted, Morgan persists,
thinking what a credit, what a fine wife she would be in
England, where "if anyone should happen to malign his name,
that torrent of vituperative metal would burst forth on the
offender." Besides, a "fat, pink god was squirming in his
chest." For an hour he compliments the lady who "flang
back strings of insults" until finally she sulled and sulked
and refused to answer. Eventually he became "nettled":
"His hand dropped and a long, thin knife came sneaking out
of its sheath on his belt." When Henry snarled "I shall
kill you if you refuse me," the lady made a large cross in
the air to shield her body, then "thriftily drew aside the

feathery lace of her mantilla that it might not be spotted
with blood. " The "dagger stopped and Henry Morgan looked
silly. "

Steinbeck interrupts now for one of several authorial
remarks: "Indecision in dealing with women always makes
men look silly. " Madame suddenly becomes joyful and the
interpreter explains that she begs Morgan to plunge the knife
into her heart, for a woman who dies protecting her honor
is transported straight to heaven. Instead, Morgan sends
her into a side room to be comfortable. While he contemplates "this black falcon of a woman" he so desires, "a
shrill nasal voice" rises from the side room. Madame is
telling her beads and continues to do so until Henry, exas-
perated with the monotonous tone, "clapped his black hat on
his head and strode from the house. " The sights, sounds,
and smells of violence bring him to himself again. He
shoots a "little pinched rat of an Englishman" and kicks him
viciously in the head. Suddenly a red horseman appears
bearing a note "written in English, " fortunately, asking the
amount of ransom for the wife of Don Manuel. Henry rushes
back and takes Madame in his arms and Steinbeck intervenes
once again to warn us: "Now there is nothing so ridiculous
as embracing a [woman] who does not wish to be embraced.
It is bound to be the most colossal of failures. She will
twist and turn in your arms and the result will be one of
two things. She will escape leaving you like a clown, or
she will faint eventually, and you are a brute. " Madame,
however, did neither; instead she attacked Henry Morgan
again with that pin. Henry, overcome with passion, slumps
to his knees and holds out beseeching hands as he pleads:
"Oh! love me, love me. Throw over those old ties, and I
will tear an empire from this new world with my hands, only
love me. " Steinbeck interrupts the tender scene to explain:
"You see, it was bad. He had so very little experience with
this sort of thing. "

When Henry Morgan's pleas were of no avail, he
"clambered up from his knees, and dragged out of the room. "
In deep sadness he contemplates becoming a hermit, giving
his money to the poor, even dying without her knowledge.
Then the ransom bearers arrive and he prepares for his
last interview with the lady. "His head hung down as though
he were in prayer. His words had a hoarse, released
fervency. " And the authorial voice informs us, or perhaps
apologizes: "So very few men make impromptu love of any
dramatic value. "

In his renunciation scene, Morgan tells Madame that
he loves her even more for her fidelity to her husband and
begs her to remember him with kindness and regard him as
a brother. He calls in the interpreter then to learn the
lady's parting words to him. It seems, perhaps, that she
can understand Morgan--or he thinks she can, though one
cannot be sure in this story. At any rate, he dreams of a
soft answer, but what he hears is that she will report to her
husband his attack on her virtue and his threat against her
life. After she rides away on her white horse with her
husband and his retinue, the "drunken messenger slave" remains. He tells Henry Morgan that his master paid the
mortgage because his wife is an heiress who will inherit
silver mines and coast land on the death of her grandfather:
"You see, that is the reason my master is willing to forfeit
sixty thousand gold dollars to regain a woman who has the
mind of a little child and ... how do you say it ... who is
not completely a woman." Then he giggles foolishly and
gallops after his party, "a shining speck in the distance."
And Steinbeck ends his story with this postscript: "Cuando
el diablo no tiene que hacer, El mata moscas."

As difficult as it is to take any of the story seriously,
one can never be sure of Steinbeck's intent. Critics have
complained of the lack of consistent tone in Cup of Gold:
perhaps the trouble began with this embryonic story. Though
the last half sounds like an undergraduate attempt at farce,
and both the title and postscript could support that interpretation, the descriptions of the river, the jungle, and of
Panama seem realistic and serious in intent, as do the accounts of the journey to the city and its destruction. Through
out the story, in addition, Steinbeck uses figurative language
to express ideas that belie levity. When Morgan leaves the
lady telling her beads, for example, he walks through Panama, where "Murdered townsmen were acting perpetually in
still pantomine their little moments of agony." Nevertheless,
his major characters, the posturing lumpish pirate and the
lady--perhaps the first of God's unfinished creatures Steinbeck was to depict--are strange precursors for the Henry
Morgan and Ysobel of Cup of Gold. Furthermore, the story
lacks the thematic substructure, the allusions, and the symbols that inform the novel.

Another version of Cup of Gold, an early revision of
approximately the first half of the text of the book, is also
housed in the Bender Room at Stanford. Though the 102-
page typescript is approximately the same length as the pub-

lished version, a comparison of the two shows that the typescript was considerably revised before publication. In addition to stylistic changes in almost every line, chapters and
sections of chapters were renumbered and sometimes rearranged, most notably the scene between John Evelyn and
Charles II, which was moved from the beginning of one
chapter and inserted within a later section. Speeches are
sometimes shifted from one character to another and entire
paragraphs are omitted in some places and new ones added
in others. The major addition, however, is the introductory
section on the buccaneers. The undated typescript contains
corrections in ink in what appears to be Steinbeck's writing;
the first chapter also contains suggested changes, in another
hand, in red pencil.

In all three versions, Steinbeck makes more than occasional reference to history. His protagonist's prototype,
Henry Morgan, was born in Wales in 1635, sailed for the
West Indies--probably in 1654--and became a leader of the
buccaneers and privateers in the Caribbean. In 1668 he was
appointed Colonel of the troops at Jamaica and in 1671 led a
band of approximately one thousand men who captured Panama and destroyed the city. Recalled to England under arrest, he was too popular a figure to remain long in disgrace
and was, in fact, knighted by Charles II and returned to
Jamaica as Deputy Governor, an office he held intermittently
until he died in 1688, a wealthy and respected citizen. He
denied the frequently reprinted reports that he was kidnapped
as a youth in Bristol and sold as an indentured servant in
Barbados. In 1684 he won a libel suit against the publishers
of these assertions and other alleged falsehoods which cast
aspersions on his character, maintaining that he was innocent
of the cruelty with which he was charged.

Henry Morgan was, then, an early "leader of the
people," a courageous tactician who became a successful
corsair. He was the nephew of Sir Edward Morgan, Sir
Thomas Modyford's Deputy Governor, who died in battle.
At about the age of thirty, Morgan married his first cousin,
Elizabeth, Edward's daughter.

In addition to Morgan, his uncle, and cousin, most
of the buccaneers Steinbeck names, the Governor and his
wife, King Charles II, and the diarist John Evelyn were
characters with historical counterparts. Others such as
James Flowers, the ship captain who sold young Morgan,
and the mysterious married woman in Panama appeared in

Morgan myth and legend.   Steinbeck's prognosticator Merlin
also has an historical counterpart in a fifth-century Welsh or
British bard whose story has been mingled with that of the
enchanter Merlin of the Arthurian romances.   Henry's parents and grandmother, Dafydd, the young Elizabeth in her
various metamorphoses, and Coeur de Gris seem to be
Steinbeck's own creations.

From Steinbeck's descriptions and depictions of his
family and from the recollection of those who knew them,
Henry's parents and grandmother could be modeled on Steinbeck's own: the quiet, supportive father whose "smile was
perplexity and a strange passive defiance" (CG, 2), strives
to understand Henry's compulsion and gives him what money
he can to support his venture; the practical, busy, brusque
mother--who feeds her family, mends their clothing, and
worries about their health--worships her son and loves her
husband "with a queer mixture of pity and contempt" (3); the
elderly, mystic grandmother, "a little wrinkled old woman
soon to die" (3), takes pride in practicing second sight.
Henry, restive as his beloved valley grows smaller, wishes
"to vault the mountains and strike about the world" (11) to
test his dreams, to begin his quest, as Steinbeck embarks
on his through lonely days and nights in his mountain retreat.
Steinbeck's own comments lend support to such autobiographical surmises, for he wrote a friend shortly after the novel
appeared:

> The book was an immature experiment written for
> the purpose of getting all the wise cracks (known
> by sophomores as epigrams) and all the autobio-
> graphical material (which hounds us until we get it
> said) out of my system.   And I really did not in-
> tend to publish it.   The book accomplished its
> purgative purpose.   I am no more concerned with
> myself very much.   I can write about other people.
> I have not the slightest desire to step into Donn
> Byrne's shoes.   I may not have his ability with
> the vernacular but I have twice his head.   I think
> I have swept all the Cabellyo-Byrneish precious-
> ness out for good (SLL, 17).

During their Stanford years, Steinbeck, Webster
Street, and their literary friends read and often discussed
Donn Byrne's and James Branch Cabell's work.   The influence of both on Cup of Gold is significant.   Both wrote
historical, romantic fiction filled with fantasy and mythical

elements. Byrne's best-known novels are <u>Blind Raftery</u>, the
story of an eighteenth-century Gaelic poet, and <u>Messer Marco
Polo</u>. Both express his most consistent theme: the world's
estimate of the good is selfish and vulgar, and is achieved
only by shallow, soulless people. Cabell's most famous
novel, <u>Jurgen</u>, contains a chapter entitled "Why Merlin
Talked in Twilight," in which Cabell describes the magician's
habitat, prophecy, and advice. Both authors loved archaic,
elaborate rhythms and symbols. Cabell's style is ornate,
often precious, and highly allusive. <u>Cup of Gold</u> is quite
obviously Steinbeck's attempt to achieve the same effect in
his choice of subject matter, theme, and style.

Much of <u>Cup of Gold</u> is a pastiche, perhaps a conscious and planned pastiche in which Steinbeck uses imitation
and allusion for his own purpose. Peter Lisca and Darlene
Eddy have noted echoes from Shakespeare's plays and other
Renaissance drama, 9 but Steinbeck has drawn far more
widely from his progenitors. <u>Cup of Gold</u> echoes much of
what must have been required reading in his recently completed English courses at Stanford: Shakespeare, Conrad,
Tennyson, Wallace Stevens, Malory, Coleridge, The Bible,
O'Neill, and Tolstoy.

A few examples must suffice here: Dafydd is a
stricken Kurtz poisoned by the horror of his own jungle's
darkness: "That soul leaks out of a man the very first
thing in the Indies, and leaves him with a dry, shrunken
feeling where it was. It's not my soul at all; it's the
poison that's in me, in my blood and in my brain" (<u>CG</u>, 7).

Henry is a young Ulysses with "a burning and a will
overpowering to journey outward and outward after the
earliest risen star" (<u>CG</u>, 16).

Merlin borrows from Stevens' "Sunday Morning" in
his description of his travels:

> We came at last on these green Indies, and they
> were lovely but unchanging. Their cycle is a
> green monotony. If you go there you must give
> up the year; must lose the pang of utter dread in
> the deep winter with its boding that the world has
> fled solar fealty to go careening into lonely space
> so that Spring may never come again. And you
> must lose that wild, excited quickening when the
> sun turns back, the joy of it flooding over you like

the surge of a warm wave and choking you with
pleasure and relief.   No change there; none at all.
Past and future mingle in an odious, eternal now.
(CG, 17)

Steinbeck's references to Arthur, Avalon, and the
circling stones (CG, 18) reflect his knowledge of Malory.
The mesmerizing words of fury delivered by the skull-faced
master of the Bristol Girl, "armed with his God," are very
like sermons preached by Jonathan Edwards:

"God has struck you with only the title of his
shattering might," he shouted.   "He has shown
you the strength of His little finger that you may
repent before you go screaming in hell-fire.   Hear
the name of the Lord in the frightful wind and
repent you of your whorings and your blasphemies!
Ah! ..." (CG, 45-46)

Tim's sea tale bears some resemblances to "The
Ancient Mariner": in both a strange woman appears on
another ship in the sea, dice are cast for possession of
another--or others, and ships sink suddenly and mysteriously
into the depths.   Coleridge's woman is the nightmare Life-
in-Death, with skin "a white leprosy."   Steinbeck's woman
"with a long white forehead" jumps overboard and disappears,
to reappear two nights later, "a white thing" swimming after
them, her long white hands reaching out "like the ship was
a lodestone and it a bit of iron."   Though the Ancient Mariner hears "nor sigh nor groan," Tim's men "cry and moan"
as their own white albatross follows in their wake.   The
next night, the bo's'n, grayed overnight, bursts out of the
hold screaming like a mad man.   Two long white hands are
ripping the planks off the ship like paper; it gives a list and
starts to settle down.   The mariner's ship also "went down
like lead."

Despite such occurrences, Steinbeck tells us, with
biblical overtones: "There is a peace in the tropic oceans
which passes a desire for understanding" (CG, 52).

The faceless little creatures, "strange beings, having
the bodies of children, and bulbous, heavy heads, but no
faces," who cluster thickly around Morgan's death bed and
question him in strident, harsh voices (CG, 196) remind one
of the little formless fears, the size of creeping children,
who crawl out of the blackness of the forest and terrify

O'Neill's Emperor Jones as they squirm toward him with
low mocking laughter.

Morgan's death bed scene with its smoldering ember
and dying light is reminiscent of Ivan Ilych's, though more
somber. When Tolstoy's protagonist saw light instead of
death, he felt great joy; when Morgan's ember is extinguished,
he sees only darkness, "no light anywhere," and for a moment hears the "deep, mellow pulsation of the Tone."

This seminal novel is most significant, however, for
its foreshadowing of the work still to be written; the early
Steinbeck above all reminds us of the Steinbeck to come.
Similarities exist in technique, structure, themes, characters,
scenes, symbols, imagery, and style.

At the time Steinbeck was composing Cup of Gold,
his favorite record was Dvořák's "New World" Symphony,
which he thought paralleled the story of the Welsh boy who
left home to seek his fortune, never to return. Steinbeck
said he planned the book to follow the symphony, regulating
pace, tonal quality, and word sounds to conform to major
changes in the music's tempo and mood. [10] He was to use
the same technique with other music for later novels: To a
God Unknown, The Grapes of Wrath, and East of Eden.

Steinbeck's journey motif in Cup of Gold is the fore-
runner of other trips in later times. Morgan's travels began as a quest for wholeness, became a search for fortune
and power, and terminated in an arrangement for comfort
and security. Counterparts are Steinbeck's accounts of both
actual and symbolic journeys in later works--the Joad's trek
west, Juan Chicoy's wayward trip, Pepé Torres' flight, as
well as the passage from innocence to awareness in initiation
or maturation stories such as Jody Tiflin undergoes in "The
Red Pony," or Cal Trask in East of Eden. Steinbeck's
nearest parallel to the protagonist of his first novel is that
of his last; Ethan Allen Hawley plunders in the modern manner and is no more content in his ill-gotten gains than was
Morgan in his.

In Cup of Gold, Steinbeck begins three of his five
chapters with prefatory sections which provide general background for his specific story of Morgan: the century-old
struggle between Spain and England for the new world and
the colonization of their possessions in the West Indies; the
origin, exploits, and members of the Free Brotherhood of

Buccaneers; and the history of Panama--all early versions
of the technique Steinbeck would apply more successfully in
Tortilla Flat and The Grapes of Wrath.

     Recurring Steinbeck themes find their roots here,
most prominently the quest for the Grail, a life-long concern
of Steinbeck's, treated most extensively in his first novel and
in his unfinished and posthumously published The Acts of
King Arthur and His Noble Knights (1976). In a letter written the year before his death, Steinbeck stated explicitly that
interest which had consumed him for "over forty years":

          All my life has been aimed at one book and I
          haven't started it yet. The rest has all been
          practice. Do you remember the Arthurian legend
          well enough to raise in your mind the symbols of
          Launcelot and his son Galahad? You see, Launce-
          lot was imperfect and so he never got to see the
          Holy Grail. So it is with all of us. The Grail is
          always one generation ahead of us. But it is there
          and so we can go on bearing sons who will bear
          sons who may see the Grail. This is a most pro-
          found set of symbols ... one must accept the fail-
          ure which is the end of every writer's life no
          matter what stir he may have made. In himself
          he must fail as Launcelot failed--for the Grail is
          not a cup. It's a promise that skips ahead--it's a
          carrot on a stick and it never fails to draw us on.
          (SLL, 859)

     Other familiar themes originate in Cup of Gold: the
necessity for exploitation in the pursuit of power and money,
mediocrity as the price for comfort and security, the loss
of dreams and illusions in a practical society, the loneliness
the artist or contemplative man pays for his transcendence
of society, the leader of the people set apart from the group
animal.

     Characters in this first novel are progenitors of other
creations: prognosticators and philosophers such as Margie
Young-Hunt and Lee are descendants of Gwenliana and Merlin; Morgan leads the buccaneers as Jody's grandfather led
his people west; Morgan and Coeur de Gris are an early, if
abortive, example of the friendship and dependency that was
to develop between Mac and Jim in In Dubious Battle and
George and Lennie in Of Mice and Men.

Scenes prefigure subsequent scenes moved to another place, another time, another character. Elisa Allen's chrysanthemums, for example, are later to receive the same loving care that Robert lavishes on his roses:

> Robert was working the soil about the roots of a rose bush with his strong brown hands. His fingers lifted the black loam and then patted it gently back into place. Now and again he stroked the gray trunk of the bush with the touch of great love. (CG, 13)

The Joads' first sight of the fertile California valley engendered the same sense of wonder as the buccaneers felt when they finally looked down on Panama:

> In the evening they came to the top of a small, round hill, and there below them was Panama laved in the golden light of the western sun. Each man searched his neighbor's face to be assured that this was not his own personal hallucination. (CG, 131)

The mountain rocks Henry passes on his climb to Merlin's Crag-top foreshadow the dark watchers in both "Flight" and The Pearl: "Upward, the strewn rocks were larger and more black and dreadful--crouched guardian things of the past" (CG, 15).

Among such symbols, the titular image, the golden cup, predominates and permeates the book. Its color is reflected in the fragile golden hair of two Elizabeths, the childhood sweetheart and the cousin/wife. Its shape is that of the earth and sky and much in between--hunger and wealth, innocence and experience. The cup of gold is Panama, the earthy repository of great treasure; the sky is a blue cup, a wine cup; the hungry buccaneers have hollow cheeks, "shallow cups under their cheek bones"; money is concentric round circles of gold; lambs of innocence, grown grotesque here, chase each other on the outer edge of a golden cup; inside, on the bottom, a naked girl lifts her arms in sensual ecstasy. Henry finds the lovely chalice he had lifted from the loot defiled by its carvings and hurls it at a "fiery pyramid of diamonds." The cup is, ultimately, the unobtainable Grail; its significance increases as the novel progresses, just as more effective and better integrated titular symbols do in The Wayward Bus and The Grapes of Wrath.

Horses whinney, birds protest, cats stalk, frogs
pound, and monkeys spit, lending color to Steinbeck's figures
of speech and visual and auditory imagery to his setting and
atmosphere. "His Honor," Merlin's great red-eared dog,
nuzzles Henry, and we meet the first of Steinbeck's ubiquitous canines. The valley and talisman symbols originate in
Cup of Gold too.

Steinbeck's style, as numerous examples quoted for
other purposes in this chapter illustrate, is at best uneven
in Cup of Gold, sometimes ornate, overwrought, and exces-
sive--sometimes simple, clear, and lyrical. His diction is
often inappropriate, sometimes incredible. After fifteen-
year-old Henry, for example, dreams of a shadowy composite
of little Elizabeth and his mother, he considers himself an
unnatural monster, and Elizabeth a kind of "succubus incar-
nate." Much later Captain Morgan thinks of "the mad incon-
gruity, the turgid stultiloquy of life." The Captain, having
read James Flower's books, might conceivably have thought
in those terms, but not the boy Henry, not when his father
talked like this: "I imagine great dishes of purple porridge,
drenched with dragon's milk, sugared with a sweetness only
to be envisioned" (CG, 12) to a mother at times "laved in a
revery of the silver past" (CG, 26).

The best passages in Cup of Gold are lyrical sections
in which Steinbeck celebrates the natural world and reveals
the relationship of man to his environment, encapsulating
inner and outer landscape in clear, objective prose. As the
young Welsh boy left his home, lonely and frightened, and
walked down the road toward Cardiff: "Horses whinnied
shrilly at him as he passed, then came close and gently
touched him with their soft noses; and coveys of birds, feed-
ing on belated night crawlers in the half dark, flew up at
his approach with startled protests" (CG, 30). And Steinbeck, with Cup of Gold, left his "purple porridge" prose for
the clear prose idiom which distinguished his fiction.

Steinbeck expressed his views on first novels before
his was even accepted for publication:

> I think all first novels ought to be burned just as
> a matter of course. Some good ones might suffer
> but so few that the practice would be justified any-
> way. I shall model a little model of mud and call
> it art. Then I shall erect an altar with horns.
> And on this pyre shall my brain child go up in
> smoke while flags wave and bands play. [11]

Fortunately that sacrificial cremation was averted,
for Cup of Gold is a vitally important first novel, as valuable for its weaknesses as for its strengths. Together with
the original short story and the earlier version of the typescript, it offers Steinbeck scholars a rare opportunity to
study the development of a novelist as he learned his craft.
Cup of Gold, in its various stages, illustrates Steinbeck's
early, often crude attempts to turn an historical account into
art. As he restructured and rearranged his materials, he
supplied a thematic substructure, created characters, and
added scenes, symbols, and imagery which were to recur
throughout his work.

NOTES

1. This letter and the letters to Robert Cathcart quoted in
   this chapter are in the Bender Room at Stanford University.

2. Elaine Steinbeck and Robert Wallsten, eds. , Steinbeck:
   A Life in Letters (New York: Viking Press, 1975),
   p. 10. Subsequent references to this book are identified as SLL, and incorporated into the text.

3. Lawrence Clark Powell, "Toward a Bibliography of
   John Steinbeck," Colophon, 3 (Autumn 1938), 559.

4. Robert van Gelder, "Interview with a Best-Selling
   Author: John Steinbeck," Cosmopolitan, 122 (April
   1947), 18, 123-25.

5. A. H. Weiler, "By Way of a Report: Steinbeck and
   Pirates," New York Times, Dec. 16, 1945, Sec. 2,
   p. 5.

6. Powell, p. 559.

7. John Steinbeck, Cup of Gold (New York: Bantam, 1962),
   p. 19. When necessary for clarity, references to the
   novel will be identified as CG and incorporated into
   the text; otherwise, page numbers alone will be paren-
   thesized.

8. Mr. Street discussed the novel with me at a party held
   at Doc Rickett's lab in Monterey on August 6, 1977.

9. See the annotated bibliography at the end of this chapter.

10. Nelson Valjean, John Steinbeck: The Errant Knight, an Intimate Biography of His California Years (San Francisco: Chronicle Books, 1975), pp. 108-09.

11. In a letter to Robert Cathcart dated March 13, 1928.

IV. APPARATUS FOR RESEARCH PAPERS

A. Ten Questions for Discussion

1. Contrast Morgan's childhood sweetheart, Elizabeth, with the Red Saint, Ysobel. How do the two differ in actual appearance and, more importantly, in Morgan's conception of them? Are both symbols? If so, of what?

2. Compare Morgan's mother, Elizabeth, with his wife, Elizabeth. Can you find common traits and attitudes between them? Are they stereotyped figures? If so, how?

3. Old Robert, Merlin, and James Flower are similar in some respects. How? How do they differ? What function does each perform in his relationship to Henry? Richard Astro argues that Steinbeck offers no meaningful alternative to Morgan's pursuit of wealth and power. Who in the novel pursues both? Who neither? Whose lives seem more meaningful?

4. Discuss Merlin and Gwenliana as prognosticators. What does each foretell for Henry? How are their prophecies fulfilled?

5. Discuss the role of religion in the novel. Consider particularly Merlin's attitude and that of the Captain of the Bristol Girl.

6. Harry T. Moore says that Morgan is the only character in the book who shows any development. Joseph Henry Jackson writes: "Morgan was a young man who knew very well what he wanted and went out and got it." What were Henry's goals? Did he attain them? If not, what did he acquire? How does he change?

7. Steinbeck tells us that Henry learned much in dealing with the slaves (CG, 61-62). Discuss the five "teachings" he lists. What do they reveal about Henry? About the slaves? About human nature?

8. Do you agree with Jackson's comment: "As you follow his [Morgan's] progress in this tale you find yourself admiring the man more than you should admire a gentleman of the ruthlessness and piratical make-up of Morgan"? Or with Richard Astro's assessment of Morgan

as "idle dreamer turned sullen bully"? In either case,
why or why not?
9. Discuss Steinbeck's color imagery in the novel, particularly green, gold, and red. Note how the color red
predominates in Ysobel's section.
10. "One is tempted to dismiss this novel as the one thoroughly bad piece of Steinbeck's apprenticeship, seeing in
it ample evidence of the thin Sierra air and 7,000 feet
of altitude," writes F. W. Watt. A book reviewer for
Newsweek, on the other hand, called Cup of Gold "a
splendid fictionalized biography of the buccaneer Morgan."
With which assessment do you agree? Why?

B. Suggested Topics for Research Papers

1. Steinbeck's subtitle for his novel is A Life of Sir Henry
Morgan, Buccaneer, with Occasional Reference to History. Read a biography of Henry Morgan and compare
it with Steinbeck's fictional account. How is Steinbeck's
protagonist like the historical figure? How does he differ? Which episodes are based on Morgan's adventures?
Which have no parallels? Which characters in Steinbeck's novel have counterparts in history? Which are
solely Steinbeck's creation?
2. Steinbeck wrote a friend, A. Grove Day, that Cup of
Gold "was an immature experiment written for the purpose of getting all the wise cracks (known by sophomores
as epigrams) and all the autobiographical material (which
hounds us until we get it said) out of my system."
Write a paper on the wise cracks--or epigrams--you
can identify in the novel.
3. Read a biographical sketch of Steinbeck's early years,
then try to identify autobiographical elements in the
novel.
4. Steinbeck acknowledges the influence of Donn Byrne and
James Branch Cabell on Cup of Gold. Read a book by
either, preferably Byrne's Messer Marco Polo or Blind
Raftery or Cabell's Jurgen, and see what influences,
particularly stylistic, you can trace.
5. Discuss the four faces of Elizabeth--mother, sweetheart,
"saint," and wife--or five if you include the ship. How
are they alike and how do they differ? What role does
each play in Morgan's life? In his imagination? Do
they merge? If so, how? Consider Morgan's four versions of the young Elizabeth in your paper.
6. Write a character sketch of Steinbeck's Henry Morgan.

Consider the assessment Steinbeck made of his own
creation shortly after he completed the novel: "Goodbye Henry. I thought you were heroic but you were
only, as was said of you, a babbler of words and rather
clumsy about it. "

7. Henry Morgan tells Coeur de Gris that there is much
   suffering in women, who "seem to carry pain about them
   in a leaking package. " Discuss Steinbeck's treatment of
   women in the novel; consider such characters as Paulette
   and Gwenliana as well as the four Elizabeths.

8. John Exquemelin's eye-witness account of the invasion
   and destruction of Panama (available in the translation
   in a number of sources, including Francis Russell Hart's
   Admirals of the Caribbean) differs greatly from Steinbeck's version. Compare and contrast the two.

9. Berton Braley consulted Cup of Gold as an historical
   source and included certain incidents in his ballad Morgan Sails the Caribbean that were Steinbeck's fictional
   inventions. Braley prints an acknowledgement of Steinbeck's contributions to his effort and includes Steinbeck's
   letter granting permission for their use as a Preface to
   his book. Read Braley's ballad and discuss his use of
   Cup of Gold as source material.

10. Defend or refute Steinbeck's own assessments of his
    novel: (A) "I finished my novel and let it stand for a
    while, then read it over. And it was no good. "
    (B) "Isn't it a shame, Duke, that a thing which has as
    many indubitably fine things in it as my Cup of Gold,
    should be, as a whole, utterly worthless?" If you con-
    sider the novel "no good" and "utterly worthless, " ex-
    plain why. If you find "indubitably fine things" in it,
    what are they? Are they sufficient to redeem its value?
    In either case, support your argument with specific
    examples from the novel.

C.   Selected Bibliography

1. Astro, Richard. "Phlebas Sails the Caribbean: Steinbeck, Hemingway, and the American Waste Land, " in
   The Twenties: Fiction, Poetry, Drama, ed. Warren French.
   DeLand, Florida: Everett/Edwards, 1975, pp. 215-33.
       Astro discusses Cup of Gold and To Have and Have Not
   as reflections of the valley of ashes depicted in T. S. Eliot's
   The Waste Land. He sees Henry Morgan as "an idle dreamer turned sullen bully whose fate seems less tragic than
   pathetic, " and argues that Steinbeck offers no meaningful
   alternative to his pursuit of wealth and power.

2. Eddy, Darlene. "To Go A-Buccaneering and Take a
   Spanish Town: Some Seventeenth Century Aspects of
   Cup of Gold," Steinbeck Quarterly, 8 (Winter 1975),
   3-12.
   Eddy examines Steinbeck's use of John Exquemeling's
   The Buccaneers of America and of other seventeenth-century
   literary and historical materials, noting "his adaption of
   sources, his evocation of Renaissance voyaging, and his ap-
   proximation of specific dramatic techniques reminiscent of
   Elizabethan-Jacobean tragedy, especially the memento mor
   and the allegorical tableau."

3. French, Warren. John Steinbeck. New Haven: College
   and University Press, 1961, pp. 31-38.
   In a chapter entitled "Gatsby Sails the Caribbean,"
   French rejects Lisca's view of Henry Morgan as a Faust
   figure, regarding him instead as an anti-Arthurian quester
   closely resembling Scott Fitzgerald's Jay Gatsby. Cup of
   Gold, then, contrasts the power-seeker who forsakes his
   illusions of unique greatness and succumbs to the mediocrity
   entailed in the pursuit of money with the artist who transcends society.

4. _____. John Steinbeck. Boston: Twayne, 2nd ed.
   rev., 1975, pp. 45-58.
   In this thorough revision of his 1961 book on Steinbeck,
   French includes Cup of Gold in a chapter called "Steinbeck
   Visits the Wasteland." He finds William the roadmender,
   Merlin, and Morgan's father suitable subjects for "naturalis-
   tic" fiction, but concentrates his discussion on Henry Morgan
   as a man who "consciously and ruthlessly exploits others to
   achieve personal security."

5. Fontenrose, Joseph. John Steinbeck: An Introduction
   and Interpretation. New York: Holt, Rinehart and
   Winston, 1963, pp. 7-13.
   In Cup of Gold, four intertwined myths--the Grail
   legend, the Faust theme, the Troy theme, and the myth of
   the dying-and-rising-god--and several minor folkloristic
   themes are set in counterpoint against a realistic narrative
   of buccaneering.

6. Gannett, Lewis. "Preface," Cup of Gold. New York:
   Covici/Friede, 1936, pp. v-viii.
   Gannett's preface, a brief biographical sketch and
   review of Steinbeck's publications before 1936, accompanies
   the first reissue of Cup of Gold, perhaps "a sort of key to
   Steinbeck himself."

7. Kingsbury, Stewart A. "Steinbeck's Use of Dialect and
   Archaic Language in Cup of Gold," Steinbeck Newsletter,
   2 (Spring 1969), 28-33.
       Kingsbury examines some of the linguistic features of
   Dafydd, young Henry, Old Robert, Merlin, William, Mother
   Morgan, Gwenliana, and Tim.

8. Levant, Howard. The Novels of John Steinbeck: A
   Critical Study. Columbia: University of Missouri Press,
   1974.
       Levant examines the materials, structure, and techni-
   cal devices through which Steinbeck attempts, unsuccessfully,
   to combine his contradictory conceptions: a study of character and a record of adventure. Cup of Gold is "an unusually
   exciting first novel," an "interesting failure," at times a
   superb panoramic narrative, at times a full realization of
   minute particulars."

9. Lisca, Peter. The Wide World of John Steinbeck. New
   Brunswick: Rutgers University Press, 1958, pp. 21-38.
       Identifying the theme of the novel as Faustian, Lisca
   discusses the symbols, which carry the theme--the cup of
   gold and the name Elizabeth--and the ending as significant
   parallels. He also considers Steinbeck's style and the ideas
   and attitudes introduced in the first novel which play important parts in later work.

10. _____. "Cup of Gold and To a God Unknown: Two
    Early Works of John Steinbeck," Kwartalnik Neofilolog-
    iczny, 22, No. 2 (1975), 173-83.
        In a chapter from his forthcoming book on Steinbeck,
    Lisca calls the life of Henry Morgan Steinbeck's vehicle for
    questioning the values usually found in historical romances of
    piracy, and finds in Cup of Gold most of the techniques and
    themes developed in his later works: sensitivity to language,
    extensive use of myth and legend, the biographical metaphor,
    and the contrasts between dream and reality and between
    escape and commitment as approaches to the relationship of
    the individual to society.

11. Marks, Lester Jay. Thematic Design in the Novels of
    John Steinbeck. The Hague: Mouton, 1969, pp. 27-33.
        Concepts which became thematic patterns in Steinbeck's
    later novels appear in embryonic form in Cup of Gold: a
    leader of men motivated by his dedication to a cause, the
    observing biologist as Steinbeck hero, the metaphor of the
    group animal, and the reverence for life that arises out of
    non-teleological thinking.

12. Moore, Harry Thornton. The Novels of John Steinbeck: A First Critical Study. Chicago: Normandie House, 1939, pp. 11-17.
Moore discusses the source, style, symbols, charac-
ters, theme, and reception of Cup of Gold, concluding that
its crudenesses were signs of promise, its streaks of poor
writing "symptoms of troubled depths and a striving for
poetry and for essential drama." In a subsequent edition
published in 1968, Moore reprints his discussion of Cup of
Gold without change.

13. Watt, F. W. Steinbeck. London: Oliver and Boyd,
1962, pp. 25-28.
After finding the lyric quality of Cup of Gold spurious,
Morgan's compulsions vague, and the final scene surprising,
Watt concludes that form and content fail to mesh in a novel
that is "an anatomising of the motives, methods, and conse-
quences of great ambition and endeavor" rather than a eulogy
of romantic adventure in a pseudo-seventeenth-century world
Steinbeck himself evidently could not take seriously.

Chapter 3

STEINBECK'S BURNING BRIGHT (1950)

by Martha Heasley Cox

I. BACKGROUND

   Steinbeck's third attempt at a play-novella was published as a book by the Viking Press two days after the play
opened at the Broadhurst Theatre on Broadway, Tuesday,
October 18, 1950, following tryouts in New Haven and Boston.
Steinbeck had written Elaine Scott more than a year before,
on October 11, 1949: "Everyman [the first of several titles
for the work] continues to grow in my mind. My Christ!
it's a dramatic thing."[1] On August 30, 1950, the week before the play was to go into rehearsal, he told Webster
Street:

> As a short novel--it has been turned down by every
> magazine in the country. The Book Clubs would
> not touch it. This makes me proud of them and
> of me. This is a highly moral story and they are
> afraid of it. It also gives me reason to believe
> that I am not writing crap. Indeed I think it might
> start a new trend in the theatre--partially going
> back to old and valid thinking and partially some-
> thing entirely new. (SLL, 408)

   New York theatre professionals had far more faith in
the play than did the magazines and book clubs, and a greater array of talent could hardly have been assembled for its
production: Producers, Richard Rodgers and Oscar Hammerstein II; Director, Guthrie McClintic; scenery and lighting,
Jo Mielziner; costumes, Aline Bernstein; cast--Kent Smith,
Barbara Bel Geddes, and Howard Da Silva, Broadway and
Hollywood stars, and Martin Brooks, an acclaimed new
talent. Elaine Anderson [Scott], soon to be the third Mrs.
Steinbeck, appears on the program as "Assistant to Mr.

Steinbeck" and in the book's dedication: "To, for, and because of Elaine. " Her enthusiasm for the stage and experience in casting and stage management with the Theatre Guild
were no doubt largely responsible for Steinbeck's renewal of
interest in the theatre. He wrote to his friends, Jack and
Max Wagner, on September 19: "Elaine is wonderful. She
has been sitting on the book. Hasn't missed a rehearsal and
my god is she good. She knows the theatre like no one I
ever met and loves it. "[2]

     In Boston Steinbeck was still working on the play,
particularly the second act, heartened by its reception there
on opening night. In the audience were Lillian Gish, who
told him not to change a line, and Katharine Cornell, who
said: "If I were 20 or even 10 years younger, you couldn't
keep me out of it" (SLL, 412).

     Despite generally favorable reviews in New Haven and
Boston, the play closed on Broadway after only thirteen performances, a great disappointment and a new experience to
Steinbeck since his first play, Of Mice and Men, had won the
Drama Critics' Circle Best Play Award and his second, more
controversial, The Moon Is Down, had enjoyed a respectable
run. Both plays were named among the ten best of their
respective years in the Burns Mantle collections. Had it not
been for what was then considered an inordinately high over-
head of $18,000 a week on the $60,000 venture, efforts
would have been made to prolong the run of Burning Bright.
When it was closed, Hammerstein said: "We are very proud
to have produced it because it's a play that should have been
done. Few plays of that type are written or presented. "[3]

     Steinbeck, dismayed by the New York reviews, wrote
an article, "in no way a criticism of the critics, " in which
he counted the score: "We had favorable notices from two
critics, a mixed review from one, and the rest gave the
play a series of negatives--from a decisive no through a
contemptuous no to an hysterical and emotional no, no, no. "[4]
To a more disinterested and dispassionate reader, the notices
do not seem so devastating. Though most flaws were found
in the script, particularly with its language and overly symbolic characters, the reviewers usually also found elements
in the production to praise--the powerfully moving last act,
the acting, direction, sets, lighting, and Steinbeck's attempt
to create serious and original drama. Reviewers were, in
fact, often kinder to the play, which has never been published, than to the book, though comments about the two are
so intermingled that they are difficult to distinguish.

Within a month after the play's closing, Steinbeck
could see Burning Bright with more perspective as he wrote
the Wagners:

> It was a good piece of work and a lot of people are
> pretty mad at the critics for destroying it. I have
> thought of this a good deal. Here is a play that I,
> Elaine, Guthrie McClintic, Oscar Hammerstein,
> Dick Rodgers and many others thought was a good
> play. And god knows they are people who know
> their theatre. You would think they would know.
> It is very easy to blame the critics. They were
> not at fault. It was not a good play. It was a
> hell of a good piece of writing but it lacked the
> curious thing no one has ever defined which makes
> a play quite different from anything else in the
> world. I don't know what that quality is but I
> know when I hear it on stage. I guess we have to
> go back to the cliché "magic of the theatre." This
> thing read wonderfully but it just did not play.
> You can't learn that. (SLL, 413-14)

In a foreword Steinbeck had written for the book, he
was more sanguine. He described the play-novelette as "a
play that is easy to read or a short novel that can be played
simply by lifting out the dialogue," and explained that he
used the form both to simplify the reading of the play and to
augment the author's meaning for actor, director, and pro-
ducer, as well as reader. He listed the difficulties of the
technique: the character's thoughts can be exposed clearly
only in the dialogue; the writer must make geographical
wanderings convincing on stage; the action must be "close-
built" and something must happen to the characters; and the
piece must be short. Its rewards include clear and concise
writing with "no waste, no long discussion, no departure
from a main theme, and little exposition"; its action must
be immediate and dynamic and "dramatic resolution must
occur entirely through the characters themselves."[5]

II. PLOT SYNOPSIS

Act I

The scene opens in the dressing tent of a circus,
where Mordeen, Joe Saul, and Victor are trapeze artists
and Friend Ed a clown. Joe Saul and Friend Ed are middle-

aged, around fifty, Mordeen and Victor much younger. With
the sounds of the calliope and merry-go-round in the background, necessary exposition is supplied in the initial dialogue between Joe Saul and Friend Ed: Joe Saul has been
married to Mordeen for three years, since shortly after the
death of his first wife; Victor has been his partner for eight
months, after Cousin Will Saul was killed when he missed
the net; though Joe, Ed, and Mordeen were circus born and
bred, scions of two ancient families of clowns and acrobats,
Victor is an outsider whose blood is not their blood; Joe is
nervous and depressed because he is failing his sacred trust
to reproduce, the charge of his grandfather to continue the
blood line; Friend Ed is the father of twins. Friend Ed
leaves and Mordeen, fair and beautiful, returns from an
errand. In a tender love scene with Joe Saul, she questions
him about his obvious unhappiness, though she already knows
the reason for it. Victor, young and strong, comes to the
tent to tell Joe Saul that he has sprained his wrist playing
touch football and can't perform their act. After Joe Saul
accuses him of lack of professionalism, Victor tauntingly
inquires if Joe Saul's young wife is too much for him. Joe
Saul strikes him in the face and leaves the dressing tent.
Alone, Victor and Mordeen discuss Joe Saul and her love
for him. Victor grabs and kisses her as Friend Ed re-
enters and orders Victor to leave before Joe Saul kills him.
Mordeen confides in Friend Ed, telling him that she knows
she is fertile, for she has had a child, now dead, that Joe
Saul once had rheumatic fever and may therefore be sterile,
and that she will do anything to give Joe Saul contentment.
Friend Ed warns her that knowledge of his sterility would
bring such self-contempt that should Joe Saul find out, she
would never again be able to reach him in his misery.
Friend Ed refuses to condone her plan to conceive a child
by another man, but agrees to look for Joe Saul and stay
with him that evening. When Victor returns to "square
things off," Mordeen apologizes for her earlier conduct and
asks for his help and understanding. After ascertaining that
he comes from a family free from all diseases except old
age, she arranges to meet him in town in an hour. After
they leave, Joe Saul enters drunk and Friend Ed returns to
take up his vigil.

Act II

In a comfortable farm kitchen, a little radio plays a
circus band recessional as Joe Saul, farmer, talks with his
neighbor, Friend Ed. We learn that Victor, a town boy and

rather unsatisfactory hired hand, no longer seems to hold a
grudge against Joe Saul for having struck him in the face
after an argument. Mordeen enters the kitchen and announces
her pregnancy. Joe Saul, overcome with emotion, walks to
the window and calls, as if to the land, "Now it's all right. "
Friend Ed suggests a party to celebrate as Joe Saul bids his
"blackness, " his desolation, farewell. When Victor comes in
for his mid-morning coffee, he hears the news and watches
Joe Saul clumsily prance about the kitchen dancing in his joy.
They drink to the child and to the mother, then Victor proposes a toast to the father. Joe Saul and Friend Ed go to
town for party supplies to celebrate and a present for Mordeen, asking Victor to care for her until they return. Victor, feeling exploited, tells Mordeen of his loneliness and
love for her. Though she pities him, she advises him to go
away. The year slips past in changing seasonal imagery as
they talk, and June becomes December; when Friend Ed and
Joe Saul return they bring a Christmas tree. The child's
birth is imminent and Victor leaves, suitcase in hand, in
frustration and despair. Joe Saul announces that he had decided to give his unborn son a present, a "gift of clean
blood, " and that he will get a thorough examination--then
hang the medical papers, tied with a red ribbon, on the
Christmas tree for his child--his father's first and best
gift--"strength and health and cleanliness. "

                Act III, Scene I: The Sea

        The sounds of the harbor and the city behind it can be
heard in the tiny cabin of an old freighter when Victor,
dressed in a blue mate's uniform and cap, enters and looks
at a Christmas tree on the mantle. Mordeen, offstage, calls
Joe Saul who, Victor tells her, has gone ashore, leaving him
to look after her. Victor pleads with Mordeen to leave with
him, since his attempt to run away and forsake her and his
child has failed. When she refuses, he threatens to tell Joe
Saul everything. Mordeen pleads for time, then tells Victor
that she will try to make him a part of the family, too, if
he remains. Friend Ed stands in the doorway in his blue
captain's uniform, concealed in the half-darkness. When
Victor, still insisting that Mordeen leave with him, goes for
her suitcase which is already packed for the hospital, she
draws a knife from a sheath, a relic hanging on the cabin
wall, and conceals it in her coat. Friend Ed takes Victor
on deck to deliver a secret message and Mordeen hears "the
crunching blow, the expelled moaning cry, and in a moment
the little splash. " As Friend Ed re-enters, Mordeen's labor

pains begin. Joe Saul appears, enraged, and reports that
he has learned he has a bad heart. Friend Ed tells him
that he is lying and must now face the truth--his sterility,
his pride, and Mordeen's great love--and that he hopes Joe
Saul has the goodness and generosity to receive her gift.
After Friend Ed leaves, Mordeen collapses in labor and Joe
Saul shouts for Victor's help.

Act III, Scene II: The Child

In a quiet hospital room, Mordeen lies in bed masked
with gauze, the child a muffled bundle beside her. Joe Saul
enters wearing a cap, long white tunic, and surgical mask
which conceals his face. He tells Mordeen that he has been
into hell and back again; that he now knows that his particular seed has no importance over other seed; that the species,
not the individual line, must go on; "that every man is father
to all children and every child must have all men as father."
When Mordeen asks him to turn up the light, he tears the
mask from his shining eyes and face, raises his head and
cries in triumph: "Mordeen, I love my son."

III. CRITICAL EXPLICATION

A consideration of the components--the structure,
characters, theme, and style--of this play told in story form
will show Steinbeck's attempts to conform to the exigencies
of both the stage and the novel, and the reasons, perhaps,
for his failure to do either satisfactorily. Some attention to
the play's production may also help to explain the critics'
reaction and Steinbeck's subsequent apologia.

More play than novel, the book is divided into acts
and scenes instead of chapters. Steinbeck provides not only
dialogue, but copious hints for set designs, lighting, and sound
plots, properties, stage business, and costuming. Mielziner
set the production against a full stage cyclorama of gray un-
bleached muslin and blue velour portal, drop, and masking
wings. He cut out the portal to indicate the scalloped fringe
of a circus dressing tent and furnished the tent with the ward-
robe trunk, pinned-up photographs, and make-up tray Steinbeck describes in the first act; the farm kitchen with its
square table, chairs, stove, cot, radio, clock, and coffee
pot of Steinbeck's second act; the freighter cabin with its
desk, mess table, chairs, Christmas tree, and wall-hung
trophies; and the hospital room with its high white hospital

bed for the two scenes in his final act. [6] Reviewers uniformly praised the sets and Steinbeck said "they would break
your heart they were so wonderful." [7] Both sound and costume plots were also closely patterned after descriptions in
the novella.

      Steinbeck did, however, make some changes as the
play went into production. He approved a new title, Burning
Bright, at the producers' suggestion, writing his editor Pat
Covici that they considered "In the Forests of the Night" too
long for a play title and a "touch literary," and added that
he hoped the book's title could still be changed also even
though it was then in page proof (SLL, 405). Another major
change occurred during rehearsals and try-outs: Joe Saul
sought his "bill of clean health" gift to the unborn child at
Victor's suggestion instead of thinking of the "present" himself. That attempt to tighten structure and motivate action
rendered Victor more villainous, Joe Saul more victim.
With less initiative and concern for his child, Joe Saul is
also less heroic.

      The time, unstated in the novel, is "Anytime" on the
playbill, lending further emphasis to the "everyman-anyman"
theme of the morality play. The duration of the play would
seem to be nine months, to coincide with the conception-
birth theme. Such a division poses no problem in the first
act when conception occurs, nor in the last act when the
child is born; but in the second act, beginning, presumably,
two months after the first, the time element causes some
confusion. The act begins in June and ends in December,
and the passage of time is revealed in an expressionistic
scene between Mordeen and Victor. Their uninterrupted conversation covers a seven-month span, creating it would seem,
almost insuperable difficulties for the pregnant actress, as
the year changes and rolls on, the thunder crashes, the baby
develops, and "the endless business of the aging earth" continues. Victor talks of the summer ending "with the stubble
on the ground and the hay brushing the ridge pole in the barn
and windfall apples on the orchard earth"; of the "fall chilling
down" with the hoar frost, yellow grasses, tattering cotton
woods, black birds, wild ducks, and burning sumac; of the
white drifts and silver ice and black branches of the pear
trees and the ice-air and blue fingernails and the acid cider.
Then it's Christmas time and Mordeen's "year of bearing is
nearly over" (86-90), as Joe Saul and Friend Ed return with
a fine fir-tree nearly large enough to fill the room.

Though the characters change professions to indicate
the universality of the people and the experience, Steinbeck
carefully integrates the action by confining the cast to the
same four characters, who retain their names; appearances,
except for clothing changes; and relationships to one another
as the story line progresses. He also provides threads of
continuity, little reminders, like the circus band's wild recessional on the radio in the farm kitchen as the circus fades
from our memory, or our recollection of the fir tree from
the forest, too tall for the farm house, when it is replaced
by the "small artificial Christmas tree decorated with tinsel
and silver and red glass balls" in the tiny freighter cabin.
The music and the tree appear, respectively, in the initial
scenes of the second and third acts, as we change place and
time. Steinbeck reorients his readers, sets the stage, describes what we see and hear, and what the characters do,
in a somewhat lengthier form and fashion than that ordinarily
employed by dramatists, who usually telescope and italicize
descriptions for the set designers and sound engineers and
parenthesize stage directions for the actors.

The characters in Burning Bright are symbolic figures,
ideas about persons, rather than individualized people located
in place and time. Both the parabolic structure and the
strictures of stage time prevent the detailed development of
the individualized characters Steinbeck could and did create
in other fiction. Though aided by uniformly excellent performances by the actors, play reviewers were not sure of
the characters' symbolic meaning. One critic suggested that
the three men might be interpreted as "the ego, carnal, and
conscience facets of man's personality."[8] Another sees the
characters as "legendary archetypes of folklore," husband,
wife, friend, and outsider.[9] Reviewers of both play and
book were puzzled by Steinbeck's choice of professions.
Maxwell Geismar took a "quick guess" that "the shifts in
scene from air to land to sea involves the three main areas
of human or animal existence in the evolutionary process."[10]
Steinbeck's explanation was much simpler: "In an attempt to
indicate a universality of experience I placed the story in the
hands of three professions which have long and continuing
traditions, namely the Circus, the Farm, and the Sea."[11]

Joe Saul, Lawrencean in his obsession with the "blood,"
is related, in his overriding concern for his life line, to
Richard Whiteside in The Pastures of Heaven and, in his love
of the land, to Joseph Wayne in To a God Unknown. Joseph
Fontenrose sees Joe Saul as both the biblical Joseph and King

Saul, with Victor as David. [12] Steinbeck depicts Joe Saul as
everyman in his various guises and, at the end, disguises
him as a masked and faceless figure, identified at first only
as "he," who perhaps transcends any man. Mordeen, still
drugged with ether, thinks that both he and the child are
dead. He reassures her: "I didn't go away, or if I did, I
came back. I'm here" (128). In his walk into the shadows
he has learned that "every man is father to all children and
every child must have all men as father" (130). This particular child, he tells her, however, is "the Child." When
Mordeen says: "Let me have light. I cannot see your face,"
he replies: "Light. You want light? I will give you light,"
and tears the mask from his shining eyes and shining face.
His final words are "I love my son" (130).

Mordeen, the mother of the Child, born at Christmas,
must in that scene then be Mary, but she is also, as others
have noted, an earth mother, whose radiating love affects her
husband, who is saved by her gift; Friend Ed, who cares
enough to commit murder for her; and even Victor, who is
somewhat elevated from his original brutishness by his love
for her and for the child she refuses to acknowledge as his.

Friend Ed is the confidant, caretaker, and counselor,
who shares their troubles and triumphs, who comforts and
protects, but also strikes out with contempt when necessary.
Friend Ed was perhaps named for Steinbeck's friend Ed
Ricketts, who was killed in a train crash less than a year
before Steinbeck began his play-novelette. Steinbeck was
writing his essay "About Ed Ricketts" while working on
Burning Bright.

Victor is the outsider, who without the proper "blood"
turns a proud profession into a craft. Insensitive and crude,
he can taunt his worried partner about age and sex; brutish,
he can make unwelcome advances to his partner's young
wife; naive, he can be exploited without suspecting the reason.
Yet he learns the difference between lust and love and what
loneliness is. His love, however, is not sufficiently enno-
bling to enable him to act unselfishly; so in the end he must
be eliminated quickly and quietly, and at some cost to the
play's theme. If "every man is father to all children and
every child must have all men as father" (130), Victor and
his son seem rather obvious and ironic exceptions.

Steinbeck gains tension with his use of dramatic irony
throughout the play as the reader and the other characters

know what Joe Saul does not: the identity of the child's
biological father; but the irony in the final scene, when Victor's demise is necessary to prevent his acting as father to
his own son, vitiates the book's theme and could hardly be
intentional.

Conflicts, both symbolic and real, are waged between
youth and age, life and death, immortality and extinction,
all thematic substructures. The dead sperm of sterility are
the only true destroyers, for age and death are meaningless
and man becomes immortal, everlastingly renewed through
his progeny--or through another's. Joe Saul learns, as did
Ma Joad, that "it is the race, the species that must go
staggering on" (129); sterility does not matter then if the
race survives.

The story's imagery, primarily sexual in Act I, becomes biological and obstetrical in Acts II and III, as the
play progresses from conception through gestation to birth.
In Act I, Joe Saul tells Mordeen that he loves her "starving-
ly" and is never satisfied (23); Mordeen says to Victor: "I
know the tricks, techniques of duration, of position, games,
perverse games to drive the nerves into a kind of hysterical
laughter" (37). As Victor waits in anticipation, she continues:

> Joe Saul knows one trick, one ingredient. You
> haven't heard about it. Maybe you never will.
> Without that trick you'll one day go screaming
> silently in loss. Without it there are no good
> methods or techniques. You know I've wondered
> how it is that one act can be so ugly and mean
> and enervating, like a punishing drug, and also
> most beautiful and filled with energy, like milk.
> (37)

That ingredient, which--Mordeen explains--few people ever
learn, is affection.

In Act II, Mordeen sits in the farm kitchen, holding
her hands in her lap, one palm in another "like a nest" (70)
as she tells Joe Saul that she is pregnant. She smiles in-
wardly, her face withdrawn in mystery, in a state which
must have been difficult at best to transfer to the stage:

> The secrets of her body were in her eyes--the
> zygote new thing in the world, a new world but

formed of remembered materials: the blastoderm,
the wildly splitting cells, and folds and nodes, the
semblance of a thing, projections to be arms and
legs and vague rays of ganglia, gill slits on the
forming head, projections to be fingers and two
capacities from which to see one day, and then a
little man, whole formed, no bigger than a stub of
a pencil bathed in warm liquor, drawing food from
the mother bank and growing. This frantic being-
ness lay under her loving hands embraced in a
slow ecstasy in her lap. (71)

In Act III, Mordeen struggles and writhes on the floor
as she screams hoarsely in labor (124). In the final scene
the child is born, and Joe Saul, having gone through his own
travail and darkness, has overcome ego and pride in his
blood line, "the long knowledge remembered, repeated," and
through love has thrown off the "icy clothes" of loneliness.
He can now affirm the species and its survival: "The spark
continues--a new human--only being of its kind anywhere--
that has struggled without strength when every force of tooth
and claw, of storm and cold, of lightning and germ was
against it--struggled and survived, survived even the self-
murdering instinct" (129).

That speech, and the preceding one in which Joe Saul
says that our "ugly little species, weak and ugly, torn with
insanities, violent and quarrelsome" will stagger on, is very
much like sections in a book published the following year:
another book containing a play within a novel, William Faulkner's Requiem for a Nun.

Steinbeck explained that he attempted to write in
Burning Bright "a kind of universal language not geared to
the individual actors or their supposed crafts" but rather
the best he could produce:

> While I had eminent authority for this method from
> Aeschylus down through O'Neill, it was still prob-
> lematical whether audiences used to the modern
> realistic theatre would accept such expression.
> This language did not intend to sound like ordinary
> speech, but rather by rhythm, sound, and image to
> give the clearest and best expression of what I
> wanted to say. The attempt was to lift the story
> to the parable expression of the morality plays.
> It is a method not without its great exponents. The

test is whether it can be found acceptable in a modern book or play or whether an archaicness in its sound cuts it off.   A number of critics both of book and play have become so enraged by the method that they have not looked beyond it at the subject matter. [13]

Few critics of book or play found the attempt success-ful, though the reader generally found it less objectionable than the theater-goer.   Compounds such as "wife-loss," "friend-right," and "laughter-starving"; the avoidance of all contradictions; the slot-slipping of words from their usual syntactical context in such expressions as "Oh, very yes"; and the undeviating use of both Joe Saul's first and last names and of Ed's appellation "Friend" make the dialogue seem artificial and stylized and sometimes embarrassingly sentimental.   Only occasionally does it approach the lyrical essence Steinbeck sought.   One reviewer, particularly bothered by the hyphenated couplings, inquires: "Have I, I wonder, the admirer-right to tell Mr. Steinbeck that this trick has set me screaming silently in my reader-loss?"[14]

Though Steinbeck thought his theme of sterility was heretofore unexamined in literature, "perhaps too terrible and secret a thing" to be discussed, [15] George Jean Nathan notes that it was "embarrassingly pointed out to him that not only did Lorca employ the idea in his play, Yerma, but that Elinor Glyn, of all people, also used it in her long ago fiction gem, Three Weeks."[16]   Steinbeck's book and play seem closer in most aspects, however, to the drama of Eugene O'Neill.   Numerous parallels exist between the characters and scenes in Burning Bright and both Strange Interlude and Desire Under the Elms.   In the former a young wife has a child by another man because of a strain of insanity in her husband's family; in the latter a young wife bears the child of her elderly husband's son.   Numer-ous parallels also exist in subject matter and technique be-tween Burning Bright and Thornton Wilder's The Skin of Our Teeth.

Despite such comparisons, however, Steinbeck's play in story form is more original than derivative, a courageous attempt to examine a serious subject through a combination of old and new techniques.   Not even in print now, it is generally regarded as an honorable failure.   A study of its structure, theme, characters, and language is instructive, however, particularly in view of Steinbeck's explanation,

written after the play's quick demise, of what he wanted to
do and how he went about doing it.

NOTES

1. Elaine Steinbeck and Robert Wallsten, eds., Steinbeck:
    A Life in Letters (New York: Viking Press, 1975),
    p. 381. Subsequent references to this work are
    identified as SLL and incorporated in the text.

2. Steinbeck's letters to the Wagners are in the Bender
    Room of the Stanford University Library.

3. Sam Zolotow, "Burning Bright Quits Tomorrow," New
    York Times, October 27, 1950, p. 24.

4. John Steinbeck, "Critics, Critics Burning Bright,"
    Saturday Review, 33 (Nov. 11, 1950), 21.

5. John Steinbeck, "Foreword," Burning Bright (New York:
    Bantam, 1962), p. 1. Future references to Burning
    Bright are identified with the page number.

6. The scenery and property plot, costume plot, and sound
    plot are in the typescript of the play entitled "In the
    Forests of the Night" in the Lincoln Center Library
    and Museum of the Performing Arts of the New York
    Public Library.

7. Nov. 28, 1950, letter to the Wagners.

8. Michael S. Willis, "Burning Bright--A Powerful
    Drama," San Francisco Chronicle, Feb. 6, 1963.

9. Alice S. Morris, "Inheritance for a Child," New York
    Times Book Review, Oct. 22, 1950, p. 4.

10. "Cosmic Mother and the Gift of Life," Saturday Review,
    33 (Oct. 21, 1950), 14.

11. "Critics, Critics Burning Bright," p. 20.

12. Joseph Fontenrose, John Steinbeck: An Introduction
    and Interpretation (New York: Holt, Rinehart, and
    Winston, 1963), p. 116.

13. "Critics, Critics Burning Bright," p. 20.

14. L. A. G. Strong, "Fiction [A Review of Burning Bright]," Spectator, 6611 (Aug. 10, 1951), 196.

15. "Critics, Critics Burning Bright," p. 20.

16. "Burning Bright," [A Review of Burning Bright], The Theatre Book of the Year (New York: Alfred A. Knopf, 1951), p. 70.

IV. APPARATUS FOR RESEARCH PAPERS

A. Ten Questions for Discussion

1. How does Steinbeck's triangle differ from that usually portrayed in film, fiction, and the theater?
2. The sea and the sailor, and the earth and the farmer seem obvious choices for professions and settings for Steinbeck's Everyman--or representative of all men. Why? Can you think of reasons why he may have included the circus? What connotations does it have? What might it represent?
3. Is Victor a villain? Why or why not? Does he develop in the play? If so, how?
4. Discuss the role of Friend Ed. Is he essential to the novel? To the play? If so, why? How would the demands of the stage make him more important to the latter than the former?
5. Steinbeck makes Mordeen pure, never prurient. How?
6. Joe Saul is, by design, universal and historical man. Through what devices does Steinbeck attempt to make him so? How successfully?
7. Two of the great commandments are shattered when the characters commit adultery and murder. The book also contains quarrels, blows, an illegitimate child. Do you consider it, then, a violent or sensational novel? If not, why not?
8. Discuss Steinbeck's depiction of love, friendship, and paternity as they develop in Burning Bright.
9. "The Theme of Burning Bright is a shocking, even sensational one," according to the publicity blurb printed inside the Bantam edition. What is the theme? Or themes?
10. A number of critics feel that Victor's murder vitiates the theme of brotherhood and universal fatherhood. Do you? Why or why not? What were the alternatives?

B. Suggested Topics for Research Papers

1. Compare Burning Bright with Eugene O'Neill's Desire
    Under the Elms. How does Mordeen's motivation to have
    a child differ from Abbie's? Consider the attitude of
    each young woman toward both her husband and the father
    of her child. Compare and contrast the husbands and
    the lovers.

2. Compare Burning Bright with another Steinbeck story or
    novel: the Whiteside saga, chapter eleven of The Pas-
    tures of Heaven; To a God Unknown; or East of Eden.

3. The title Burning Bright is taken from William Blake's
    poem "The Tyger," which begins: "Tyger! Tyger!
    burning bright / In the forests of the night," and was
    printed in the play program. One reviewer said: "I
    have not yet worked out its connection with the play."
    Study Blake's poem and see if you can. Note particu-
    larly Steinbeck's use of burning, brightness, night and
    darkness. Can you find other echoes from the poem in
    the novella? A thematic correspondence between the
    two?

4. Read the account of Saul in the Old Testament (1 Samuel
    9-15), then discuss possible parallels between the bibli-
    cal account and Steinbeck's book. Note particularly
    parallels between Joe Saul and King Saul, and between
    David and Victor.

5. Steinbeck wrote that he made his characters speak in a
    universal language. Most critics, however, found the
    dialogue stilted, artificial, and highly stylized, unlike
    anything spoken any time, anywhere. Analyze some of
    the dialect and discuss its linguistic features. Note
    choice of diction--archaisms, coinages, compounds--
    sentence patterns and rhythms, and idiosyncrasies. Do
    you find it successful? Give the reasons for your opin-
    ion.

6. Discuss Steinbeck's use of dramatic irony in Burning
    Bright.

7. Examine Steinbeck's handling of time in Burning Bright,
    both between and within the acts.

8. Trace the bright and dark imagery throughout the book.

9. Discuss Steinbeck's use of parallelism throughout the
    book: Consider settings, sounds, characters, scenes
    and ideas.

10. Read Lorca's Yerma and compare it with Burning Bright.

11. Discuss Burning Bright in the light of Steinbeck's fore-
    word: Does he fulfill all of the qualifications he lists
    for a piece of dramatic literature? If not, where, and

how does he fail? Where does he succeed? How?
12. Write a review of <u>Burning Bright</u>. You may wish to
consult the reviews of professionals before--or after--
writing your own.

C. Selected Bibliography

1. Ditsky, John M. "Steinbeck's <u>Burning Bright</u>: Homage
to Astarte." <u>Steinbeck Quarterly</u>, 7 (Summer-Fall 1974),
79-84.
     Ditsky considers evolution of the human family the
main theme of <u>Burning Bright</u> and says that all four characters progress upward. He finds a deeper set of meanings,
however, in the character of Mordeen: as Astarte-Ishtar,
lover and destroyer, she becomes "the Great Mother who
exploits sacrificed youth so that mankind may progress, and
so that the seasons may resume their course."

2. Fontenrose, Joseph. <u>John Steinbeck: An Introduction</u>
<u>and Interpretation</u>. New York: Holt, Rinehart and
Winston, 1963, pp. 115-17.
     Fontenrose sees Joe Saul as both the biblical Joseph
and Saul, and Victor as David in an unsound parable in which
the characters' speeches are sentimental and unreal.

3. French, Warren. <u>John Steinbeck</u>. New Haven: College
and University Press, 1961, pp. 148-52.
     French calls <u>Burning Bright</u> "pure allegory that is
artistically negligible, but important to an understanding of
the author's ideas" and finds counterparts for each of the
four characters in Steinbeck's other works.

4. _____. <u>John Steinbeck</u>. 2nd ed. rev. Boston:
Twayne, 1975, pp. 138-40.
     Remembered today only for its relationships to Stein-
beck's efforts to create a convincing drama of consciousness,
<u>Burning Bright</u>, with its unimpressive and confusing gimmicks,
was unrelieved moralizing, hardly a stimulating theater experience.

5. Levant, Howard. <u>The Novels of John Steinbeck: A</u>
<u>Critical Study</u>. Columbia: University of Missouri Press,
1974, pp. 158-63.
     Levant argues that <u>Burning Bright</u> "is the exemplifica-
tion of a structural crisis, a concentration of external form
imposed on materials for its own sake, which distorts them

in the process of manipulation or the denial of all other
novelistic considerations. "

6. Lisca, Peter. The Wide World of John Steinbeck. New
   Brunswick: Rutgers University Press, 1958, pp. 248-60.
   After a brief discussion of the play's critical reception and Steinbeck's reaction to that reception, Lisca comments on deficiencies in theme, structure, and language as
   reasons for the failure of the play-novelette, concluding,
   however, that Burning Bright, while not aesthetically significant, is interesting because it reveals in positive terms
   Steinbeck's "mystic conception of the unity of life in the group
   animal. "

7. Steinbeck, John. "Author's Foreword, " in Burning
   Bright: A Play in Story Form. New York: Bantam,
   1962, pp. 1-3.
   Steinbeck describes the play-novelette form, explains
   why he chooses to use it, and discusses its difficulties and
   advantages.

8. _____. "Critics, Critics Burning Bright, " Saturday
   Review, 33 (Nov. 11, 1950), 20-21.
   The author discusses the hazards of Burning Bright--
   its subject, sterility; its method, shifts in background; and
   its language, an "attempt at the parable expression of the
   morality plays"--and the reaction of audiences and critics
   to its production.

Chapter 4

STEINBECK'S EAST OF EDEN (1952)

by Richard F. Peterson

I. BACKGROUND

As early as November, 1947, John Steinbeck was writing to his friends about a projected long novel. The setting for the novel, tentatively entitled The Salinas Valley, was "to be the region between San Luis Obispo and Santa Cruz, particularly the Salinas Valley," the narrative time "between 1900 and the present."[1] He told Pascal Covici that the book would be about "the whole nasty bloody lovely history of the world" (SLL, 304). By 1948, he was telling people that The Salinas Valley was the book he "had been practicing to write" (SLL, 310) all his life. All his other novels were merely training for the one big book.

Unfortunately, at the very moment that John Steinbeck was beginning the greatest literary project of his career, he was staggered by two tragic events in his personal life. In May 1948, Ed Ricketts, Steinbeck's close friend and spiritual adviser for nearly thirty years, was killed in an automobile-train accident. Deprived of the friendship and advice of "the greatest man I have known and the best teacher" (SLL, 312), Steinbeck suffered a second major setback a few months later when his second wife, Gwyndolyn Steinbeck, asked for a divorce. While trying to recover from losing both his closest friend and his family, Steinbeck found it impossible to start on his new book: "I have not worked on The Salinas Valley. I don't want to now until everything is clear because I think I am about ready for it and I'm letting it stew. It would be bad if the whole conception turned out no good. But I'll do it anyway. I am really looking forward to the doing of it, good or bad" (SLL, 334).

The desire to do the book, good or bad, became a

vital part of Steinbeck's struggle to survive his personal
ordeals.   Fearing that his life and talent might "dribble away
like piss in the dust" (SLL, 339), he associated the recovery
of his emotional health with "my big train of a book" (SLL,
343).   To begin the book would mean that the energy to
create had not been destroyed by his terrible losses.   In a
letter to John O'Hara, Steinbeck described his seven months
at Pacific Grove as an effort to reduce his emotional "mael-
strom to tea kettle size" (SLL, 359).   During that time, he
discovered "there are two things I cannot do without.   Crude-
ly stated they are work and women, and more gently--crea-
tive effort in all directions" (SLL, 359).   In the same letter,
Steinbeck also stated in the strongest terms a belief at odds
with his Phalanx or Group Theory: "I think I believe one
thing powerfully--that the only creative thing our species has
is the individual, lonely mind" (SLL, 359).   Though he did
not specifically tie this belief to his planned book, Steinbeck
followed his brief discussion of the uniqueness of the human
mind with a comment on his great project: "I've been practicing for a book for 35 years and this is it" (SLL, 360).

        Steinbeck proved his own best prophet.   Before be-
ginning his book, he found a loving and creative relationship
with Elaine Scott.   They met during a Memorial Day weekend
in 1949.   At the time she was unhappily married to the actor
Zachary Scott and Steinbeck was going through a painful
divorce procedure with Gwyndolyn.   Within a short time, the
relationship grew in intensity and intimacy, so that when the
final break came with her husband in November, Elaine Scott
agreed to marry Steinbeck when both divorces became final.
By August 1950, Steinbeck was writing to friends again about
the "long novel--the one I have been practicing for all of my
life" (SLL, 408).   In a letter to Bo Beskow, he linked his
plans for a December wedding to a commitment "to get a
great piece of my novel done" (SLL, 411) during their first
winter together.

        In one sense, Steinbeck began his novel on January
29, 1951.   Though he did not write his first line until
February 15, he started his work by writing two long letters
in a notebook to his editor and good friend, Pascal Covici.
In his first letter, dated January 29, he wrote about his
original plan, what he thought would be two books in one--
"the story of my country and the story of me."[2]   His intention was to address the book to his two sons, to "tell them
one of the greatest, perhaps the greatest, story of all--the
story of good and evil, of strength and weakness, of love and

hate, of beauty and ugliness" (JN, 4). He repeated what he
had been saying to his friends since 1947, that this book
would be his greatest challenge. Not only did he feel that
it was to be the most difficult of all he had ever attempted;
he viewed the book as both a personal and epic project: "I
think perhaps it is the only book I have ever written. I
think there is only one book to a man. It is true that a man
may change or be so warped that he becomes another man
and has another book but I do not think that is so with me"
(JN, 5).

In his second letter to Covici, dated February 12,
Steinbeck formally announced the beginning of his book.
Rather than actually starting, however, he wrote about his
physical and emotional condition and his basic strategy for
the novel. His description of his condition reads like a
blend of Catholic's confession and fighter's boast. While
admitting that, two weeks before becoming 49, he was short
of breath, overweight, and "drinking too much" (JN, 5),
Steinbeck claimed that he felt young, strong, and elastic.
His sexual drive, which he equated with his creativity, was
"stronger than ever" because "it is all in one direction now
and not scattered" (JN, 5). His thinking, while suffering
occasionally from confusion and lack of concentration, was
still active and flexible. His strategy for the actual writing
was "to keep a double-entry book--manuscript on the right-
hand page and work diary on the left" (JN, 5). Thus each
day, before starting on his manuscript, he would write an
entry, in the form of a letter to Covici, in his work diary.
While the manuscript would proceed at a pace of about two
pages a day on the right-hand side of the 10 3/4" x 14"
notebook given to him by Covici, the work diary would give
him a chance to loosen up like a baseball pitcher before
entering the big game.

The diary entries, published in 1969, after Steinbeck's
death, as Journal of a Novel: The "East of Eden" Letters,
cover the full range of Steinbeck's experiences during the
writing of the novel. His early letters are about the design
of the book, still called The Salinas Valley and addressed to
his sons, Tom and John. They also reveal his personal
hopes, frustrations, and disappointments as he set his early
schedule and established his writing patterns. His first
chapter, after addressing itself to his sons, was to establish
the physical background of the book with a detailed description of the Salinas Valley. It would, then, introduce his
grandfather's family, the Hamiltons, and their neighbors, the

Trasks. The second chapter would begin the actual plot with
the story of the Trasks. His original plan, to alternate the
chapters between the Hamiltons and the Trasks, had been
abandoned, but he still hoped to continue his letter to the
boys in every other chapter: "Such readers as only like
plot and dialogue can then skip every other chapter and meanwhile I can take time for thought, comment, observation,
criticism, and if it should seem a good thing to throw it out,
I can do that too" (JN, 7).

    Steinbeck's feeling that "a great deal" of his continuing
letter to his sons "may be thrown out" proved entirely accurate. As a matter of fact, the entire concept of the letter
to his sons was removed from the first draft after it was
completed. Meanwhile, Steinbeck, after a few false starts,
plunged ahead with his book about "a universal family living
next to a universal neighbor," a book so large and important
he would "write this one as though it were my last ..." (JN,
8). Though a great deal of Steinbeck's diary entries have to
do with his writing eccentricities, his new life with Elaine
Steinbeck, and his worries about his sons, the letters occasionally yield some insight into the novel and Steinbeck's
general attitude toward writing. His style for the book, for
example, like the style in all his works, was to be as simple and warm as possible. This way he could establish the
familiar tone and manner as a way of overcoming the differences between individuals, of meeting his readers on a common ground. Thus, in a few statements, he set down the
key to his success with so many readers. No matter what
his views, Steinbeck's style constantly stresses the human
experience, uniting narrative view and reader sympathy in a
common cause, the revelation of the simple desires, failures,
and triumphs of the human spirit.

    Once Steinbeck turned to the story of the Trasks, he
began to stress their "symbol meanings" and a buried key
and "many leads" (JN, 16) to the meaning of the symbols.
He now saw the book more as a history rather than a novel:
"And while its form is very tight, it is my intention to make
it seem to have the formlessness of history" (JN, 17). This
"formless" form would reveal itself in the symbolic patterns
of the book, and these patterns would give the book its special identity. The book, then, that Steinbeck had been practicing to write all his life would have the pace of "an old-
fashioned novel," achieving "any effect it has by accumulation
rather than by quick and flashing periods" (JN, 20).

As he progressed through the early chapters, Steinbeck noted that his own voice would be more apparent in this
book than in any other because he wanted it to contain everything he remembered and knew to be true. Rather than hide
his voice for the sake of literary technique or personal
squeamishness about appearing in his own book, he would be
in this one and not "for a moment pretend not to be" (JN,
24). For the first time he wrote openly about his symbolic
key, the relationship between the Trask narrative and the
story of Cain and Abel, wondering whether the reader would
generally understand the purpose of the parallels. The work
diary also correctly anticipates that the book "is going to
catch the same kind of hell that all the others did and for
the same reasons. It will not be what anyone expects and
so the expectors will not like it" (JN, 26). With the unerr-
ing vision of a man who knows his enemy, Steinbeck felt the
Hamilton sections in particular would be attacked as slipshod
because "the Trask chapters flow along in chronological story
while the Hamilton chapters which play counterpoint are put
together with millions of little pieces, matched and discarded"
(JN, 31). Expecting the criticism that the Hamiltons have
no place in the book "because they do not contribute directly
nor often to the Trask development," Steinbeck argued that
"this is not a story about the Trasks but about the whole
Valley which I am using as a microcosm of the whole nation.
It is not a romanza. I know I will have that war to fight"
(JN, 65).

After completing his first major part of the novel and
introducing Cathy and Lee, two of his most controversial
characters, Steinbeck still puzzled over the book's title. He
liked My Valley because it was "a wonderful-looking title"
(JN, 82) and had warmth and simplicity. A few days later,
however, he rejected the title because it was too close to
How Green Was My Valley (he seemed oblivious to the fact
that he had already used The Long Valley as a title) and because Pascal Covici apparently disapproved of it. Frustrated,
he suggested Valley to the Sea as a possible title, but at
this point he claimed he did not "give a damn what it is
called" (JN, 86). All statements to the contrary, the title
of the book still bothered him. Several days later, he finally closed in on something suitable. He realized that the book
should have a general rather than a specific title because
rather than being solely about the Salinas Valley or its local
history and people, its "framework roots" were from the
story of Cain and Abel in Genesis: "Now since this is indeed
my frame--is there any reason to conceal it from my reader?

Would it not be better to let him know even in the title what
the story is about?" (JN, 90).

    Steinbeck's re-reading of the story of Cain and Abel
inspired Cain Sign as the new title for the book.   Three
weeks later, however, while working on the critical discussion in Chapter 22 of the story of Cain and Abel, he knew
he had found the perfect title: "And I think I have a title at
last, a beautiful title, EAST OF EDEN.   And read the 16th
verse to find it.   And the Salinas Valley is surely East of
Eden" (JN, 104).   He went on in the entry to discuss the
reason why "this story," more than any other, had tremendous significance for the psychological history of the human
race.   It embodied the basis of all human neurosis "--and
if you take the fall along with it, you have the total of the
psychic troubles that can happen to a human" (JN, 104).
Steinbeck wanted the discussion to illuminate the entire book.
Risking the danger of critical disapproval for interrupting
his plot for "a discussion of Biblical lore," he committed
himself to making the discussion the pivotal point for the
entire novel because he was "using the Biblical story as a
measure of ourselves" (JN, 105).

    A few days later, Steinbeck gave some idea of how
the Hamilton parts worked within the structure of the novel.
The story of Tom Hamilton, rather than being a diversion
or a departure from the plot, "bears out the thesis of guilt--
carries it to its logical conclusion so that he must sacrifice
himself" (JN, 106).   This thesis of guilt was becoming more
and more important to Steinbeck as he turned from Adam
Trask to his son, Caleb.   He was particularly concerned
about the meaning of the Hebrew word, timshel, which "has
been variously translated 'do thou,' 'thou shalt' and 'thou
mayest'" (JN, 108).   He preferred "thou mayest" so that he
could stress the concept of free will in the book.   The struggle and choice between good and evil was taking on new directions and complexities.   He attached great importance to
the death of Samuel Hamilton.   His death should not be mistaken as the end of something good in the novel.   Rather
Samuel's spirit should reign throughout the rest of the novel
as "one of those pillars of fire by whom little and frightened
men are guided through the darkness" (JN, 115).   Perhaps
anticipating the criticism of Samuel's death coming in the
middle of the novel, he asked Covici if he could feel the
change in Adam Trask: "I have repeated that good things do
not die.   Did you feel that Samuel had gotten into Adam and
would live in him?   Did you feel the rebirth in him?   Should

I make it clearer or were you aware of it? Men do change,
do learn to grow" (JN, 124).

          As Steinbeck worked on the second half of the novel,
he reaffirmed his faith in East of Eden as The Book. No
creative work had given him as much pleasure and joy. He
repeated that all his other books were preparation for the
one, big novel. He felt that he had spent a lifetime writing
East of Eden, and yet he regretted the fact that he was near-
ing the end of his work. The novel's "formless" form was
developing according to Steinbeck's original strategy: "On an
impulse I just went back and read the opening notes addressed
to you. I wanted to see whether I have failed in any part to
carry out my intention and I do not think I have. The direction has not changed a bit and this book which seems to
sprawl actually does not at all. It is almost as tight as a
short story. And I am pleased about that" (JN, 149).

          Now that Steinbeck's thesis had been clearly stated
and developed, events assumed greater importance and time
moved more quickly. The basic point of view in the novel
now reversed itself. The first part of East of Eden was
seen through the eyes and emotions of Adam. Charles, the
dark principle, remained in the background. In the last
part of the novel, Caleb, the Cain principle, now dominated
events and provided the perspective. To balance this dark
burden placed upon the novel, Steinbeck introduced "the
principle of Abra" (JN, 146). New to the book, this "strong
female principle of good" (JN, 146) would also counter the
monstrous Cathy. With all the pieces finally in place, East
of Eden was ready to move ahead to its conclusion: "We
have a new kind of world in the Salinas Valley and our time-
less principle must face a new set of facts and react to
them. Are you interested to see what happens? I am" (JN,
146).

          As Steinbeck neared the completion of the book, the
possibility of failing or falling short of his goal became a
persistent theme in his work diary. It was still The Book,
but sometimes it seemed to have "the high purpose" set for
it and at other times it seemed "pedestrian and trite" (JN,
157). He now feared that the book had shrunk into a small
thing rather than the large book he had planned. One thing
was certain--he had found in the character of Cal "his baby.
He is the Everyman, the battleground between good and evil,
the most human of all, the sorry man" (SLL, 429). The
novel's climax worried him, too, because it was to be "a

quadruple climax" (JN, 159). At the end of the book "two
lives are lost and two changed ... " (JN, 159). The last
scene in particular was to be "the most violently emotional
scene I have ever attempted and I am frankly afraid of it"
(JN, 164).

In the final weeks of the book, he worried about the
critics' attacks on his work. He was sure that East of Eden
was going to take a beating because it was full of ideas and
speculations. Unfortunately, American critics, Steinbeck
felt, often showed a fear and hatred of ideas in their reviews. Realizing that his job was to finish the book, not to
defend it, he moved into the last week fearing only that the
thunder of the past several months may have produced a
mouse. When he finally wrote his last line, he finished his
hidden correspondence with Covici by writing a "dedication,
prologue, argument, apology, epilogue and perhaps epitaph
all in one" (JN, 179). Though the dedication never appeared
in the book, except in a shorter and more personal form,
it contained Steinbeck's expression of the gladness and terror
of the creative act. He acknowledged the times he "held
fire in my hands" and the times he "never lost the weight
of clumsiness, of ignorance, of aching inability" (JN, 179).
Reluctantly he surrendered his book, his child, to the literary lions waiting to tear it to pieces. Next would come the
reader--"He'll take from my book what he can bring to it.
The dull witted will get dullness and the brilliant may find
things in my book I didn't know were there" (JN, 182).

II. PLOT SYNOPSIS

Steinbeck made two critical changes in his basic plan
for East of Eden, eliminating the concept of the letter to his
sons and the strategy of alternating chapters between the
Hamiltons and the Trasks. The effect was to release the
novel from any obvious and artificial narrative constraints.
What emerges is a sprawling multileveled narrative of three
generations of the Trask family, counterpointed by the appearance of the Hamiltons and enriched by a narrative voice
commenting on the flow of American history from the Civil
War to World War I.

Part One of the novel opens with an evocation of the
Salinas Valley and a description of its earliest settlers,
leading up to the arrival of the Hamiltons and, later, the
Trasks. Once Adam Trask is mentioned as one of the in-

dividuals coming to the Salinas Valley with the money to begin a new life, the actual plot of East of Eden begins.
Framed by the perspective of the historical voice of the narrator and the spiritual goodness of the Hamiltons, the story
of Adam Trask opens with his early years "on a farm on the
outskirts of a little town which was not far from a big town
in Connecticut."[3] Though the narrative, as Steinbeck indicated in his work diary, is controlled by Adam's perspective,
the narrative events of Adam's youth are dominated by his
militant and Satanic father, Cyrus Trask, his dark and sar-
donic brother, Charles, and the most purely evil character
Steinbeck ever invented, Cathy Ames, Adam's eventual wife.
The first part of the novel, then, is an odyssey of a basically decent human being through a world of oppression, violence,
and evil. Surviving his brother's beatings and the military
service imposed upon him by his father, Adam still falls
prey to the evil machinations of Cathy. After the death of
Cyrus Trask, he leaves for California to begin a new life in
the company of the woman he falsely perceives as a symbol
of purity and goodness.

     Part Two of East of Eden opens with a half nostalgic,
half critical evocation of the year 1900. The beginning of
the new century coincides with the great physical change in
Adam Trask's life and his moral and spiritual struggle between good and evil. The forces of goodness actively enter
the novel in the form of Samuel Hamilton, who replaces
Cyrus Trask as the paternal figure, and Lee, the Chinese
servant and sometimes philosophical surrogate for Steinbeck
himself. Once Adam purchases the old Sanchez place, his
personal choice for Eden, Samuel becomes a vital part of
Adam's life, drilling for water, delivering Cathy's twins,
and generally offering Adam the chance to share his cosmic
vision of life. Opposed to Samuel, however, is Cathy, who
warns Adam that she intends to leave "Eden" as soon as she
has the opportunity. Later, after the twins are born, she
shoots Adam in the shoulder when he tries to stop her from
leaving. While Cathy, now Kate, becomes a whore in a
Salinas brothel, Adam, wounded psychically more than
physically by Cathy's evil, withdraws into a gray spiritual
death. Only Samuel has the strength and imagination to stir
Adam back into responsibility. When he learns from Lee
that Adam has not named the twins in the three months since
Cathy's departure, Samuel turns on him, forcing him through
a combination of physical and moral blows to return to life
by accepting his sons. Thus Part Two ends with Adam,
Samuel, and Lee resisting the urge to name Adam's twins

Cain and Abel, even if they find the story itself irresistible,
and giving the boys the names, Caleb and Aron.

        Thematically, Part Three of East of Eden is the most
important section of the novel.   It contains the critical discussions among Adam, Samuel, and Lee about the Cain and
Abel story and the meaning of the word, timshel, which
Lee's four Chinese scholars interpret as "thou mayest."
There are also several critical narrative events in Part
Three, including Adam's confrontation with Kate, Cal and
Aron's first meeting with Abra, and, the most important
event of all, the death of Samuel Hamilton. [4] Samuel's death
actually hovers over the entire section, suggesting that his
departure brings an end to much of the wonder and joy of
the novel.   Steinbeck, however, as he noted in the work
diary, wanted Samuel's spirit to pass on to Adam, thereby
creating a rebirth in him.   This is accomplished in the narrative through Samuel's departing "gift" to Adam, the knowledge that Kate is now the madam of a Salinas brothel.   After
Samuel listens to Lee's story about the scholarly investigation of the meaning of timshel, he decides to give Adam the
choice between spiritual life and death by forcing him to confront the truth about Cathy.   His decision, based on his
faith in the individual human soul to overcome evil, is the
right one, for after Samuel's death, Adam visits the brothel,
resists Kate's advances, and releases his soul for the first
time in his life from the influences of violence and death:
"I'm free, I'm free.   I don't have to worry any more.   I'm
free.   She's gone.   She's out of me.   Oh Christ Almighty,
I'm free!" (EE, 330).

        In Part Four, the narrative events move quickly and
freely compared to the earlier sections of East of Eden.
Eleven years had elapsed between the naming of the twins
(Part Two) and the departure of Samuel Hamilton (Part
Three).   Now the narrative moves rapidly through the period
just before World War I, focusing on Adam Trask's disas-
trous experimentation in refrigeration, and on to the early
war years, with the emphasis on Adam's appointment to the
draft board, Cal's speculation in beans, Adam's rejection of
the profits, and, finally, Kate's suicide, Aron's death, and
Adam's paralyzing stroke.   The only diversion in the narrative, except for an opening evocation of the theme of Part
Four--the terrible and desperate human need for love and
acceptance--is the narrator's occasional comment on the
Valley's reaction to the War.   The chief narrative interest
is Cal's struggle between good and evil for his self-identity.

This struggle reaches its crisis when Adam refuses to accept Cal's gift, thereby setting in motion the series of
events, specifically triggered by Cal's decision to show
Aron his mother, which end with Kate's and Aron's death
and Adam's paralysis. Cal, however, is able (no pun intended) to overcome his Cain heritage through Lee's spiritual guidance and Abra's love. The climax of East of Eden,
what Steinbeck described as "the most violently emotional
scene" he had ever attempted, is a powerful and intense
scene, in which Cal receives his timshel blessing from
Adam, who can barely utter the word. The blessing releases Cal from his guilt and gives him the chance to choose
freely between the forces of good and evil--and it also re-
asserts Steinbeck's basic theme in East of Eden: the importance of the individual human soul.

III. CRITICAL EXPLICATION

    East of Eden is a natural ground of controversy be-
cause the book seems to contain the best and the worst of
Steinbeck's writing. Since Steinbeck proclaimed East of Eden
as The Book, the critics have not been reluctant to use it as
measurement of what Steinbeck hoped to achieve in his career
and the reasons for his failure. Except for an occasionally
enthusiastic and unqualified study like John Ditsky's Essays
on "East of Eden," the critiques of The Book have woven the
thread picked up and continued by Howard Levant: "the real
importance of East of Eden does not lie in Steinbeck's mistaken claim to greatness, revealing as it is, but its testi-
mony--much like a completed blueprint--to the author's en-
during difficulty in fusing structure and materials into a
harmonious whole."[5]

    The most consistent critical view of East of Eden,
then, is that Steinbeck's grand design produced a flawed epic.
As to the seriousness of the book's defects, whether it be a
flawed masterpiece like Moby Dick or a literary disaster like
Faulkner's A Fable, most critics view East of Eden negatively. Peter Lisca offers perhaps the most unrelenting and
complete examination of East of Eden's stylistic, structural,
and thematic problems. After noting the awkward and
twisted syntax and the baroque language that plague the narrative, Lisca states that the novel fails because Steinbeck
lost control of his original plan to write a book to his sons
about his maternal family, the Hamiltons. Once Steinbeck
introduced his universal neighbors into East of Eden, "he

soon found himself at the mercy of his materials," and as
"the importance of the Trask family grew," he "realized that
he had a far different book on his hands from what he originally conceived, one which centered on the Trasks and not
on the Hamiltons, Steinbeck's maternal family."[6] According
to Lisca, Steinbeck, once caught in the dilemma, was unable
to find a design or purpose for the shifts back and forth between the families. The end result was an awkward, dis-
tracting narrative to go along with an inflated language.

    Lisca points out several other serious problems in
East of Eden related to the Trask material. One of the most
irritating and confusing is the "I" narrator who appears occasionally to comment on the passing historical scene in the
Salinas Valley. Unfortunately, this narrator gets confused
with the character "John" and the collective "we" and the
personal "me" because it "is plainly a vestigial element
from the first draft of the book as a family saga addressed
to his children, and is ill-mated to the 'I' as narrator."[7]
Even more irritating, if less confusing, is Steinbeck's C-A
strategy in naming characters and forming relationships. By
branding all Cain characters with the letter "C" (Cyrus,
Charles, Cathy, Caleb) and his Abel characters with the letter "A" (Adam, Aaron, and Abra), he seriously strains the
credibility of the novel. This naming process becomes painfully embarrassing in the scene in which Samuel, Adam, and
Lee give names to the twins. Rejecting the obvious names
of Cain and Abel for the sons of Adam, they select Caleb
and Aaron--and never notice the C-A connection. There are
also several extremely obvious parallels with the story of
Cain and Abel in East of Eden as well as two long discussions of the meaning of the sixteen verses in Genesis, which
at one point are read aloud. Both Charles and Cathy have
bad scars on their foreheads that appear to the eye as long
finger-marks. On separate occasions covering two generations, God's rejection of Cain's gift is acted out in Cyrus'
preference for Adam's puppy over Charles' pocketknife and
Adam's rejection of Cal's gift of the money made in bean
speculation. Added to these parallels are the excessive
goodness associated with the "A" characters and the dark
evil of the "C" characters.

    While the parallels with the story of Cain and Abel
are so obviously planted in East of Eden that they intrude
upon the narrative by creating forced comparisons, Lisca
further notes that the characters most responsible for examining the Biblical story and discovering its meaning are

questionable creations in themselves. Samuel Hamilton,
Steinbeck's pillar of fire, is simply too good to be real.
Moral and mystical by nature, he seems more divine than
human. Lee, Steinbeck's alter ego, is too convenient to be
real. Both servant and philosopher, he seems too much of
a conduit for Steinbeck's views and judgments to have any
organic role in the novel. Cathy Ames, Steinbeck's monster,
is too evil to be real. Misshapen and horrible in spirit, she
seems, more than any other character, to defy Steinbeck's
doctrine of timshel because of her unrelievedly evil actions.

Lisca's criticism of East of Eden is well supported
by the novel's form and content. The flaws in language,
structure, and character are simply too obvious to be ig-
nored--and the critics of East of Eden have had no trouble
doing their job. Curiously, though, the first critic to identify the problems in East of Eden was John Steinbeck. His
work diary clearly indicates that he knew exactly what the
critics would find objectionable in his novel. The major
battle to be fought with the critics would be over East of
Eden's "formless form"--the constant shifts in language,
point of view, and structure. Specifically, he felt that the
critics would aggressively attack the structural relationship
between the Hamiltons and the Trasks because they would
fail to understand his strategy of counterpointing the Hamilton sections, while developing the chronology of the Trask
family through three generations. The work diary also
anticipates critical attacks on point of view, symbolic structure, and character development. Steinbeck readily admitted
that his own voice would be more apparent in East of Eden
than in his previous novels, arguing that he wanted the opportunity to express openly his own observations and criticisms of the history of the Valley and its relevance to
American history. Though the work diary does not specifically comment on possible criticism of the symbolic design
of the book, it does give ample evidence of Steinbeck's great
interest in his symbol story and characters. It also shows
why Steinbeck wanted to emphasize symbolic meaning over
narrative description. As much as Steinbeck feared and
fretted about the critics, he wrote East of Eden for the common reader. His primary aim, therefore, was to illuminate
the book, not for the symbol hunters, but for the reader
interested in measuring human behavior in terms of one of
the greatest stories of all time.

Steinbeck's comments do not erase the flaws of East
of Eden, but they do suggest that critics have leaped upon

the obvious, the "formlessness" of the novel, while saying
little about its form and patterns except where they are contrived and intrusive.   Either that or Steinbeck, while recognizing the areas of controversy and weakness, was helpless
to do anything about them.   This view is shared by Lisca
and Levant, but for different reasons.   Lisca argues that
Steinbeck lost control of the narrative form of the novel because of the demands of the Trask material, while Levant,
who believes that Steinbeck lacked a coherent sense of structure, concludes that Steinbeck badly mixed allegory and "is"
thinking.

        Another possibility is that Steinbeck, while recognizing
that his basic strategy would violate critical standards for
narrative form and character development, followed his own
instincts and experience and wrote the book he had been preparing to write all his life.   Very early in the work diary
indications are that Steinbeck, rather than losing control of
his narrative form, had devised the strategy of using the
Hamiltons in "little pieces" to "play counterpoint" (JN, 31)
to the chronological story of the Trasks.   What Steinbeck
does not say in his work diary is why he made this decision--
what purpose the Hamilton pieces have in the narrative--and
why most of the pieces appear in the first half of the novel.

        The key to the Hamilton parts of the narrative ob-
viously is Samuel Hamilton.   His role in East of Eden suggests that the Hamilton family functions as a principle of
universal goodness to counterbalance the evil forces acting
upon Adam Trask.   Even though the perspective of the first
half of the novel belongs to Adam, the chief influences upon
his life, until he meets Samuel Hamilton, are dark and
dangerous--Cyrus, Charles, and Cathy.   The presence of
Samuel Hamilton and the legends about the Hamilton family,
including Olive's plane ride, are designed to elevate the
novel above the realistic level.   Even Samuel's speech,
attacked for being unrealistic, is elevated to the level of
music to counterbalance the realistic narrative of the Trasks.
Thus Samuel functions more on the level of epic or myth
than on the realistic level.   His divine presence in the nar-
rative--Steinbeck had earlier described the Valley as the
Pastures of Heaven--establishes the epic tone and mythic
character of the first half of East of Eden.   Approached as
an epic event, Samuel's death or departure has tremendous
significance in the novel.   Rather than an awkward, bumbling
indication of Steinbeck's failure to control his narrative,
Samuel's death clearly signals the departure of the miracu-

lous from human affairs. Even though he leaves behind his
testament in Lee and his faith in Adam, his death concludes
the Age of the Gods in East of Eden. Not surprisingly,
Samuel's last scenes have the same meaning as the final
appearance of the Grail before it is taken away from the
eyes of the world. Both signify the end of God's visible
presence on earth, and the beginning of the Age of Man.

Most of the attacks on East of Eden have focused on
problems in the first half of the novel. The structural im-
balance between the Trask and the Hamilton sections, the
shifting identity of the "I" narrative voice, the heavy and
obvious symbolism, and the unrealistic characterizations, all
are prominent in the part of the novel dominated by Adam's
journeys and trials. The reason for the excesses in each
case, however, is to elevate the first half of East of Eden
to the level of epic and myth. The "I" narrator, for example, properly functions on a national and racial level.
Thus his identity encompasses character (John Steinbeck),
family (the Hamiltons), nation (America), and God (legends
and miracles). The weighted symbolism--the C-A pattern,
in particular--is also related to Steinbeck's purpose in the
first half of the novel. The obviousness of the parallels with
the story of Cain and Abel is part of a deliberate attempt to
raise the level of the narrative from the realistic to the epic.
The narrative manipulation of characters and events suggest
a world in which large and unexplainable forces are at work.
The signs, particularly the Cain sign, are visible evidence
of these forces.

Interestingly, those who have complained so vehemently
about Steinbeck's heavy-handedness in using symbolic parallels
with the Cain and Abel story have ignored the parallels with
Paradise Lost. John L. Gribben, in his essay on Steinbeck
and Milton, offers a refreshing perspective on the moral
theme in East of Eden by pointing out the similarities between Steinbeck's and Milton's doctrine of free will. [8] Though
Gribben is reluctant to claim influence, the specific parallels
with Paradise Lost are evident very early in East of Eden.
The militant Cyrus, in particular, owes his conception to
Milton's Satan in Book I. The first sentence introducing
Cyrus describes him as "something of a devil" (EE, 14).
When Adam, as a child, realizes that Cyrus is not a great
man, his discovery is described in Miltonic terms: "And
there is one sure thing about the fall of the gods: they do
not fall a little; they crash and shatter or sink deeply into
green muck" (EE, 19-20). Later, when Cyrus tells Adam

about the military life, his vision of the army resembles
Satan's anguished memory of heavenly glories, of what he
lost in his epic rebellion against God: "you will know a
holy joy, a companionship almost like that of a heavenly
company of angels. Then you will know the quality of men
even if they are inarticulate. But until you have gone way
down you can never know this" (EE, 26).

Cyrus Trask is only one of several characters in the
first half of East of Eden whose role is more epic than
realistic. Judged from the standard of realism, of "is"
thinking, Samuel Hamilton, Cathy Ames, and Lee are contrived and embarrassing creations. Seen from the perspective of Steinbeck's design, each character has a vital role
in the mythic reality of East of Eden. Samuel, as already
discussed, is the God presence. Representing the miracu-
lous and divine, he functions as a symbol of the aspirations
of the human soul. Levant sees Samuel "transformed into
a kind of human divinity or an expression of the divine in
man," and points out that "his last phrase recalls God's
language in the Garden of Eden after the Fall ('Here am
I). . . ."9

Cathy Ames functions as the mythic counterpoint to
Samuel Hamilton. Representing the demonic presence in
East of Eden, she is Steinbeck's "psychic monster," determined by her very nature to commit evil in the world:
"There was a time when a girl like Cathy would have been
called possessed by the devil. She would have been exor-
cised to cast out the evil spirit, and if after many trials
that did not work, she would have been burned as a witch
for the good of the community" (EE, 73). The narrator's
description of witch burning as an act "for the good of the
community" is particularly significant because Cathy, unchecked by any witch or monster hunts, eventually reigns
over the secret sins of Salinas from her position as madam
of a brothel. After an incredible history of corruption and
murder, including the near destruction of Adam's soul,
Cathy, now called Kate, sits at the very core of all the evil
the human mind can imagine and commit. Samuel's last act
in the novel is to give Adam, inspired by Samuel's spiritual
goodness, the knowledge of Kate's evil so that he may be
able to choose between the two.

Lee, Steinbeck's Chinese philosopher-servant, is the
most difficult character to accept because he is a bridge between the human and the divine. His specific role in the

first half of East of Eden is the translator of the mythic
into human terms. His four ancient Chinese philosophers
are symbolic of the four gospel writers in the Bible. He
acknowledges the divine in Samuel, and, after Samuel's departure, functions as a spiritual guide in a too human world.
Lee's role as Steinbeck's spokesman is clearly indicated in
the work diary. Most of Steinbeck's discussions of the Cain
and Abel story in the diary, including his investigation of
timshel, find their way into the novel through Lee. Steinbeck
saw his character as an objective vantage point for himself:
"he is going into the book because I need him. The book
needs his eye and criticism which is more detached than
mine" (JN, 73). Lester Jay Marks, evaluating Lee's role
in the thematic design of East of Eden, sees him functioning
as a non-theological spokesman for the novel's theme of the
individual's struggle between good and evil. [10]

The second half of East of Eden, dominated by the
Cain principle, has very little of the epic about it. Samuel
Hamilton has departed, and the only Hamilton who plays any
significant role in the narrative is the worldly and mundane
Will, the one Hamilton capable of making money because he
lacks his father's imagination. Cathy Ames, now Kate,
gradually changes from a psychic monster into a physical
one. She becomes twisted and tormented by an arthritic
condition and her growing fear of being discovered and pun-
ished for past crimes. Like her imaginary Alice, she
grows smaller and smaller until she finally disappears from
view. Lee's function, as already indicated, is to act as a
disciple of Samuel Hamilton. He is present at several crucial moments to translate human conflict in terms of the
words and wisdom of the divine Samuel.

Steinbeck's description of Caleb as "the Everyman,
the battleground between good and evil, the most human of
all, the sorry man" is the key to the changes in the second
half of East of Eden. Steinbeck's epic narrative, no longer
viable, is replaced by a realistic narrative more suitable to
the inner struggles between good and evil that now dominate
the novel. Conceptually and structurally, the epic dimensions of East of Eden are now reduced to a realistic framework to accommodate Cal's moral drama.

Steinbeck's major theme now becomes clearer in East
of Eden because it is reduced to human terms. The discussions of the story of Cain and Abel earlier in the novel are
now fleshed out in Cal's struggle with his almost overpower-

ing sense of guilt. The philosophical word-splitting of Lee's
ancient Chinese scholars is acted out in Cal's effort to
understand the nature of this guilt, whether it be an inheritance or something he has some control over. Gribben
points out that the basic difference between Paradise Lost
and East of Eden is that whereas "Milton's epic is an attempt to justify the ways of God to man," Steinbeck's novel
is more intent on "justifying the ways of man to men and of
each individual to himself."[11] Actually, what Steinbeck tried
to write was a story that would have both mythic and human
value, that would establish a universal and eternal framework for the story of Cal's struggle with his own sense of
guilt and his eventual recognition of his freedom of action.
Marks points out the consistency of Steinbeck's non-teleological system once the universal truth of the novel is established
through the story of Cain and Abel ("These old men believe
a true story, and they know a true story when they hear it")
(EE, 304). According to Marks, "Steinbeck's non-teleological
system works this way: It examined in scrupulous detail the
human condition under which man is perpetually embroiled in
the war between good and evil.... Once this condition is
faced and accepted ... then the individual can exercise his
power of choice and attempt to rule over sin...."[12]

Significantly, Steinbeck's large moral theme, played
out upon the background of epic and myth and consistent with
his non-teleological point of view, is also relevant to his own
time (the post-World War II period) and the contemporary
period in American literature. Coming out of his own dangerous period to write East of Eden, Steinbeck noted in his work
diary that "writers of today, even I, have a tendency to celebrate the destruction of the spirit and god knows it is destroyed often enough" (JN, 115). Recognizing that "it is the
fashion now in writing to have every man defeated and destroyed," Steinbeck insisted that "the beacon thing is that"
the human spirit survives sometimes and "I think I can take
time right now to say that" (JN, 115). These lines were
written as Steinbeck was preparing to end the first part of
East of Eden with the death of Samuel Hamilton. They found
their way into the text, in an abbreviated form, in Samuel's
parting words to Lee. He tells Lee that, for a while, he,
like so many others, "conceive[d] of a life as ending in de-
feat" (EE, 308). But the two-word translation of timshel as
"thou mayest" convinced him that he does "not believe all
men are destroyed.... It is true that we are weak and sick
and quarrelsome, but if that is all we ever were, we would,
millenniums ago, have disappeared from the face of the
earth" (EE, 308-09).

"Thou Mayest"--this is the blessing that Cal receives
from Adam.   Within the framework of the universal truths
established early in East of Eden, the non-teleological narrative of the second part of the novel leads up to the moment
when the individual is released from and denied the belief in
predetermined sin by the blessing of Adam, who benefits
from the teachings of Samuel, but still must find the deter-
mination in himself to raise his hand and speak the word.
In the background are Lee, the link between the divine word
and human experience, and Abra, who represents the natural
goodness, rather than the evil, of the physical world.   Thus
Cal, free of the sins of the past and in close contact with
the natural harmony of his world, has the path open to choose
between good and evil: "And it occurs to me that evil must
constantly respawn, while good, while virtue, is immortal"
(EE, 415).

The significance of Steinbeck's effort in East of Eden
is that he wrote a book about what is true and constant in
the world and in the individual mind at the beginning of a
literary period that would produce Tommy Wilhelm (Seize
The Day), Yossarian (Catch-22), Billy Pilgrim (Slaughter-
house-Five), and other Sad Sacks of the American literary
scene.   That he found a theme large enough for his purpose
is hardly debatable, but whether he had the mastery to handle
his theme is another matter.   Critics have had no trouble
identifying the unevenness in East of Eden--Mark Schorer,
after writing a favorable review of Steinbeck's novel, refused to allow Tedlock and Wicker to publish his comments
in Steinbeck and His Critics because he regretted his own
first judgment.   Curiously, however, the structural and
thematic flaws that the critics have identified in East of Eden
are similar to the flaws noted numerous times in Moby Dick.
As a matter of fact, the contemporary reviews of Moby Dick
closely resemble the criticism of East of Eden in their
eagerness to point out the botched job that Melville did in
trying to write a whaling story and an allegorical romance
at the same time.   Levant's view that Steinbeck botched
some fine narrative moments of "is" thinking by wrapping
"incredible or forced allegorical elements" around them is
particularly relevant here. [13]

This is not to say that East of Eden is the great
modern epic that Steinbeck thought it would be.   It falls far
short of the mastery of the strategy T. S. Eliot defined as
the mythic method, a method used with great range and
depth in Joyce's Ulysses.   On the other hand, East of Eden

is far superior to Faulkner's A Fable, which is little more
than an awkwardly mechanical attempt to turn Humphrey
Cobb's Paths of Glory into a modern version of the story of
Christ's passion and resurrection. Whether East of Eden is
comparable in value to Moby Dick is questionable, but the
thematic and formal similarities between the two books need
be more fully explored. 14

The criticism of East of Eden has done a thorough
job in drawing attention to the obvious flaws in the novel,
many of which Steinbeck identified in his work diary. Ditsky's point is well taken that "John Steinbeck's own humility
was, perhaps, his own worst enemy. "15 Warren French has
argued that the next step in Steinbeck criticism should be in
the direction of structural studies. 16 Hopefully, however,
this means that critics interested in evaluating the structure
of Steinbeck's novels will not insist on imposing predetermined notions of form upon his works, but, instead, will
study his novels in terms of what Steinbeck tried to accomplish in each one. This approach should yield a great deal
of new insight into Steinbeck's craftsmanship, particularly in
East of Eden.

NOTES

1. Steinbeck: A Life in Letters, eds. Elaine Steinbeck and
    Robert Wallsten (New York: Viking, 1975), p. 303.
    All subsequent quotations from Steinbeck's letters are
    taken from this edition, identified as SLL in the text.

2. John Steinbeck, Journal of a Novel: The "East of
    Eden" Letters (New York: Viking, 1969), p. 3. All
    subsequent quotations from Steinbeck's work diary are
    taken from this edition, identified as JN in the text.

3. John Steinbeck, East of Eden (New York: Viking, 1952),
    p. 14. All subsequent quotations from the novel are
    taken from this edition, identified as EE in the text.

4. The shift in the spelling of "Aaron" to "Aron" comes
    about through Aron's insistence that this name be
    spelled in the latter way.

5. Howard Levant, The Novels of John Steinbeck, with an
    introduction by Warren French (Columbia: University
    of Missouri Press, 1974), p. 234.

6. Peter Lisca, The Wide World of John Steinbeck (New Brunswick: Rutgers University Press, 1958), p. 263.

7. Ibid., p. 266.

8. John L. Gribben, "Steinbeck's East of Eden and Milton's Paradise Lost: A Discussion of Timshel," in Steinbeck's Literary Dimensions: A Guide to Comparative Studies, ed. Tetsumaro Hayashi (Metuchen: Scarecrow Press, 1973), pp. 94-104.

9. Levant, p. 241.

10. Lester Jay Marks, Thematic Design in the Novels of John Steinbeck (The Hague: Mouton, 1969), p. 130.

11. Gribben, p. 99.

12. Marks, p. 131.

13. Levant, p. 256.

14. See, for example, Warren French's comparison in John Steinbeck (New York: Twayne, 1961), pp. 152-53.

15. John Ditsky, Essays on "East of Eden" (Steinbeck Monograph Series, No. 7) (Muncie: Steinbeck Society, Ball State University, 1977), ix.

16. Warren French, "Introduction" to Howard Levant's The Novels of John Steinbeck, pp. ix-xii.

IV. APPARATUS FOR RESEARCH PAPERS

A. Ten Questions for Discussion

1. The translation of timshel as "thou mayest" establishes the concept of free will in East of Eden. How might other American writers--Hawthorne, Dreiser, Faulkner, Vonnegut--interpret timshel?

2. Is the idea of timshel ("thou mayest") applicable to other Steinbeck novels?

3. What scenes in East of Eden best illustrate Steinbeck's timshel? What scenes seem to contradict the idea?

4. Are there times in East of Eden when visible signs of goodness hide evil? What purpose does this strategy serve in this novel?

5. What view of American history emerges from the narrator's comments--nostalgic, realistic, romantic, deterministic?
6. Is Cathy-Kate's role in the novel too large? Are all her evil machinations necessary to the theme and structure of East of Eden?
7. Is Adam any less of an Everyman than Cal? Why does Steinbeck identify Cal as his Everyman even though he is a Cain figure?
8. Is Lee too artificial to have any real narrative value in East of Eden?
9. Abra, Adam, and Aron represent goodness in East of Eden. What specific element of goodness does each character represent?
10. Cyrus, Charles, Cathy, and Caleb represent sinfulness in East of Eden. What specific element of sin does each character represent?

B. Suggested Topics for Research Papers

1. Cyrus Trask, Samuel Hamilton, and Adam Trask as paternal figures in East of Eden.
2. A comparison of Adam Trask in East of Eden and Adam in Milton's Paradise Lost.
3. The function of the Hamilton pieces in the narrative structure of East of Eden.
4. A comparison of the Cain-Abel relationships (Charles-Adam, Caleb-Aron) in East of Eden.
5. The clashing roles of Cathy-Kate and Abra in East of Eden.
6. The role of miracle, legend, and myth in the first half of East of Eden and their influence, if any, upon the second half.
7. The gospel according to Lee and Samuel Hamilton: the interpretations of the story of Cain and Abel in East of Eden.
8. The validity (or lack of validity) of Steinbeck's psychological explanations of Cathy-Kate's monstrous character.
9. Cal as Everyman: the second half of East of Eden as morality play.
10. East of Eden and Moby Dick: the American novel as epic in the 19th and 20th century.

C. Selected Bibliography

1. Ditsky, John. Essays on "East of Eden" (Steinbeck

Monograph Series, No. 7). Muncie: Steinbeck Society,
Ball State University, 1977.
An imaginative and enthusiastic study of East of Eden.
The essays are "Toward a Narrational Self," "Outside of
Paradise: Men and the Land in East of Eden," and "The
'East' in East of Eden."

2. Fontenrose, Joseph. "Another View of James Gray's
   John Steinbeck," Steinbeck Quarterly, 8 (Winter 1975),
   19-22.
   This short essay notes that there was no scholarly
controversy over the meaning of timshel or Steinbeck's spelling of the word. Gray's view to the contrary, Steinbeck's
spelling of Timshol as Timshel was nothing more than "Steinbeck's slip."

3. _____. John Steinbeck: An Introduction and Interpretation. New York: Holt, Rinehart, and Winston,
   1963.
   Still the best critical study of Steinbeck's use of
myth. Chapter on East of Eden concentrates on Steinbeck's
use of the story of Cain and Abel and concludes that the
myth fails to support the narrative events.

4. French, Warren. John Steinbeck. New York: Twayne,
   1961; revised edition, Boston: Twayne, 1975.
   The starting place for the beginning scholar interested
in John Steinbeck. In the 1961 edition, though he hesitates
to compare East of Eden and Moby Dick, French does suggest that Steinbeck's problem in working with two separate
forms resembles Melville's struggle in Moby Dick. Also
offers a comparison of Cathy-Kate and Captain Ahab as
studies of the self-destructive tendencies of monomaniacs.
Regrettably, the discussion of Steinbeck and Melville and the
comparison of East of Eden and Moby Dick do not appear in
the revised edition.

5. Gribben, John L. "Steinbeck's East of Eden and Milton's
   Paradise Lost: A Discussion of Timshel," in Steinbeck's
   Literary Dimension: A Guide to Comparative Studies,
   ed. Tetsumaro Hayashi. Metuchen: Scarecrow Press,
   1973, pp. 94-104.
   The essay focuses on the subject of free will in East
of Eden and Paradise Lost. Gribben does not offer any
material on the possibility of influence, but his discussion of
timshel adds a new dimension to the views of Steinbeck's
moral vision in East of Eden.

6. Levant, Howard. The Novels of John Steinbeck: A
    Critical Study. Introduction by Warren French. Colum-
    bia: University of Missouri Press, 1974.
        The thesis of Levant's book is that Steinbeck's bril-
    liance was flawed by his lack of an intelligent and coherent
    understanding of structure. East of Eden is critical to this
    thesis because Levant argues that it contains the best and
    the worst of Steinbeck's work. French's introduction is an
    excellent review of Steinbeck scholarship.

7. Lisca, Peter. The Wide World of John Steinbeck. New
    Brunswick: Rutgers University Press, 1958.
        The most thorough study of the apparent inconsisten-
    cies in East of Eden. Concentrates on problems of language,
    point of view, structure, characterization, and theme.

8. Marks, Lester Jay. Thematic Design in the Novels of
    John Steinbeck. The Hague: Mouton, 1969.
        One of the few sympathetic studies of East of Eden.
    Marks offers an interesting study of the relationship between
    mythic and non-teleological thinking in the novel.

Chapter 5

STEINBECK'S THE LOG FROM THE SEA OF CORTEZ (1951)

by Richard F. Peterson

I. BACKGROUND

In 1951, ten years after the publication of John Steinbeck and Edward F. Ricketts' Sea of Cortez: A Leisurely
Journal of Travel and Research, the Viking Press published
a modified version of the same book under the title, The Log
from the Sea of Cortez. The first book, also published by
the Viking Press, is the record of a six-week exploration of
the Gulf of California, once called the Sea of Cortez--"a
better-sounding and a more exciting name."[1] Organized by
Steinbeck and his close friend, Ed Ricketts, the trip con-
sisted of a series of stops "in many little harbors and near
barren coasts to collect and preserve the marine inverte-
brates of the littoral."[2] Though the observing, collecting,
and recording of marine life was the main reason for the
trip and elevated it to the level of a scientific expedition,
the larger purpose, which inspired the narrative form of the
book, was "to see everything our eyes would accommodate,
to think what we could, and out of our seeing and thinking,
to build some kind of structure in modeled imitation of observed reality."[3]

The Log from the Sea of Cortez is a re-publication
of the narrative portion of Sea of Cortez (1941). Absent
from the Log is the Annotated Phyletic Catalogue and Bibliography which makes up the second half, or three hundred
pages, of the first book. The only additional material added
to the Log is a sixty-page essay, "About Ed Ricketts,"
written by Steinbeck. The chief purpose of the essay, which
functions as an introduction to the narrative portion of the
Log, is to offer the reader an informal and loving portrait
of Ed Ricketts, who had died in a car-train accident on May
11, 1948.

Ironically, Steinbeck had become less dependent upon Ed Ricketts' friendship and guidance in the period just before Ricketts' death. Their personal and philosophical intimacy, reflected in their collaboration on the Sea of Cortez expedition and the subsequent publication of their research and the record of their travels, had gradually diminished because of Steinbeck's decision to live permanently in New York and his reluctance to become involved in an extensive collecting trip to the Queen Charlotte Islands that Ricketts had been planning. [4] Ricketts, who had already made two trips to Vancouver Island and the Queen Charlottes, had sent the records of these earlier expeditions to Steinbeck in the hope of drawing him into a sequel to Sea of Cortez. [5] Richard Astro believes that "having completed preliminary work on a 'giant novel' tentatively titled 'Salinas Valley,' Steinbeck felt that an interruption of the type the marine biologist had in mind would impede his drive for artistic independence."[6]

According to Astro, rather than liberating Steinbeck from the influence of his long time friend and teacher, Ricketts' death re-established the biologist's mode of seeing and thinking upon Steinbeck's work, first affectionately in Burning Bright and "About Ed Ricketts," then critically in Viva Zapata![7] Astro points out that "finally, in Sweet Thursday, Steinbeck severed the cords completely by stating that the hard facts of modern existence made Ricketts' life-style utterly intractable."[8]

Whatever the pattern of Steinbeck's treatment of Ricketts' memory, "About Ed Ricketts" clearly establishes Steinbeck's deep love and respect for his friend. As an introduction to The Log from the Sea of Cortez, the essay also creates the appearance that Steinbeck is both the author of the essay and the narrator of the entire log of the expedition. The implication of the Steinbeck essay and the Steinbeckian narrative voice is that the metaphysical speculation in the Log also belongs more to Steinbeck than to Ricketts.

Even the title page, if not read carefully, creates the illusion that Steinbeck is the author or controlling agent of the Log. The title of the book, The Log from the Sea of Cortez, appears in large print. Beneath the title, in much smaller print, are the words, "The narrative portion of the book, Sea of Cortez, by John Steinbeck and E. F. Ricketts, 1941, here reissued with a profile 'About Ed Ricketts.'" Beneath these words, in the same large type as the title are the words, "by John Steinbeck." Read carefully, the

title page acknowledges that the narrative portion of the book
was a collaboration of Steinbeck and Ricketts, while noting
that the essay "About Ed Ricketts" obviously was written by
Steinbeck. The appearance of the title page, however, strongly suggests that Steinbeck is the author of the entire work
because "The Log from the Sea of Cortez by John Steinbeck"
is what boldly confronts the reader on the title page. Ironically, until recently Steinbeck's critics have turned the title
page into a prophecy, and have interpreted the materials in
the Log, particularly the materials on non-teleological thinking, as Steinbeck gospel. Extensive research on the Steinbeck-Ricketts relationship, however, has well illustrated that
this has been an unfortunate and misleading interpretation.

II. SYNOPSIS

The format and structure of the narrative portion of
The Log from the Sea of Cortez has been summarized by
Richard Astro in A Study Guide to Steinbeck (Part I). [9]
Worth noting specifically in the Log is the long discussion
of non-teleological thinking that appears in the March 24,
Easter Sunday chapter. This is the essay that has been
used to support the argument that Steinbeck's thinking is
basically non-teleological. The premise of the chapter is
"that non-teleological or 'is' thinking might be substituted in
part for the usual cause-effect methods." [10] Non-teleological
ideas come about through "is" thinking, which "concerns itself primarily not with what should be, or could be, or
might be, but rather with what actually 'is'--attempting at
most to answer the already sufficiently difficult questions
what or how, instead of why" (135).

The greatest objection to teleological thinking is that
the answers or ideas derived teleologically are often a reflection of the beliefs of a mind dogmatically opposed to any
way of thinking that might offer different or alternative ideas.
On the other hand, the objection to non-teleological thinking
is that it is too "detached, hard-hearted, or even cruel"
(146). Arguing the former while rejecting the latter, the
narrative states that "non-teleological methods more than any
other seem capable of great tenderness, of an all-embracing-
ness which is rare otherwise" (146). More a method of
handling material than an intellectual or thinking process, it
accepts rather than blames or apologizes for life: "The
method extends beyond thinking even to living itself; in fact,
by inferred definition it transcends the realm of thinking
possibilities, it postulates 'living into'" (147).

Steinbeck's essay, "About Ed Ricketts," which was
added as a long introduction to the reissue of the log portion
of Sea of Cortez, is an excellent example of an attempt at a
non-teleological narrative. To seek out the essence of his
friend, Steinbeck rejects the idea of simplifying the many
paradoxes of his life and offering a definition and judgment
of the man. Instead, he decides that "it would be better to
put down the mass of material from our memories, anec-
dotes, quotations, events" (xi). Rather than deriving some
formula to understand and evaluate Ricketts, "the simplest
and best way will be just to remember--as much as I can"
(xii). By accepting the facts, stories, and legends about the
man and by acknowledging the profound and loving emotions
he evoked in his friends, Steinbeck can "live into" Ricketts,
and write truly about his life.

What emerges in "About Ed Ricketts" is a series of
stories about the marine biologist that are intended to reveal
the truth about him by functioning as keys to his personality
and life. The stories in themselves are wonderfully told,
but, ironically, reveal more about Steinbeck's genius as a
storyteller than Ricketts' genius for living. As Steinbeck
moves from story to story "so that from all the bits a whole
picture may build itself for me as well as for others"
(xxxix), he creates a warm, vital, and comic world out of
Ricketts' habits, mannerisms, passions, and biases, which
seems much larger than the truth each story contains about
the man. At the end of the essay, Steinbeck claims that
Ricketts' greatest gift was his ability "to receive anything
from anyone, to receive gracefully and thankfully and to
make the gift seem very fine" (lxiv). Actually, it is this
very quality in Steinbeck's writing, that of receiving material and turning it into something fine, that distinguishes the
essay and elevates it to the level of myth in spite of Steinbeck's feeling that the remembering "has not laid the ghost"
(lxvii).

III.   CRITICAL EXPLICATION

In the decades since the publication of The Log from
the Sea of Cortez, Steinbeck's critics have recognized the
importance of the ideas developed in the narrative portion of
the book, but until recently they have failed to understand
completely the relationship between Steinbeck and Ricketts
and the role Ricketts played in the composing of the book.
Richard Astro's comprehensive research into this key friend-

ship in Steinbeck's life has uncovered the history of the ideas in the Log and dispelled "certain myths which have grown up around Sea of Cortez" by "examining the facts about the Gulf of California expedition and by noting how the book was written."[11]

Astro has pointed out that the major assumption about the Log, that Steinbeck wrote the narrative of the trip and Ricketts the phyletic catalogue, is incorrect, as is the belief that both Steinbeck and Ricketts kept journals during the expedition: "There were two records kept during the voyage but neither was written by Steinbeck. Rather they were kept by Ricketts and by Tony Berry (captain of the boat which Steinbeck chartered for the trip), and Steinbeck composed the narrative almost entirely from Ricketts' journal."[12] When Pascal Covici wanted the title page of the 1941 publication to read,

The Sea of Cortez

By John Steinbeck

with a scientific appendix comprising materials for a source-book on the marine
animals of the Panamic Faunal Province

By Edward F. Ricketts

Steinbeck objected on the grounds that the substance of the book was the production of the thinking of both of them and only the structure of the book was mostly his doing.[13]

The danger of assuming that Steinbeck developed and wrote down the central ideas of the Log is that Steinbeck's novels can (and have been) "interpreted according to premises stated in Sea of Cortez believed to be his, but actually developed by Ricketts."[14] The most glaring misinterpretations have been based upon the view that Steinbeck wrote the Easter Sunday chapter on non-teleological thinking. Ironically, the chapter was "lifted verbatim," not from Ricketts' journal of the expedition, but from essays written by Ricketts as early as 1939. Thus, the Easter Sunday chapter and other philosophical sections of the Log contain "many of Ricketts' beliefs about life (some of which Steinbeck shared, others he rejected)," while the book itself "is a sincere statement of Steinbeck's affection for his greatest friend."[15]

Out of his research into the friendship between Steinbeck and Ricketts and his close study of the influence of
Ricketts' ideas upon Steinbeck's writing, Astro has concluded
that Steinbeck discovered the advantages of non-teleological
thinking as a way of approaching a problem or situation, but,
because of his social concern, could not accept non-teleological living as an end in itself. The substance of Steinbeck's
fiction clearly shows his commitment to "a teleological program of meaningful social action."[16]

Astro's research and conclusions are a major event
in Steinbeck criticism because they attempt to reconcile
Steinbeck's interest in non-teleological thinking with his
phalanx theory. By arguing that Steinbeck's fiction is goal-
oriented, but balanced by a non-teleological method of observation, Astro has offered Steinbeck's critics a way of recon-
ciling what appears to be a major flaw or inconsistency in
Steinbeck's art. Unfortunately, there is also a potential pit-
fall for critics who take advantage of Astro's work. What
they may see is a ready formula not only for understanding
Steinbeck's fiction but for evaluating and judging it, a formula
that states that Steinbeck's best work uses a non-teleological
fictional method to illustrate the need for a group-oriented
program of social change, while his worst deviates from
this norm and therefore is poorly conceived and executed.
The trap awaiting Steinbeck's critics is quite similar to the
one that caught Hemingway critics who exploited the idea of
the physical wound and divided his characters into Hemingway heroes and code heroes. The method simplified Hemingway's art, but in the process focused on the limitations of
Hemingway's vision. It would be unfortunate if Steinbeck's
critics, after laboring long and hard to restore Steinbeck's
reputation, were to accept a ready-made formula which,
while simplifying their task, greatly underestimates the dimensions of Steinbeck's art.

In her essay in the Steinbeck Quarterly on the form
of the narrative section of Sea of Cortez, Betty L. Perez
shows the advantage of an open-minded and open-ended approach to Steinbeck's work. Noting that "Sea of Cortez has
been viewed exclusively in its philosophical relation to Steinbeck's fiction," she counters that the book has its own
unique form, which is more than its visible structure as a
ship's log.[17] By comparing Sea of Cortez to Hemingway's
Green Hills of Africa and Thoreau's Walden, she finds that
it shares with the latter two the quest "for a living reality"
and the method "of adventure and discovery."[18] Though

well aware of the non-teleological implications of the narrative, Betty Perez also notes that Steinbeck's "holistic concept
of interrelated units forming a whole with greater significance
than the sum of its parts" points the way to seeing Sea of
Cortez as a symbolic journey in which the microcosmic
world of the expedition has macrocosmic significance as "a
voyage of the mind over uncharted waters--which explores
the relationship of man to all his worlds."19 This view of
Sea of Cortez incorporates the essay on non-teleological
thinking into the form of the book--which grows beyond
scientific inquiry and philosophical tract and finally becomes
mythic voyage. Like Homer's The Odyssey, Dante's The
Divine Comedy, and Joyce's Ulysses, Steinbeck's Sea of Cortez develops the motif of the journey into man's everlasting
search for the truth of his world and his place in it.

       The value of Betty Perez's essay is that it examines
and evaluates Sea of Cortez as a work in itself without first
imposing a formula upon it or ignoring the book's structure
for the sake of a philosophy stated in a single chapter. By
doing this, she is free to trace the intrinsic patterns of the
book and discover the essential truth about a literary work--
what the writer has intended to execute or accomplish. She
is also free to compare the form of the work to similar
forms, thus placing the work within a literary tradition and
gaining an objective perspective from which to view and
evaluate its significance.

       Perhaps the most important function of Betty Perez's
essay, besides offering an original and comprehensive study
of the form of Sea of Cortez, is to show Steinbeck critics a
way of accepting the chapter on non-teleological thinking as
an integral part of the narrative without allowing the chapter
in itself to supplant the general intention and pattern of the
book. On a larger scale, it illustrates the value of approaching Steinbeck's work without any set anticipation based upon
a philosophical or political position or a scientific or biological point of view. Much of the history of Steinbeck criticism has been plagued by anticipatory criticism. Some of
the most severe attacks on Steinbeck's reputation, even those
attempts to belittle his work as sentimental, have been
mounted from a political or philosophical base. Steinbeck
detractors often accused him of going too far in his attitude
toward group man and neglecting the individual. Others
agree that he fails to go far enough and falls back upon a
sentimental acceptance of laziness and gross sensuality.
One of the most interesting negative views of Steinbeck is

that his flaws in attitude and characterization were acceptable
in the 1930s because of the power and versatility of his work,
but after that, his flaws became so excessive that he failed
as a novelist. This view seems to suggest that a single
novel is not an entity in itself, that its value is dependent
upon other works, particularly those that follow it. Here is
Steinbeck's holistic concept of life applied to literary criticism with a vengeance. Very few literary reputations, including Hemingway's, Fitzgerald's, and Faulkner's, could
hold up under a similar critical view.

Most of the positive studies of Steinbeck share an
interest in the social, biological, and mythic patterns that
emerge out of his individual works and the way in which
these patterns continue or vary during his career. They
also attempt to place Steinbeck's works not only within a
contemporary context but within some literary tradition as
well. Thus, Steinbeck, influenced by his biologist friend,
Ed Ricketts, and aware of the difficult position of being an
artist in an age crying out for some affirmative political or
social action, also shares an American literary tradition
with Emerson, Thoreau, and Whitman. Captivated by biological and social realities and the interrelatedness of the
two, Steinbeck also was intrigued by the ideas and patterns
that he discovered in literature ranging from the Bible and
Milton to J. G. Frazer and D. H. Lawrence.

Astro's research on the Steinbeck-Ricketts friendship
has cleared up several misconceptions about their working
relationship and the influence of the biologist upon the writer.
His book on the subject offers a comprehensive study of the
appearance of the Ricketts hero in Steinbeck's fiction and the
ways in which Ricketts' non-teleological thinking influenced
the shape more than the substance of Steinbeck's art. Astro'
view that Steinbeck developed non-teleological thinking into a
fictional method rather than theme does, however, raise
some questions because it seems to argue that the most
valuable novels or short fiction done by Steinbeck are those
most concerned with Ricketts and his way of thinking. At
issue here is the narrative voice in Steinbeck's fiction and
how consistent or varied that voice is in his novels. Astro's
view suggests that in the ideal Steinbeck novel the narrative
(non-teleological) is one with the novel's hero (non-teleological thinker) even if the novel turns out to be a criticism or
rejection of non-teleological living. Rather, Steinbeck's
narrative voice often shifts not only from novel but also
within the novel itself. Moving from personal comment to

realistic description to mythic parallel and alternating between detachment and commitment as well as between humor
and criticism, the narrative structure of Steinbeck's fiction
is one of the most interesting and diversified elements in
his art.

Astro's conclusions bring us back to the major
dilemma for Steinbeck's critics, that of attempting to understand and evaluate the form of Steinbeck's art by formulariz-
ing the criticism. The new information about Steinbeck's
interest in biology and his collaboration with his biologist-
friend, Ed Ricketts, opens new doors for Steinbeck's critics
but in no way should it suggest closing doors already opened
by Warren French, Peter Lisca, Joseph Fontenrose and
other leading Steinbeck scholars, or ignoring the possibility
of opening further doors that would lead to a more exact
appraisal of Steinbeck's language, style, and structural devices. One of the most illustrative books on Steinbeck in
recent years is Steinbeck's Literary Dimension, edited by
Tetsumaro Hayashi. It offers no less than eleven comparative essays which range from considerations of Steinbeck's
literary relationships with Faulkner, Hemingway, and Salinger
to those with Dickens, Zola, and Kazantzakis.

In the Introduction to Tedlock and Wicker's Steinbeck
and His Critics, the editors claim that the serious student
of Steinbeck criticism may "feel like a sober late arriver at
a cocktail party" as he struggles with the "comedy of critical disagreement" surrounding Steinbeck's career. [20] A fate
worse than this would be to arrive at a party and discover
that everyone looks the same, sounds the same, and that
only one refreshment (barley water?) is being served and
only one narrow subject discussed. At the end of their summary of the Steinbeck criticism appearing in the volume,
Tedlock and Wicker return to the metaphor of the lively and
confusing cocktail party to report that they "came home late
at night not entirely sure what all the talk was about but
determined to think clearly about it some other and soberer
day."[21] Fortunately, one thing remembered by the editors
now that, metaphorically speaking, a "soberer day" has come,
is that too many Steinbeck critics "show themselves unable or
unwilling to follow the old, sane, fundamental rule which ob-
ligates critics to try to understand the author's intention and
to judge his success or failure in realizing it before they
shift to more universal and--wry thought in an eclectic age--
controversial considerations."[22]

Steinbeck criticism has struggled through many controversial periods. Its latest direction, toward a more
biologically oriented view of Steinbeck, certainly promises
another season of controversy. Already, we have learned
much about Steinbeck's knowledge of biological theories and
their influence upon his work. The information has already
added a new and vital perspective to Steinbeck criticism.
Exploited into a formula, however, it will eventually impose
a new restriction upon Steinbeck's art and create another
distraction in the efforts to appreciate properly this controversial American writer.

NOTES

1. John Steinbeck and Edward F. Ricketts, Sea of Cortez:
   A Leisurely Journal of Travel and Research (New
   York: Viking, 1941), p. 1.

2. Ibid., pp. 1-2.

3. Ibid., p. 2.

4. Richard Astro, John Steinbeck and Edward F. Ricketts:
   The Shaping of a Novelist (Minneapolis: University of
   Minnesota Press, 1973), pp. 178-79.

5. Ibid., p. 179.

6. Ibid.

7. Ibid., p. 180.

8. Ibid., pp. 180-81.

9. Richard Astro, "Steinbeck's Sea of Cortez," in A Study
   Guide to Steinbeck: A Handbook to His Major Works,
   ed. Tetsumaro Hayashi (Metuchen, New Jersey:
   Scarecrow, 1974), pp. 170-73.

10. John Steinbeck, The Log from the Sea of Cortez (New
    York: Viking, 1951), p. 132. All subsequent quota-
    tions from the Log will be taken from this edition.

11. John Steinbeck and Edward F. Ricketts, p. 13.

12. Ibid., p. 13. See also "Steinbeck's Sea of Cortez,"
    p. 174.

13. Ibid., p. 14.

14. Ibid. See also "Steinbeck's Sea of Cortez," p. 173.

15. Ibid., pp. 18-19. See also "Steinbeck's Sea of Cortez," p. 179.

16. Ibid., p. 126.

17. Betty L. Perez, "The Form of the Narrative Section of Sea of Cortez: A Specimen Collected from Reality," Steinbeck Quarterly, 9 (Spring 1976), pp. 36-37.

18. Ibid., pp. 37-39.

19. Ibid., p. 41.

20. E. W. Tedlock and C. V. Wicker, eds., Steinbeck and His Critics: A Record of Twenty-five Years (Albuquerque: University of New Mexico Press, 1957), p. xi.

21. Ibid., p. xl.

22. Ibid.

IV. APPARATUS FOR RESEARCH PAPERS

A. Ten Questions for Discussion

1. How reliable and valid are an author's works of non-fiction in interpreting his fiction?
2. Does the content of The Log from the Sea of Cortez suggest that it is a collaboration or the work of one author?
3. Does the style of The Log from the Sea of Cortez suggest that it is a collaboration or the work of one author?
4. What is the structural design of The Log from the Sea of Cortez?
5. Do the individual chapters function as separate units or are they vitally interrelated to each other?
6. Is there a structural design within each chapter that is consistently developed throughout The Log from the Sea of Cortez?
7. Is non-teleological thinking a balance of detachment and great tenderness?

8. Is there any blaming or apologizing in The Log from the
    Sea of Cortez that contradicts the non-teleological ap-
    proach discussed in the Easter Sunday chapter?
9. What role do the members of the Western Flyer play in
    the narrative of The Log from the Sea of Cortez?
10. What are the key symbols in the narrative of The Log
    from the Sea of Cortez?

B. Suggested Topics for Research Papers

1. A comparison of Steinbeck's The Log from the Sea of
    Cortez and Hemingway's Green Hills of Africa.
2. The non-teleological characters in Steinbeck's fiction.
3. The function of humor in The Log from the Sea of Cor-
    tez.
4. A holistic approach to Steinbeck's career.
5. The role of non-teleological thinking in Steinbeck's
    proletarian novels.
6. The conflict of non-teleological and teleological thinking
    in Steinbeck's works.
7. The Easter Sunday chapter in The Log from the Sea of
    Cortez as a critical standard for Steinbeck's fiction.
8. Steinbeck's moral novels and non-teleological thinking.
9. Cannery Row and Sweet Thursday as portraits of the
    non-teleological hero.
10. The Easter Sunday Chapter and the structure of The Log
    from the Sea of Cortez.

C. Selected Bibliography

1. Astro, Richard. "Steinbeck's Sea of Cortez, " in A
    Study Guide to Steinbeck: A Handbook to His Major
    Works, ed. Tetsumaro Hayashi.   Metuchen, New Jersey:
    Scarecrow, 1974, pp. 168-86.
        Though the essay is on the 1941 publication, its main
    concern is The Log from the Sea of Cortez.   Contains ex-
    cellent material on the background, purpose, and value of
    The Log.   Also has a valuable selected bibliography of the
    reviews of the 1941 book and the evaluation of Sea of Cortez
    in critical articles and books on Steinbeck.

2. _____ . John Steinbeck and Edward F. Ricketts: The
    Shaping of a Novelist.   Minneapolis: University of Min-
    nesota Press, 1973.
        A comprehensive study of the influence of Ed Ricketts'

thinking on Steinbeck's--essential reading for scholars interested in Steinbeck. It attempts to trace the effect of the
friendship upon Steinbeck's major works. Also points out
the major disagreement between the two men and concludes
that Steinbeck used a non-teleological fictional method but
created a goal-oriented fictional world.

3. Benton, Robert M. "A Scientific Point of View in
    Steinbeck's Fiction," Steinbeck Quarterly, 7 (Summer-
    Fall 1974), 67-73.
        Essay focuses on Cannery Row and Sweet Thursday
in its discussion of Steinbeck as an ecologist who sees man
as "just one more entity dependent on the rest of the life
continuum."

4. Hedgpeth, Joel W. "Genesis of the Sea of Cortez,"
    Steinbeck Quarterly, 6 (Summer 1973), 74-80.
        Traces the history of Sea of Cortez (1941) from its
inception to its completion. Discusses the work being done
by Ricketts and Steinbeck at the time of their decision to
undertake the expedition and the manner in which the book
was prepared for publication.

5. Perez, Betty L. "Steinbeck, Ricketts, and Sea of Cor-
    tez: Partnership or Exploitation?" Steinbeck Quarterly,
    7 (Summer-Fall 1974), 73-79.
        The essay offers a strong argument for Sea of Cor-
tez as a partnership between Steinbeck and Ricketts. By
comparing selected passages from the journal kept by
Ricketts during the expedition and the text of Sea of Cortez,
it establishes the dependency of the book's structure and
content upon the journal material.

6. _____ . "The Form of the Narrative Section of Sea
    of Cortez: A Specimen Collected from Reality,"
    Steinbeck Quarterly, 9 (Spring 1976), 36-44.
        A companion piece to the earlier essay on the part-
nership of Steinbeck and Ricketts. This essay shows the
way in which Steinbeck developed the form of the narrative
section of Sea of Cortez from "factual narrative to mythic
saga." Here Steinbeck is more guiding force than partner.

Chapter 6

STEINBECK'S THE MOON IS DOWN (1942)

by Charles J. Clancy

I. BACKGROUND

Various terms have been applied to Steinbeck's The
Moon Is Down: play-novelette, novel, novella, and novelette.
In fact, the work exists in two forms, that of a play which
was written first and opened in New York in 1942, and that
of a novella, also published in 1942. The first phrase, one
used by Steinbeck, can and has been applied to two other
works by the author--Of Mice and Men (1937) and Burning
Bright (1950). Since the play and the novella are so close
in content, if not correspondent in form, it might be worthwhile to discuss their origins simultaneously.

The success of Of Mice and Men, in print and later
on the stage, made possible Steinbeck's first trip to Europe
in 1936-37.[1] He traveled on a Swedish ship and developed
a fondness for Scandinavia, Norway in particular. This suggests at least some personal familiarity with the small village in an unnamed democratic eastern European country that
he later depicts in the novella.

Before American entry into the second World War,
attempts were made to enlist the talents of American writers
in the cause of the allies. After America's declaration of
war against the Axis powers, Steinbeck was encouraged to
contribute to the war effort. Bombs Away (1942), a kind of
pictorial version of a training exercise exposing the Army
Air Corps to the American populace, was Steinbeck's first
such effort. In 1941, Steinbeck had conversations with Col.
William J. Donovan, head of the Office of Strategic Services
(the precursor of the CIA). They discussed resistance movements in Eastern Europe and the value of propaganda by
American writers to those groups. One result, as suggested

100

by a number of critics, was The Moon Is Down, both play
and novella. 2

The first mention of the play occurs in a letter by
Steinbeck in September of 1941: "I may write my play [in
New York]. "3 Before its completion in play form on Decem-
ber 8, 1941, with its present title (SLL, 238), Steinbeck
wrote about its nature and his intentions to his friend, Webster
F. Street on November 25, 1941:

> The play? It's about a little town invaded. It has
> no generalities, no ideals, no speeches, it's just
> about the way the people of a little town would feel
> if it were invaded. It isn't any country and there
> is no dialect and it's about how the invaders feel
> about it too. It's one of the first sensible things
> to be written about these things and I don't know
> whether it is any good or not. (SLL, 237)

Some of the suggestions Steinbeck makes belie his effort,
and certainly pale in relation to the conflict critics would
generate concerning anonymity and systems of belief, reward,
and punishment present or absent in the two works.

Early academic/professional reviews of the play were
fairly positive. John Gassner, in Current History (1942),
speaks of it as good theatre, if a better novelette than what
he calls a sketch of a play. 4 Rosamond Gilder, in Theatre
Arts Monthly (1942), is more enthusiastic. She praises its
microcosmic vision, its fairness to the humanity of both
sides, and its dramatic immediacy. 5 Henrich Straumann
reports Eastern European reaction to the novella as a powerful piece of propaganda, 6 while James W. Tuttleton states
that it was "met with general disappointment"7 in Russia because Steinbeck was thought to be too compassionate to the
Germans. However, James Thurber was more vitriolic in
the New Republic of March 16, 1942, and it was denounced
in both the Saturday Review and Newsweek.

The play was selected for inclusion in The Best Plays
of 1941-42, and The Year Book of the Drama in America,
edited by Burns Mantle. 8 It achieved a respectable run on
the New York stage, opened at the Whitehall Theatre in London on June 8, 1943, 9 and ironically, as Steinbeck was
leaving Moscow in 1963 after his part in a cultural exchange
program, The Moon Is Down opened to favorable reviews by
Tass (Tuttleton, 89).

Although sales of the novella were brisk, and its
stage history positive, professional critics of the theater
and of literature since 1943 have generally joined in its
disparagement. It is of interest to hear Steinbeck's reaction to its vilification. In an essay for the English
Journal of 1954 entitled "My Short Novels," Steinbeck had
this to say:

> I wrote The Moon Is Down as a kind of cele-
> bration of the durability of democracy. I
> couldn't conceive that the book would be de-
> nounced. I had written of Germans as men,
> not supermen, and this was considered a very
> weak attitude to take. [10]

Here the novella's "invader[s]"[11] are identified as Germans,
as if Steinbeck, after the passage of twelve years, was able
to temper his original reaction to the work's savaging by
critics he had earlier termed "Park Avenue Commandos"
(O'Connor, 80). In a letter to Pascal Covici in 1957, Steinbeck satisfyingly reports an anecdote that seemed at least to
bear out Colonel Donovan's desires for the work. Steinbeck
had met an Italian who, during the war, has translated and
run off 500 copies of the novella for resistance fighters in
Italy. The individual was fascinated by it because it "so
exactly described Italy" (SLL, 590). So much, Steinbeck
crows, for the critics. Despite the sense of vindication,
and Steinbeck's suggestion that critics themselves need to be
reviewed, [12] The Moon Is Down has received scant praise, if
a fair amount of space, in the literary criticism devoted to
Steinbeck's works.

II.   PLOT SYNOPSIS

Steinbeck's novella, The Moon Is Down (1942), is
divided into eight chapters, his play of the same name into
eight scenes. The correspondence between the two are
quite close, with the exception of the stage directions and
business of the latter. Each chapter/scene recounts the
events of the occupation of a village by an invading force
described in Chapter One as the "invader[s or] foreign
soldiers" (MID, 1, 3). For convenience, the cast of characters is first listed, and then a chapter-by-chapter summary of the novella follows.

Villagers   Invaders

Mayor Orden   Col. Lanser, commandant
Madame Orden   Major Hunter, engineer
Dr. Winter   Capt. Bentick, first to die
Joseph⎱ servants of the Mayor   Capt. Loft, ideal soldier
Annie ⎰   Lt. Prackle
Alexander Morden, first to   Lt. Tonder, second to die
  be executed   Sgt. and enlisted men
Molly Morden, his widow
Mr. Corell, collaborator
William Deal   ⎫
Walter Doggel   ⎬ escapees
Will and Tom Anders   ⎭ to England

Chapter One: Four hundred years of democratic
government is ended in a little less than an hour. The invaders, in battalion strength, take the town, neutralize the
local troops, and bury the town's dead. They play band
music and obtain quarters as their commander, Col. Lanser,
arrives at 11 a. m. to discuss the new order with Mayor
Orden. He arrives promptly, after Captain Bentick has
everyone searched and the Mayor's weapons seized. He
also tells Dr. Winter the identity of the local quisling, Mr.
Corell. The Mayor's servants, Joseph and Annie the cook,
are present. After Corell's work has been revealed to the
Mayor, he is forced to leave, and Lanser asks for coopera-
tion. Annie scalds some soldiers on the rear porch, and
Lanser excuses her conduct in an effort to get Orden's co-
operation. The Mayor will remain in office in return for
order, fish, and coal. Lanser "requests" the Mayor's house
for staff billeting, and leaves.

Chapter Two opens in the invaders' headquarters
room at the Mayor's home. Here Steinbeck sketches rapidly
the members of the military staff. Major Hunter, a model
railroad buff, is an "arithmetician rather than a mathemati-
cian" (MID, 22); Captain Bentick is a gentle anglophile;
Captain Loft, a Hitler youth type; while Lieutenants Prackle
and Tonder are respectively a snot-nosed artist and a darkly
romantic, if naive poet. Col. Lanser is the only one presented as knowing "what war really is in the long run" (MID,
25). He is older, more experienced, and the center of
strength and weakness for the invaders. Hunter works on
designing a siding for the mine. Loft gives manual-of-arms
lectures, until he is sent to relieve Bentick at the coal mine.
Hope for a quick end to the war and return home fades

quickly.   After Corell and Lanser argue privately about
measures for the control of the village and the new role of
the quisling, Loft then returns to report the death of Captain
Bentick at the hands of a miner, Alex Morden.

   Chapter Three: The news of Morden's act spreads
and the novocaine mood of earlier reactions begins to dis-
sipate.   Escapes to England begin, as well as plots against
the life of Corell.   Molly arrives and Orden tells her that
he will not sentence her husband.   Lanser follows to ask
Orden to participate in Morden's trial, to keep order and
appearances.   The Mayor denies the validity of martial law
built upon the murder of six of the town's inhabitants.   He
then tells the Colonel that he has embarked upon an impossible job: "to break man's spirit permanently" (MID, 54).

   Chapter Four opens with an early snow and a gray
sky.   The military trial is conducted, and Morden is found
guilty and sentenced to death.   He expresses no remorse,
despite the record, and Orden makes his first clear public
act.   He tells Morden and the court, "You will make the
people one" (MID, 59).   He then kisses Morden on the cheek,
and listens as his execution takes place in the town square.
Immediately, reprisals begin as Lt. Prackle is wounded by
a shot through a window of the Mayor's house.   Violence,
emotion, and destruction all start to accelerate.

   Chapter Five: As time passes into winter, the air of
victory changes to one of entrapment and terror as "slow,
silent waiting revenge [brings] death in the air [and the]
conqueror[s find themselves] surrounded" (MID, 61) and
afraid.   Sabotage wracks the mine, and lanterns are used to
supply light at military headquarters.   Tonder, already upset, loses control and suggests to Joseph that the "leader"
is crazy, that the war will never end, and hysterically avows
that the "flies conquer the flypaper" (MID, 73).   Loft strikes
Tonder as the chapter ends.

   Chapter Six: Repressive measures grow.   Annie announces to Molly that the Mayor and the Anders boys will
visit her home before the Anders flee to England.   Annie
leaves, Lt. Tonder arrives and pleads his case with Molly.
She offers herself to him for "two sausages" (MID, 82).   He
leaves, and the Mayor and the others arrive.   They plot to
kill Corell, and to secure dynamite for the village from the
English.   As Tonder returns, the others flee.   Molly hides
a pair of scissors in her dress, which she will later use to
kill the lieutenant.

Chapter Seven opens as "In the dark, clear night a
white half withered moon [yields] little light" (MID, 92).   Two
bombers circle and drop packages of dynamite.   By 9 a. m.,
Loft brings samples of the packages to Col. Lanser.   They
are addressed "to the unconquered people" (MID, 100), and
are provided with instructions for sabotage.   Counter measures are discussed, as Corell arrives with new authority.
He demands that Orden be held hostage for order in the village.   Tonder's death is revealed, and Lanser must stiffen
the will of the despondent Prackle, exhorting him to duty,
since "We can't take care of your soul" (MID, 106).   Orden
and the Doctor are both arrested and held as hostages.

Chapter Eight: Orden's arrest becomes known, and
the townspeople continue to hide the air-lifted packages.
Orden displays "a fierce little jubilance" (MID, 109), and
Dr. Winter announces to the Mayor that "we have as many
heads as we have people, and in a time of need leaders pop
up among us like mushrooms" (MID, 112).   The Mayor admits his fear and repeats Socrates' speech before his death
from The Apology, which he had recited at his high school
graduation.   Lanser enters and hears it through.   The Mayor,
wearing his chain of office, tells the Colonel that:

> Free men cannot start a war, but once it is
> started, they can fight on in defeat.   Herd men ...
> cannot do that, and so it is always the herd men
> who win battles and the free men who win wars.
> (MID, 118)

Lanser re-affirms his fidelity to his role--"I will carry out
my orders no matter what they are ..." (MID, 119)--as
explosions are heard in the background.   After the 11 a. m.
deadline set by the Colonel, Orden kisses his wife, and
quotes Socrates' farewell to Crito: "I owe a cock to
Asclepius' (MID, 120).   As he leaves to be executed, he is
answered by Dr. Winter: "The debt shall be paid" (MID,
120).

III.   CRITICAL EXPLICATION

The Moon Is Down, the play and the novella, has
been roughly handled by the critics since its first stage
performance and its publication.   It is characteristically
judged a failure for moral, political, social, and intellectual
reasons.   When it is examined without any overt assertions

of failure, it is usually described as either a transitional or link work, most frequently flawed by its form, or by Steinbeck's intentions.

Blake Nevius considers the portrayal of Col. Lanser, and a denial of "the moral dilemma"[13] between his roles as a soldier and as a human being, revelatory of Steinbeck's "sentimental evasion" (Nevius, 310) of the tragic irony of the novella. Reloy Garcia feels that attempting to contribute to the war effort prompted Steinbeck to "narrow moralizing and thin propaganda; [thus, he became] a disseminator of parables, of thin moral tracts."[14] For Edwin Berry Burgum the same tension indicates that Steinbeck "broke under the strain in The Moon Is Down."[15] It takes no political sides: "Instead it advocates by inference a third system which is neither Nazism nor democracy but a vague kind of aristocratic government" (Bergum, 117). For Peter Lisca it is a political failure, as well as an artistic one, and "a better play than it is a novel."[16] It lacks the tension of real experience, is too abstract and teleological, and lacks both effective characterization and a "significant structure" (Lisca, 190-91). Lisca concludes that "the main failure of The Moon Is Down is that it carries stylization beyond the limits where it emotionally concerns us, to the point of dehumanizing his materials" (Lisca, 196).

In his 1955 dissertation, Lisca had noted that the novella's system had submerged its characters, to the detriment of both.[17] Critical ascription of design imposed, if not successfully executed, introduces Warren French's reading of the novella as an unsuccessful Faustian allegory, in which story and moral fail to coalesce.[18] In his essay on Steinbeck, in American Winners of the Nobel Literary Prize (1968), French concludes that the didactic impulse of the fabulist (moralist) in the novella forced Steinbeck "to strain too hard to make his points."[19] Joseph Fontenrose interprets it as "a parable of democracy against tyranny"[20] in which the false humanity of the Germans, and a flawed structure, reveal "plainly the inadequacies of Steinbeck's interpretation of society and history" (Fontenrose, 101). John Clark Pratt considers the novella's "Parabolic structure ... its characterizations and situation ... contrived,"[21] and the result is an unsuccessful allegory.

Howard Levant begins his discussion of the novella by demolishing Steinbeck's assertions about the nature of the play-novelette as a literary form.[22] He then denies it effective structure, characterization, and a consistent logic or morality (Levant, 146-57). Finally, Roy S. Simmonds judges it flawed as a novel because of its over-dependence upon stage technique, flawed as a play because of its lack of flexibility and experimental design, and concludes that it "made a far better film than it did a play."[23]

Three critics have considered the novella as primarily significant because of its linking or transitional relationship to the earlier and later fiction of Steinbeck. Lester Jay Marks notes that it "defies classification as either a contribution to the war effort or as critical commentary on war [although] it represents the most reliable link between his pre- and post-war fiction."[24] Robert E. Morsberger considers In Dubious Battle, The Grapes of Wrath, and The Moon Is Down as the root studies of leadership for Steinbeck's Zapata.[25] Thus, the novels and the novella alike "reveal a continuity in Steinbeck's intellectual concerns" (Morsberger, 59). Lawrence William Jones suggests that Steinbeck's career falls into two parts: first "the pre-war work [which] represents experiments with the form of the novel, [and second] the post-war work [which represents] an experiment with the form of parable."[26] The Moon Is Down is transitional, that is, between these two stages, because it is non-teleological in morality and because intellectually an unresolved conflict between Steinbeck's biological theory of group man and his artistic theory of the play-novelette animates the works (Jones, 18).

The Moon Is Down may be all that the critics suggest, and yet aspects of its meaning have not been fully explored. One such aspect is the theme of love in the novella. It is a theme both literal and metaphoric which re-appears in Steinbeck's work, his fiction in particular. Beneath the sun and the moon in his novels, from Cup of Gold to The Winter of Our Discontent, love animates the characters and activities of Steinbeck's fictional world. Whether it be love unrequited or fulfilled, love absent or present, Steinbeck examines the humanizing, singular faculty which unites and divides people.

The title The Moon Is Down evokes archetypal suggestions about the moon and its associations with love, and fulfillment or betrayal. Both Hyman and Fukuma have commented on its meaning here and in other fiction by Steinbeck.[27] In the novella the moon barely shines and the sun is soon obscured by snow and grey clouds. Because of the selection of the title, and because of the physical characteristics of its setting, Steinbeck intends the reader to view the

time of the novella as a stasis.   In it love is suspended
from nature and perverted into revenge.   It becomes an
abstraction given form by the deaths inflicted on both sides
in the village.   Thus, he depicts the neutral space that is a
world war.   It is a null set which epitomizes the paradoxical
naturalness or humanness of murder and destruction.

        Steinbeck consciously avoids an in-depth approach to
his characters, for both dramatic and intellectual reasons.
The characters function in a morality, not a parable or an
allegory, a bare-surfaced recounting of human foibles and
virtues placed in a time period when the loss of life, on
either side, is pointed to as demonstration of the fitness or
unfitness of a political philosophy or system.   Steinbeck's
point is that however natural war may be to the human
species, Huxley's argument in "War as a Biological Phen-
omenon" aside, the actions and thoughts it engenders reveal
more than who wins and who loses.   It touches upon what
Plato calls the pursuit of the one, the sense of integrity and
fitness, this side of the grave/veil, which animates life.

        If one considers a sampling of Steinbeck's novels
with regard to the theme of love, it is possible to see The
Moon Is Down in a new light.   To a God Unknown presents
the love of a man for the land and for fertility taken to such
an extreme that self love's perfect act is self-sacrifice.
Joseph Wayne commits a ritual suicide, and his blood renews
the land.   In Dubious Battle shows the divisiveness of political and social love of ideas or concepts in conflict not only
with the status quo, but with real human need.   Marxist
epistemology is as sufficient unto itself as bigoted hatred
for the have-nots, but neither nourishes understanding, nor
brings about a better future.   In The Grapes of Wrath, famil-
ial love represented by the extended Joad family carries with
it the code or ritual of strength and compassion in numbers.
The family may be splintered, part dead, and part-hunted,
yet it leaves traces of its efficacy, while those who seek to
destroy it leave only empty forms, the kind transferred from
one era to another, by mindless violence, fascism, totali-
tarianism, and also democracy.   George and Lennie, in Of
Mice and Men, illustrate more than the truth of platitudes
such as Robert Burns' line about plans and reality.   In the
novella George's intellectual and emotional love for Lennie,
who loves him in return on a visceral and a cerebral level,
cannot compete with or remain strong in a world that judges
by appearance and deals with cripples with a gun.   George's
intellect can grasp the problem, but he cannot overcome the

obstacles to a fruitful life and love when the object of the
love possesses what the majority considers a deficient
intellect. George must kill Lennie as an act of love, just
as Joseph Wayne must kill himself to bring rain.   Closer to
the experience of most middle-class Americans is the plight
of Ethan Allen Hawley in The Winter of Our Discontent.
Ethan returns betrayal for confidence, death for weakness,
and almost flees life. He is called back by the insight and
tenacity of his daughter. Ethan's lonely self, the talisman,
and his view of the future embodied by his daughter make
possible his final reclamation. He has been transformed by
the power of love, and there is hope for his further development. Tentative as the application of the thesis of love is,
it is clear that Steinbeck feels there is a force capable of
binding and destroying individuals and groups.   Love is also
an important theme in The Moon Is Down.

      Steinbeck intends the title of the novella and the names
of a number of its characters to be significant posts for
meaning and association. Thus, the title, The Moon Is Down,
is a rhetorical question and a metaphoric statement. It asks
and the novel suggests such questions as why is the moon
down? when will it rise? what will the day be like after it
reappears? and what kind of period before dawn does it
represent here and now? The correspondence between setting
and time of year also relates to the moon.   Its time frame
is fall and early winter. These represent more than just a
temporal setting; they also represent the time of life and the
part of the sensuous cycle closest to death, and therefore to
rebirth, both literally and metaphysically.   In the novella,
death is the emblem of action, life is in the future.   Dr.
Winter, the sage physician-scientist, is an emblematic character. He no longer delivers babies, but sees to the dead
and dying. Mayor Orden's name singularly introduces the
paradox of order before the invasion and during it, and by
his death as a part of the new order, he reveals the nature
of life in the present and expectations for the future.   Captain
Loft in conduct and speech represents the pragmatic military
idealist. He is cruelty and simple-mindedness given the
trappings of the status quo of force. Finally, Col. Lanser's
name is both a military and a Christian emblem. He is the
military man in the costume and abnegated will. He is also
a New Testament symbol for the acid test of life and death,
as at the Crucifixion. The cast and the setting, the time of
year and the exemplary role it plays in relation to individual
man, all combine in Steinbeck's effort to portray the sub-
lunar landscape of a lazar house of madness and death, in
which love is functional and not liberating.

On the surface of the morality, Steinbeck seems to
be suggesting a conflict within human society between a
series of interdependent units capable of love and sacrifice
and an integer society strong because of its willed oneness
of purpose and action. The basic thesis seems to be that
man, who is not a self but a function, must fall before Dr.
Winter's mushrooms. Yet what is really the same about the
two sides is what Burgum points to: "Nazi and underground
alike share the same pathology, though to highly varying
degrees; just as high principle, whether in German or native
ranks, is stained with the same tincture of impotent com-
pliance" (Burgum, 118). Thus both causes and sides succumb and share a repugnance for compassion and human
heartedness. If the Colonel is repellent and sad because he
has his position in the interest of an order based upon witless
violence, the same is ultimately true of both the Mayor and
the Doctor. If we are all equally replaceable, and if the
roles of represser and revenger continue unchecked into the
future, they both reinforce Steinbeck's point. The moon is
down here because the archetypal explanations for cycle, for
human life, and for continuance have been voided.

The novella primarily focuses upon the old. The
Mayor and his wife, the Doctor, the Colonel, Annie, and
Joseph are all past their prime. Captain Bentick is a
dreamer who dies unconsciously, Captain Loft is hopelessly
violent and impotent, and those who are younger are equally
limited, like Molly and her husband, a "stillborn" couple
reverting to mother and child roles as the death of Alex
approaches. This is also how he is remembered, like a
hurt child leaving for school/execution for the first and last
time. The two young lieutenants are characterized early as
types of the artist and poet--both out of place and time in
this era--one close to madness and the other close to a
death which is hardly military. The village has no literal
children, there is no procreation, and Dr. Winter delivers
no babies. Sex, as in the case of Lt. Tonder, leads to
death, not new life, and Colonel Lanser's message to Lt.
Prackle is millennially explicit. You may love or rape a
girl here if you choose, but you must kill her when ordered.
The kinds of love, and their illustration of a lack of com-
munication, even a feeling for words or their literal accura-
cy, are seen in a number of instances. There is class and
station love--Lanser's love of role rather than of self or of
another, Loft's love of leader and of power, Tonder's love
of pastoral beauty even in a subjugated land, and the Mayor's
love of the emblem of his office--that is, he wears his chain

of office to his death.   Thus, the thesis of love in war and
its association with the thoughts that Steinbeck seeks to
communicate are more important to the author than the
setting of the novella in Scandinavia or Italy.   The village
might as well be on a different planet for all the prospect
significance The Moon Is Down contains.

Love in The Moon Is Down is inadequate.   There is
both no time and no world for its enactment.   As Marvell's
"To His Coy Mistress" suggests, the characters of the
novella are within "the iron gates of life" (1.44), entombed
where "none, I think, do [there] embrace" (1.32).   The
novella continues to raise other questions.   Is it appropriate
to choose the courage you prefer, for philosophical, political, or ethical reasons?   Or, should there be a universal
definition for it, a point to which it is put and which transcends the particular?   Steinbeck asks the reader to ponder
the questions and the answers.   It is therefore easy to
understand the dismay and anger of the critics of the
novella/play.   There are no easy answers; there is no cer-
titude since the novella possesses a juggernaut-like consistency in putting at center stage, or at the center of thought,
the archetypal dissatisfaction with a world and its events
during a war.

Socrates not only helps place the theme of love and
its relationship to life in a humanistic tradition, he is the
appropriate figure for allusion in the novella.   He is a pre-
Christian martyr, a self-motivated lover of intellect and life
who further emblemizes the suggestions about setting and
character in the novella.   He is old, poor, and a victim of
the society he brought light and meaning to.   His death
amply illustrates the poverty of spirit which suggests tire-
lessly that humans kill and rekill that which they fear, and
therefore seek to destory.   It is further ironic that Orden
quotes Socrates' speech correctly, despite Winter's and the
Colonel's comments.   Socrates did say "after my death [not
departure (MID, 115)] punishment far heavier than you have
inflicted on me will surely await you."[28]   Socrates' legacy
to his children, his own, was to hope that they would remain
poor.   Orden's legacy to the village and to the invaders is
a poverty of spirit illustrated by the quote from the Phaedo
that Winters hears and responds to (MID, 120).   The killing
will continue, and the moon is still down.   It is not a
Christian nor a Socratic world, but an anthropomorphic one
of lost souls and values.   There is courage, it is true, but
it is partisan; it is not the transcendental emotion that love

is, nor is it Hyman's sense of the transcendent strength of
the free man overcoming the mindless invader (Hyman, 164).

NOTES

1. Lewis Gannet, "John Steinbeck's Way of Writing," in
   Steinbeck and His Critics: A Record of Twenty-Five
   Years, eds. E. W. Tedlock, Jr. and C. V. Wicker
   (Albuquerque: University of New Mexico Press, 1957),
   p. 31.

2. See Warren French, John Steinbeck (New York: Twayne,
   1961), pp. 126-27; F. W. Watt, Steinbeck (London:
   Oliver and Boyd, 1962), p. 77; James Woodress,
   "John Steinbeck: Hostage to Fortune," South Atlantic
   Quarterly, 43 (Winter 1964), p. 392; Richard O'Con-
   nor, John Steinbeck (New York: McGraw-Hill, 1970),
   p. 78; for an exception to the above, see Stanley
   Edgar Hyman, "Some Notes on John Steinbeck," in
   Steinbeck and His Critics: A Record of Twenty-Five
   Years, p. 153.

3. John Steinbeck, Steinbeck: A Life in Letters, eds.,
   Elaine Steinbeck and Robert Wallsten (New York:
   Viking, 1975), p. 237. Hereafter references appear
   in the text prefaced by SLL and the page number.

4. John Gassner, "The Moon Is Down as a Play," Current
   History, 2 New Series (May 1942), 236.

5. Rosamond Gilder, "Moon Down, Theatre Rises,"
   Theatre Arts Monthly, 26 (May 1942), 187-89.

6. Heinrich Straumann, American Literature in the Twentieth Century (1951, rpt. New York: Harper and Row,
   1965), pp. 115-16.

7. James W. Tuttleton, "Steinbeck in Russia: The Rhetoric
   of Praise and Blame," Modern Fiction Studies, 11
   (Spring 1965), 82.

8. John Steinbeck, "The Moon Is Down [play]," in The
   Best Plays of 1941-42 and the Year Book of the
   Drama in America, ed. Burns Mantle (New York:
   Dodd, Mead, and Company, 1942), pp. 72-108.

9. Roy S. Simmonds, "John Steinbeck's World War II Dispatches: An Annotated Checklist," Serif, 11 (Summer 1974), 22.

10. John Steinbeck, "My Short Novels," English Journal, 43 (March 1954), 147.

11. John Steinbeck, The Moon Is Down [novella] (1942; rpt. London: William Heinemann, Ltd., 1971), p. 1. Hereafter references appear in the text prefaced by MID and the page number.

12. John Steinbeck, "Critics--A Writer's Viewpoint," in Steinbeck and His Critics: A Record of Twenty-Five Years, p. 51.

13. Blake Nevius, "Steinbeck: One Aspect," Pacific Spectator, 3 (Summer 1949), 309.

14. Reloy Garcia, Steinbeck and D. H. Lawrence: Fictive Voices and the Ethical Imperative (Steinbeck Monograph Series, No. 2, 1972), p. 27.

15. Edwin Berry Burgum, "The Sensibility of John Steinbeck," Science and Society, 10 (Spring 1946), 133.

16. Peter Lisca, The Wide World of John Steinbeck (New Brunswick, N.J.: Rutgers University Press, 1958), p. 186.

17. Peter Lisca, "The Art of John Steinbeck," Ph.D. diss., University of Wisconsin, 1955, in John Steinbeck: A Guide to the Doctoral Dissertations (Steinbeck Monograph Series, No. 1, 1971), ed. Tetsumaro Hayashi, p. 3.

18. French, p. 32, p. 115.

19. Warren French, "John Steinbeck," in American Winners of the Nobel Literature Prize, eds., W. G. French and W. E. Kidd (Norman, Oklahoma: University of Oklahoma Press, 1968), p. 216.

20. Joseph Fontenrose, John Steinbeck: An Introduction and Interpretation (New York: Barnes and Noble, 1963), p. 99.

21. John Clark Pratt, John Steinbeck: A Critical Essay.
     (Grand Rapids, Michigan: William B. Eerdmans,
     1970), p. 78.

22. Howard Levant, The Novels of John Steinbeck: A Crit-
     ical Study (Columbia, Missouri: University of Mis-
     souri Press, 1974), pp. 130-31.

23. Roy S. Simmonds, Steinbeck's Literary Achievement
     (Steinbeck Monograph Series, No. 6, 1976), pp. 24-25.

24. Lester Jay Marks, Thematic Design in the Novels of
     John Steinbeck (The Hague: Mouton, 1969), pp. 99-
     100.

25. Robert E. Morsberger, "Steinbeck's Zapata: Rebel
     vs. Revolutionary," in Steinbeck: The Man and His
     Work, eds., Richard Astro and Tetsumaro Hayashi
     (Corvallis, Oregon: Oregon State University Press,
     1971), p. 44.

26. Lawrence William Jones, "John Steinbeck as a Fabulist,"
     ed. Marston LaFrance (Steinbeck Monograph Series,
     No. 3, 1973), p. 3.

27. Stanley Edgar Hyman, in Steinbeck and His Critics: A
     Record of Twenty-Five Years, pp. 153-57; Kin-ichi
     Fukuma, "Man in Steinbeck's Works," Kyushu Ameri-
     can Literature, 7 (1964), pp. 21-30.

28. Plato, The Apology, tr. Benjamin Jowett, in The Har-
     vard Classics, ed. C. W. Eliot. Plato, Epictetus,
     Marcus Aurelius, II (New York: P. F. Collier,
     1909), p. 26.

IV. APPARATUS FOR RESEARCH PAPERS

          A. Ten Questions for Discussion

1. What is a play-novelette? (According to Steinbeck?
     According to the critics?)
2. Discuss initial critical reaction to: a. the play (1942);
     b. the novella (1942); c. the movie (1943).
3. In light of the war protest movement of the 1960s,
     ascertain Steinbeck's attitude toward World War II as
     evidenced by The Moon Is Down.

4. What is the significance of the work's title?
5. Relate the play to Greek, Roman, Elizabethan, European, and American drama. Is it a tragedy, or a melodrama?
6. Discuss narrative technique, imagery, style, tone, characterization, and structure in both versions of the work.
7. Relate Steinbeck's sense of group or herd man, and his sense of the importance of the individual (i. e., see SLL, 354) to the propagandistic level of the work.
8. Apply Aquinas' four-fold exegetical method to the novella. Apply E. M. Forster's distinction of flat and round fictional creations to it.
9. How realistic are Corell's (the quisling) expectations after the invasion?
10. Why is the theme of religion either absent or muted in the novel? Is there humor in the work?

B. Suggested Topics for Research Papers

1. Relate the novel to post-World War II fiction by Americans on the same subject.
2. Relate the terms non-teleological or objectivity, by Steinbeck, to "Negative Capability" or "Wise-Passiveness," by Keasts, in relation to the style of the novella and Keasts' sense of a musical scale applicable to language and emotion.
3. Compare and contrast the play-novelettes of Steinbeck with the dramas of Sir Walter Scott.
4. Relate, stylistically and thematically, The Moon Is Down to Steinbeck's Once There Was a War.
5. Relate the theory of the four elements/humors to the characters and setting of The Moon Is Down.
6. Compare and contrast The Moon Is Down with the battle of Ismail in Byron's Don Juan with regard to the statement each author makes about war.
7. Relate Yeats' "Second Coming" to the novella in view of the order before, during, and after the invasion that Steinbeck suggests.
8. Does The Moon Is Down represent Steinbeck's view of the world in 1942? Does it approach the world view presented in Auden's "The Shield of Achilles"? Relate the two worlds in terms of myth, or the lack of myth, in each work.
9. If comedy, according to Suzanne Langer, is a "green world of the imagination," how would you describe in colors, and in relation to faculties, what this novel represents?

10. Suppose the inhabitants of the village occupied the coun-
    try of the invaders. What would this relationship be
    like? Would it merely be a reversal of roles?

                    C. Selected Bibliography

1. <u>Texts</u>

Steinbeck, John. <u>The Moon Is Down</u> [novella]. London:
William Heinemann, 1942; rpt. 1971.

Steinbeck, John. <u>The Moon Is Down</u> [play]. In <u>The Best</u>
<u>Plays of 1941-42 and the Year Book of the Drama in</u>
<u>America</u>, ed. Burns Mantle. New York: Dodd, Mead,
& Co., 1942 (pp. 72-108).

2. <u>Letters</u>

Steinbeck, John. <u>Steinbeck: A Life in Letters</u>, eds. Elaine
Steinbeck and Robert Wallsten. New York: Viking, 1975.

3. <u>Bibliographical Material</u>

Beebe, Maurice, and Jackson R. Bryer, eds. "Criticism
of John Steinbeck: A Selected Checklist." <u>Modern Fic-</u>
<u>tion Studies</u>, 11 (Spring 1965), 90-103.

Bryer, Jackson R., ed. <u>Fifteen American Authors: A Sur-</u>
<u>vey of Research and Criticism</u>. "John Steinbeck," by
Warren French. Durham, N.C.: Duke University Press,
1969, pp. 369-87. <u>Sixteen American Authors....</u> Durham, N.C.: Duke University Press, 1974, pp. 499-
527.

Hayashi, Tetsumaro. <u>A New Steinbeck Bibliography, 1929-</u>
<u>1971</u>. Metuchen, N.J.: Scarecrow Press, 1973.

Steele, Joan. "John Steinbeck: A Checklist of Biographical,
Critical and Bibliographical Material." <u>Bulletin of Bibli-</u>
<u>ography</u>, 24 (May-August 1965), 149-52, 162-63.

Plato. <u>The Apology Phaedo</u>, tr. Benjamin Jowett, in <u>The</u>
<u>Harvard Classics</u>, ed. C. W. Eliot. <u>Plato, Epictetus,</u>
<u>Marcus Aurelius</u>, II. New York: P. F. Collier & Son,
1909.

4. Criticism

(a) Reviews of the Play:

Gassner, John. "The Moon Is Down as a Play," Current
History, 2 New Series (May 1942), 228-32. A favorable
review.

Gilder, Rosamond, "Moon Down, Theatre Rises." Theatre
Arts Monthly, 26 (May 1942), 287-89. Favorable, but a
catalogue of its failures as a play.

(b) Criticism of Secondary Importance

Burgum, Edwin Berry. "The Sensibility of John Steinbeck,"
Science and Society, 10 (Spring 1946), 132-47. The
novella is the evidence of Steinbeck's failing as a critic
of society, since it advocates not Nazism, or democracy,
but "a vague kind of aristocratic government" (rpt. in
Tedlock, p. 117).

Corin, Fernand. "Steinbeck and Hemingway," Revue des
Langues Vivantes, 24 (1958), 60-75, 153-63. Some interesting remarks on their two styles, but nothing directly
about the novella.

Davis, Robert Murray, ed. "Introduction," Steinbeck: A
Collection of Critical Essays. Englewood Cliffs, N.J.:
Prentice Hall, 1972. The novella is overwritten politi-
cally, with undeveloped characters.

Eisinger, Chester E. Fiction of the Forties. Chicago:
University of Chicago Press, 1963. Its failure as a
novella is not political but aesthetic and psychological--
indicative of the fact that Steinbeck had lost his creative
ability in the 40s.

Fukuma, Kin-ichi. "'Man' in Steinbeck's Works," Kyushu
American Literature, 7 (1964), 21-30. Dr. Winter is
Steinbeck's ideal humanist-scientist.

Hayashi, Tetsumaro, ed. John Steinbeck: A Guide to the
Doctoral Dissertations (Steinbeck Monograph Series, No.
1, 1971). See Lisca and Wallis.

Jackson, Joseph Henry, ed. The Shorter Novels of John
Steinbeck. New York: Viking, 1953; rpt. 1965. Critical

furor caused by Steinbeck's avoidance of extremes in the
novella.

Levidova, I. "The Post-War Books of John Steinbeck"
    (Voprosy Literature, No. 8, 1962), Soviet Review, 4
    (Summer 1963), 3-13. The novella focuses on the strug-
    gle between good and evil in moral conduct.

Lieber, T. M. "Talismanic Patterns in the Novels of John
    Steinbeck," American Literature, 44 (May 1972), 262-75.
    Interesting study of pattern and structure that might be
    applied to the novella.

Lisca, Peter. "Escape and Commitment: Two Poles of the
    Steinbeck Hero," in Steinbeck: The Man and His Work,
    eds. Richard Astro and Tetsumaro Hayashi. Corvallis,
    Oregon: Oregon State University Press, 1971. Orden is
    committed to the status quo, not the future, and his base
    is neither Christian nor symbolic, but only slightly
    Socratic.

Morsberger, Robert E. "Steinbeck on Screen," in A Study
    Guide to Steinbeck: A Handbook to His Major Works, ed.
    Tetsumaro Hayashi. Metuchen, N. J. : Scarecrow Press,
    1974, 258-98. The novella's screen version seen in the
    context of Steinbeck's other efforts in films.

_____. "Steinbeck's Zapata: Rebel vs. Revolutionary,"
    in Steinbeck: The Man and His Work, eds. Richard Astro
    and Tetsumaro Hayashi. Corvallis, Oregon: Oregon
    State University Press, 1971. One of Steinbeck's studies
    in leadership revealing "a continuity in Steinbeck's intel-
    lectual concerns" (p. 59).

Nelson, Harland S. "Steinbeck's Politics Then and Now,"
    Antioch Review, 27 (Spring 1967), 118-33. His political
    beliefs have not changed.

Nossen, Evon. "The Beast-Man Theme in the Work of John
    Steinbeck," Forum (Ball State University), 7 (Winter
    1966), 52-64. Applications to the novella are obvious,
    point is that human values, etc. , necessitate the control
    of the beast in man.

Ross, Woodburn. "John Steinbeck: Earth and Stars,"
    University of Missouri Studies in Honor of A. H. R.
    Fairchild, 1946, pp. 177-91.

_____. "John Steinbeck: Naturalism's Priest," College
English, 10 (May 1949), 432-38. Considers it an unusual
illustration of a democracy occupied and run by a totalitarian group.

Shively, Charles. "John Steinbeck: From the Tide Pool to
the Loyal Community," in Steinbeck: The Man and His
Work, eds. Richard Astro and Tetsumaro Hayashi. Corvallis, Oregon: Oregon State University Press, 1971. A
comparison of the ideas of Steinbeck, the naturalist, and
Josiah Royce, the neglected American absolute idealist.
Group man vs. individuality at an impasse.

Woodress, J. "John Steinbeck: Hostage to Fortune," South
Atlantic Quarterly, 43 (Winter 1964), 385-97. Sees the
novella as a factor of Steinbeck's journalistic bent, and
his major contribution to the war effort.

(c) Criticism of Primary Importance

Bracher, Frederick. "Steinbeck and the Biological View of
Man," Pacific Spectator, 2 (Winter 1948), 14-29. Group-
individual conflict reveals the Nazi evil to be a collective
force, and a destroyer of individuality.

Fontenrose, Joseph. John Steinbeck: An Introduction and
Interpretation. New York: Barnes and Noble, 1963.
The novella was intended to be a "parable of democracy
against tyranny" (p. 99). The Germans display a false
humanity, and the novella is a failure because Steinbeck
inaccurately represents both society and history.

French, Warren. John Steinbeck. New York: Twayne,
1961. The novella is a Faustian allegory inadequately
realized aesthetically.

_____. "John Steinbeck," in American Winners of the
Nobel Literary Prize, eds. W. G. French, and W. E.
Kidd. Norman, Oklahoma: University of Oklahoma Press,
1968. Strained failure as a fabulist/moralist.

Hyman, Stanley Edgar. "Some Notes on John Steinbeck," in
Steinbeck and His Critics: A Record of Twenty-Five
Years, eds. E. W. Tedlock, Jr. and C. V. Wicker.
Albuquerque, N. M. : University of New Mexico Press,
1957. Interesting, controversial article tracing the sig-
nificance of the title through Steinbeck's other works, and

suggesting that it represents a dialogue of Steinbeck's
ideas on the group and the individual.

Jones, Lawrence William.   John Steinbeck as a Fabulist,
   ed. Marston LaFrance.   (Steinbeck Monograph Series,
   No. 3, 1973.) The novella is transitional and not a
   parable because it is non-teleological and represents an
   unresolved conflict between biological and aesthetic theory.

Levant, Howard.   The Novels of John Steinbeck: A Critical
   Study.   Columbia: University of Missouri Press, 1974.
   Attacks Steinbeck's concept of the play-novelette and crit-
   icizes the play for not being organic in structure and effective in character or ideals.

Lisca, Peter.   The Wide World of John Steinbeck.   New
   Brunswick, N.J.:   Rutgers University Press, 1958.   The
   novella is a failure because it lacks tension, credibility,
   effective characterization, a significant structure, and a
   humanization of its materials.   Lisca prefers the play
   version.

Marks, Lester Jay.   Thematic Design in the Novels of John
   Steinbeck.   The Hague: Mouton, 1969.   A link between
   Steinbeck's pre- and post-war fiction, the novella is
   neither propaganda nor critical commentary on war.   It
   is a defense of democracy and an examination of the
   moral responsibility of individuals confronted with a
   totalitarian group.

Nevius, Blake.   "Steinbeck: One Aspect," Pacific Spectator,
   3 (Summer 1949), 302-10.   The novella is a moral and
   intellectual failure since Steinbeck's sentimentalism in his
   characterization of Lanser reflects his own uncertainty
   about the theme of the novel.

Pratt, John Clark.   John Steinbeck: A Critical Essay.
   Grand Rapids, Michigan: William B. Eerdmans, 1970.
   It has an unsuccessful parabolic structure, which presents
   characters rather than people and excessive moralizing
   rather than a realized allegory.

Simmonds, Roy S.   Steinbeck's Literary Achievement.
   (Steinbeck Monograph Series, No. 6, 1976.)   It explores
   "communal unity" (p. 9) and follows the basic structure
   of a stage play, which indicates its lack of success as a
   novella, and since it is not experimental enough, and has

limitations as a stage play.   He concludes "It is generally
agreed ... that The Moon Is Down made a far better film
than it did a play" (p. 25).

Watt, F. W. Steinbeck. London: Oliver and Boyd, 1962.
   It is a qualified failure because "it has the dangerous
   facility of a 'well-made play', though its simplicity and
   dignity can still be moving" (p. 78).

Chapter 7

STEINBECK'S A RUSSIAN JOURNAL (1948)

by Charles J. Clancy

I. BACKGROUND

Steinbeck's A Russian Journal was the result of a
trip he and Robert Capa, a professional photographer, took
to Russia in the summer and early fall of 1947. The trip
would have been undertaken earlier, except that Steinbeck
was injured at home that spring, and was unable to leave
New York until late July. As Steinbeck describes the cir-
cumstances, he had been unable to finish a play, probably
Burning Bright, and Capa was out of a poker game and had
just published Slightly Out of Focus (1947). [1] They met in
the bar of the Bedford Hotel, on East 40th Street, in New
York. At the suggestion of Steinbeck, and with the encour-
agement of Capa and the bartender, Willy, Steinbeck con-
tacted George Cornish of the Herald Tribune (RJ, 4), the
newspaper that had sent him to Europe in 1944. (His dispatches had resulted in Once There Was a War, 1958.) He
broached the subject of the paper's supporting a project of
travel to Russia to record, in words and pictures, their
experiences. Cornish agreed, and the trip, delayed as it
was, was undertaken. Steinbeck and Capa arrived in Moscow
on August 1, 1947, and remained in Russia until September
9-10, 1947, returning via Prague. As Richard O'Connor
notes, neither spoke Russian. [2]

Steinbeck was no stranger to the Soviet Union, having
visited it and Scandinavia, England, and Ireland in 1936-37
with his first wife, Carol. [3] He returned for the stage production of Of Mice and Men, the work whose profits had
financed the trip. The travelogue format appealed to Steinbeck: witness the Sea of Cortez (1941) and Travels with
Charley (1962). But this was an effort perhaps before its
time in the use of photographs to illustrate or comment on

the text.   Warren French praises it as "... a beautifully
written and illustrated book that ... failed to appeal to the
public. "4

Its media presentation is interesting because, as
Steinbeck says in the text of the journal, the camera was a
device which aroused suspicion and fear not only in the minds
of its subjects and their political representatives (RJ, 5),
but for personal reasons, in Steinbeck himself.   In a letter
of June 10, 1932 to his friend Robert O. Ballou, Steinbeck
had stated: "I hate cameras.   They are so much more sure
than I am about everything" (SLL, 63).   Steinbeck had evidently overcome this phobia, although the most frequent
criticism of the narrative portion of the journal has centered
around its tentativeness and lack of focus.   Concomitantly,
the photos have received greater praise as well as a wider
currency apart from the text.

Sixty-nine photos were selected and published from
an estimated 4,000 developed negatives (RJ, 8) that Capa
brought out of Russia, only a handful having been removed
before the two left Kiev.   Since a great deal is known about
Steinbeck, it might be worthwhile to include some information about Robert Capa, ně André Friedman, the photographer and author of "A Legitimate Complaint," part of this
journal.   Capa was born in Budapest, Hungary in 1913.   He
attended Berlin University, and became a professional photographer.   In 1935, in Paris, he adopted the name Capa,
a "successful European" and later "American photographer,"
to increase his business opportunity.   His photos of pre-
World War II Europe, particularly during the Spanish Civil
War (1936-39), gained him international recognition.   He
visited and photographed the early conflict between China and
Japan in 1938, and worked in Italy, England, and France,
participating in the Normandy invasion for Life in 1944.   His
friendship with Pablo Picasso produced some remarkable
photos, and he visited the U.S.S.R. in 1947 (with Steinbeck),
and Israel in 1948.   He died, as the first "American" correspondent casualty, in Indochina in 1954, the victim of a
landmine. 5

The collaboration in A Russian Journal is an interesting one, although neither Capa nor Steinbeck elected to
include a photo of either, or of both, in the text.   A Russian
Journal has elicited little detailed critical commentary until
fairly recently.   The reasons for that and for its re-assess-
ment will be discussed.   In addition, commentary by a pro-

fessional photographer on Capa's contributions to the journal
will be included.

II. SYNOPSIS

        A Russian Journal is comprised of nine chapters by
John Steinbeck, a three-page "Legitimate Complaint" by
Robert Capa, and sixty-nine photographs by Capa interspersed
throughout the text. Since it is a journal reconstructed from
notes, and presented in chronological fashion, a summary by
chapter will mimic its attempt to recreate the period spent
in Russia from August 1, 1947 to September 9-10, 1947.
Exact dating, that is, a day-by-day entry format, is not possible because the dates in the text are occasional in nature
rather than systematic. Where appropriate, the dates present
in the journal will be included.

        Chapter One details the circumstances that led to the
joint effort. It gives examples of the reactions of enlightened
and unenlightened friends and acquaintances to the projected
work, and introduces its thesis--to see and photograph the
Russian people, to "avoid politics and the larger issues" (RJ,
4), "to report what Russian people were like, and what they
wore, and how they acted, what the farmer talked about, and
what they were doing about rebuilding the destroyed parts of
their country" (RJ, 7). Steinbeck and Capa were to return
with over 4,000 negatives, and several hundred pages of
notes reduced in Chapters 2-9 as "A Russian Story" (RJ, 8)
as it happened.

        Chapter Two: Steinbeck and Capa flew from Stockholm
to Helsinki where they boarded a "Russian" C-47 for the
flight to Leningrad and then Moscow. The center of the
journal is Moscow, since all of their journeys started and
ended in the capital. After customs inspection at Helsinki,
and a view of the destroyed Stalingrad from the air, the
travelers arrived at Moscow on August 1, 1947. Unmet,
they were taken to the Hotel Metropole by a French courier.
They appropriated the room of Joe Newman, the Herald
Tribune reporter in Moscow, and proceeded to drink all of
his whiskey.

        Chapter Three finds Steinbeck and Capa trying to
establish their identity in the Soviet Union so as to be able
to travel beyond Moscow. Voks, the cultural relations
organization of the U.S.S.R., gets them a room in the Savoy

Hotel and assumes responsibility for them.   They travel in
Moscow, visit both ration and commercial restaurants, become accustomed to the office schedules there (noon to mid-
night), learn about the rouble-dollar rates of exchange, visit
stores, and are interviewed by Mr. Karaganov of Voks, who
promises to try to help them.   He asks them to tell the
truth, to tell what they see, and notes that "Stalin has said
that writers are the architects of the human soul" (RJ, 27).
Newman returns and they meet the American ambassador,
General Smith.   Voks then provides an interpreter and guide,
a University of Moscow American history major, Svetlana
Litvinova, afterwards known as Sweet Lana.   They visit the
Lenin Museum, an Air Show, and then, after seven days in
Moscow, they leave on August 8 for Kiev.

Chapter Four.   They are accompanied by Voks representative Mr. Chmarsky, renamed the Kremlin Gremlin, a
student of American literature.   They notice the prevalence
of statues of Lenin and Stalin in Moscow and all over Russia--
"a frightening thing and a distasteful one" (RJ, 51).   They
fly over the grain belt of the Ukraine to the Dnieper and Kiev.
They view the destruction wrought by the Germans--"Here
German culture did its work" (RJ, 53)--and are asked what
becomes a representative question: Will the U. S. attack the
U. S. S. R. ?   They visit the city's museum, which Capa describes as "the Church of the Russians" (RJ, 62).   They
attend a performance of a nineteenth-century melodrama,
Storm, and Steinbeck observes: "It seemed odd to us that
the people in the audience, who had known real tragedy,
tragedy of invasion, and death, and desolation, could be so
moved over the fate of the lady who got her fingers kissed
in the garden" (RJ, 65).   After a visit to the ubiquitous
Russian circus, and to a night club called The Riviera, the
chapter ends.

Chapter Five.   On August 9 they ride out to visit a
collective farm, Shevchenko I, almost totally destroyed by
the Germans and now being rebuilt.   It is the first good
harvest since 1941 and the farm has little machinery and few
livestock, but great hope.   The beekeeper has just received
six California queens, and he is proud of them.   Meals,
toasts, and political and social conversation (e. g. , how do
American farmers live?) end the day.   The next day they
visit a second and more prosperous collective farm,
Shevchenko II, which is electrified.   They eat, see a revolutionary play ("naive and charming, " RJ, 100), and are
asked about Roosevelt and atomic power.   Again they see

many women, few men, and notice the lack of prosthetic
devices for many of the living. Returning to Kiev, they visit
a bakery factory which produced while being bombed. "To
them mechanization means ease and comfort, and plenty of
food, and a general richness. They love machinery as much
as Americans do" (RJ, 110). Finally, Steinbeck is interviewed by a representative of a Ukranian literary magazine,
and fields questions about Simonov's play about American
journalism, The Russian Question. This line of questioning
is finally answered here and elsewhere by Steinbeck's satiric
outline of The American Question.

At the start of Chapter Six, Steinbeck and Capa return
to Moscow and a party. Capa makes an important contact
for developing his film in Russia, since they later learn it
would have been unlikely that they would be allowed to re-
move undeveloped film. They go out sightseeing again and
then fly to Stalingrad. They view the twenty miles of destruction on the Volga, visit the battlefield, a tractor factory, ride the Volga, and see the plans for the new city.
Since there is no city museum, only a plan for one, gifts to
the city from all over the world are brought to their hotel
room. Steinbeck says what they really need is "half a dozen
bulldozers" (RJ, 135). They tour an apartment complex and
get a sense of salaries and of the cost of things. (Skilled
workers earn 2,000 roubles a year, semi-skilled 1,000, un-
skilled 500; a new car costs 10,000 roubles, and a cow between 7,000 and 9,000.) They again board a plane for Moscow.

Capa's "Complaint" (RJ, 146-49) catalogues his dissatisfaction: he is not happy with Steinbeck, his negatives,
or the dull Russian people. He notes that he had been
denied entry to Russia in 1937.

Chapter Seven. Steinbeck and Capa fly to Georgia,
over the Caucasus, on the Black Sea. It is the Florida and
Southern California of Russia, and its gay, cheerful people
are the envy of all other Russians. The Germans never got
there. They visit Tiflis, the first clean Oriental city that
Steinbeck has ever seen.

Chapter Eight opens with Steinbeck attending the Tiflis
writer's reception at which he hears a history of Georgian
literature and answers questions about the role of the American writer and the literary tastes of its citizens. The next
day they visit Gori, the birthplace of Stalin, and then attend

championship wrestling matches. Near the Black Sea and at Batum they visit rest and vacation homes provided by labor unions and the government. They tour a tea farm and its completely mechanized factory, fly to Sukhum and then back to Moscow.

In Chapter Nine, Moscow is lit up for the celebration of the 400th anniversary of the city. Steinbeck covers it for Newman and the Tribune, since the reporter is in Stockholm. They again tour the city, observing the celebration. By September 6, it is getting cold in Moscow. They take a side trip to the home of Tchaikovsky, attend the Bolshoi, and see The Russian Question at the Moscow Art Theater. They dine with Simonov and tour the Kremlin, and Steinbeck refers to its artifacts as "the incredible claptrap of monarchy" (RJ, 213). At the Moscow Writers' Union dinner, a near-riot erupts about truth, literature, and the responsibility of the writer, until Karaganov calms everyone. With three days of their stay remaining, they go to two parties and to the Bolshoi again. Capa's box of developed negatives is taken for examination, and then returned. The Russians stipulate that it must remain sealed until they are off the ground at Kiev and on their way to Prague. They leave on Sunday, reach Kiev and find that only a few negatives have been removed (e. g. , a photo of the mad child of Stalingrad). On September 10, 1947, they arrive in Prague.

III. CRITICAL EXPLICATION

One point often repeated about Steinbeck is his sense of the relationship between the parts of a thing and the entity they comprise. In regard to the earth and its human inhabitants, Steinbeck is frequently read as one who examines the species for its herding instincts as well as for those particular factors which animate the herd(s) and, of necessity, isolate the individual. A Russian Journal is a continuation of this concern, an acting out of non-teleology, or objectivity, which points to what Byron had noticed 125 years before, that there is nothing human which is truly objective. Even the Republic uses the techniques of the poet-artist to castigate the bad artist. The point here is that the Journal, balanced by its photos of a people strange to most Americans in 1947-48, strikes one as an attempt to pose for a different camera. It does not quite work, and yet the effort is worthy of consideration. It is a personal view of and by two men, primarily by Steinbeck, and it provides his sense

of the order of things.   It is also an exercise in self-censor-
ship or self-control which is not always successful.   It asks,
if not answers, fundamental questions about not only reporting
what one sees, but about what is truthful and what art has to
do with truth.

For some of the reasons suggested above, I find it
difficult to do a great deal with most of the published criticism devoted to A Russian Journal.   That is, I find much of
it either academic in the strict sense, an exercise whose
purpose is publication, or thesis-oriented, the finding of a
work's place in a regimen of ideas by rules of inclusion or
exclusion.

A Russian Journal has been treated cursorily with the
rhetoric of both praise and blame.   Peter Lisca refers to it
as "an interesting piece of reporting,"[6] and interesting reading;[7] for Levidova it is a timely, necessary, "artless record";[8] and O'Connor notes "the intensity of [Steinbeck's]
curiosity."[9]   Joseph Fontenrose comments that it and Once
There Was a War "... although pleasant reading, add nothing
to Steinbeck's stature and are not significant, as was Sea of
Cortez, for an understanding of his fiction,"[10] and John Gray
suggests, on the basis of its alleged flaccid style, rambling
structure, and lack of pointed emphasis that it is "not one of
his most impressive achievements."[11]

The two most recent and longest critiques follow the
pattern illustrated above.   One is laudatory, if arch, and the
other more caustic at the expense of both the journal and its
author.   Both articles demonstrate contemporary attempts to
see all of Steinbeck in context.   Richard Astro censures the
Journal because it displays no curiosity which leads to discovery and knowledge.[12]   Its style, a "tired prose" (41), its
"steady tone" (42), and its preoccupation with facts "to the
exclusion of everything else" (44) indicate its flawed structure
and lack of insight into either its authors or its subject (41).
The redeeming feature of the Journal is its "fine photos" (41)
by Capa.   In essence, A Russian Journal does not do what
Astro wants it to do, and therefore it is a failure.   John F.
Slater's essay praises the work as a "delicate performance."[1]
But the article is written in a style difficult to evaluate, and
advances a thesis that nebulously traces its roots to the fiction and non-fiction of nineteenth- and twentieth-century Ameri
can authors who traveled in the world, principally Irving,
Twain, Crane, and Henry James.   The resemblances pointed
to are tenuous, and the purpose of this evocation remains

unclear at the end of the essay. Some of the difficulties of
its style and point are illustrated by the following:

> [The Journal is] a study in dualities that converge
> on the common center of Steinbeck's personal bias
> (99). [It contributes to] a systematic network of
> spirited references that participate in or contribute
> to the organic nucleus of Steinbeck's writing (99-
> 100). The molecular ingredients of Steinbeck's
> language in A Russian Journal spring from the
> dynamics of contrast (101).

Slater praises its "buoyant tone" (99) and notes that its
dominant stylistic technique is the simile (102). He concludes that "A Russian Journal often resembles a partially
inhibited debate between immobilizing bureaucracy and subversive, deadpan irony" (103).

It is more useful to examine the Journal as a unique
performance by Steinbeck than to compare it to the kinds of
precedent that Slater advances. That is, although it has its
roots in the literature of the past, whether American, or
English, or Russian, its point resides in what relationship
it evinces between what Steinbeck tried to do and what he
accomplished. In this light, Steinbeck's letter of June 8,
1949 to John O'Hara is germinal:

> I think I believe one thing powerfully--that the only
> creative thing our species has is the individual,
> lonely mind. Two people can create a child but I
> know of no other thing created by a group. The
> group ungoverned by individual thinking is a hor-
> rible destructive principle. The great change in
> the last 2,000 years was the Christian idea that
> the individual soul was very precious (SLL, 359).

The previous mention of Lord Byron was not accidental. It
seems to me that Steinbeck echoes here, and in his fiction,
his letters, and other journals a remarkably Romantic and
modern notion of the value of the individual and that which
identifies him as a member of a group. As Byron does in
his journals, Steinbeck plays a conscious role in this work.
Whereas Byron's roles are multiple, dependent upon occasion
and anticipated audience, Steinbeck's is more singular and
the result of a predisposition directly stated in the Journal
as its thesis and guiding force stylistically, rhetorically, and
ideationally. Steinbeck is attempting a tone of style and con-

ception that follows a median of both experience and expression. He wants to reach and touch the minds of those he observes in Russia and those who observe Russia through Capa's camera and his writing. He wants not to judge, but to show the thing for what it is. This, needless to say, is difficult and it runs counter not only to more contemporary efforts in journalistic reporting, but to Steinbeck's efforts in both fiction and non-fiction in works such as Sea of Cortez and Travels with Charley. This difference helps explain A Russian Journal and its cursory, caustic dismissals as well as its ultimate failure.

It might be suggested that Steinbeck attempts what Chesterfield accomplished in his Letters to His Son. Steinbeck is writing a book about conduct and the nature of a quest in an effort to bring the stranger and the resident together for a time. Mandeville's presence in Chapter One is also important, not because the inhabitants of Russia, or of the United States, are actually the curiosities that each frequently assumes the other to be, but because rumor and suspicion are frequently more forceful than the truth. John Stuart Mill suggests in On Liberty that the truth will not out if it is voiceless. If a photo does not lie, a great deal of its message may still be related to its method of preparation. In this context, Steinbeck is trying a didactic exercise aimed at being non-didactic, an exercise involving seeing before judging, and communicating before impressing, either negatively or positively. Steinbeck and Capa are not ugly American tourists, they are people; and the Russians are not representative of a Red Menace--they too are people. This, I believe, is Steinbeck's message, conveyed in a controlled style and vocabulary, with occasional lapses in form, insight, and taste. It is, however, generally focused upon exploring the bonds between people. It is about them as individuals and as members of a species--concentrating on concerns for birth, death, pain, joy, hospitality, hypocrisy, and nourishment, both real and imaginary.

In this record of forty days in Russia--centering in Moscow and radiating to the Southwest to Kiev, to the Southeast to Stalingrad, and to the deep South to Russian Georgia--Steinbeck and Capa attempt to recreate their trip, emphasizing throughout the surface upon which they travel, its reality. This encourages its readers, first, as Slater notes, to review their expectations (96), and then to wonder, to extrapolate, for example, to caption the photos for themselves as they read the text, and to go with their very human guides,

both Russian and American, on the journey itself.   Here we
confront the paradox of a belief in "the individual, lonely
mind" (SLL, 359) viewed inseparably from the herd which
surrounds and sustains it.   We must see both to notice
either.

What we find in A Russian Journal are not surprises
in themselves, but what Wordsworth and Coleridge para-
phrased would have referred to as seeing in a new light and
with different coloration things from our own environment,
that which we see so often and which we no longer notice.
Thus family love for the living and the dead, illustrated by
the little Russian boy who speaks every evening with his dead
father, the disassociated humanity of the mad girl of Stalingrad, the desire to share good food and drink, to wear our
best clothes and to clean house as marks of hospitality, love
for the circus, for the ballet, for art, for the theater, and
for sports are not striking in and of themselves, and yet
they are striking because we forget that our love and enjoyment of such things are not distinctly ours.   We have not
invited the pleasure or the pains of life, and what A Russian
Journal attempts is to cast a new look, not colored by imagination but by objectivity, on the substance of life within any
culture or national boundary.   One of the most striking things
about the Russians, their hope and confidence is what the
future will provide, by means of hard work, technology, and
an abundant nature, echoes too familiarly perhaps the American Dream.

In order to see what is underfoot, sometimes that
which directly confronts us must or will be ignored.   In this
case, questions about such subjects as politics, religion,
minority problems, and the repatriation of the German
prisoners of war seen in all the major cities visited here
go unasked as well as unanswered.   This absence erodes
one aspect of the substance of the work, but does not totally
invalidate it.

Despite its self-consistency and its success in ad-
hering to the thesis Steinbeck advances for A Russian Journal,
it is not a work likely to be considered major in his canon.
This is so not for most of the reasons suggested by its
critics, but rather because he could not carry off what he
attempted.   A Russian Journal is a prologue or an introduction to an unwritten work.   Its controlled style, in descriptions and conversations, verges on not only the repe-
titious, but the innocuous.   It is a little like trying accurately

to reproduce the speech of a bore; if successful, the attempt
overreaches itself and bores the reader.   Here the desire to
report trammels Steinbeck's identity, while Byron's extem-
poraneous and personal reflections release him.   Byron in
his journals conveys his impressions of mankind by his manipulation of reality.   Steinbeck tries to control reality, to
focus it, and the result is a sense of the physical background
prodded to center stage, a background that Byron carried with
him, within his thoughts and style.   Steinbeck has his own
background with him, but he tries to conceal or reduce it in
favor of a common denominator prospect he felt necessary
because of his subject matter.

Thus what is cause for praise in A Russian Journal
is also cause for blame.   It is not unique enough in the information it provides, although this is part of Steinbeck's
message; and similarly, it is not personal in what it reveals
about Steinbeck, although this is also Steinbeck's intention.
Thus, like Storm, the nineteenth-century melodrama that
Steinbeck viewed in Russia, his Journal is a period piece,
not for all time.   It is important, however, in Steinbeck's
canon because it demonstrates a unique approach to a series
of difficult questions about being human and a writer.   Although some of Capa's photos are already classics, A Russian Journal will likely remain interesting as an experiment,
if not as an accomplishment.

Commentary by Alan Harkrader, Jr. ,
Professional Photographer and Artist

The first difficulty in commenting about the photographs
is caused, not by the photos or their contents, but by the
many changes that have taken place in the photographer's
craft since Capa made them some thirty years ago.   Since
1947 there have been many improvements in films and
cameras.   Thus, when a photographer looks at a thirty-year-
old photograph, he must make a conscious attempt to avoid
applying today's technical standards.   Of course, a reader
without any knowledge of photography would not have this
compulsion to compare photographic eras.

When A Russian Journal was published in 1948 the
"picture book" fad had not yet been born.   Life and Look
magazines were beginning to give the reading public the
picture story in weekly magazines, but a hard-cover publication using the photojournalist's technique was seldom used.

As one consequence, today's media would not reduce Capa's "nearly 4,000 negatives" (RJ, 8) of the Russian trip to the sixty-nine photographs used to accompany the text.

From a technical standpoint, a few of the photos suffer from the small size in which they were reproduced, especially those with vast amounts of detail, such as the city and landscapes. All photographs lose both some detail and some tone when they are translated into halftones for mechanical reproduction; this loss is amplified when they are printed on uncoated, non-white stock. In the case of this first edition, the text of the reverse page tends to bleed through the photos, causing a further degradation of the image.

The photographs are well placed with Steinbeck's text, so that they do read well with the narrative, but many of the photographs leave the reader with unanswered questions. Rare is the photo that can stand by itself, without some explanation. Very basic questions are raised by Capa's photos that are not answered by Steinbeck's copy; many people are introduced in the written journal, but one is never sure of the identity of the people in many of the illustrations. Simple captions accompanying the photos could have been used to answer these questions, and very likely would have made an even more direct link between the photographs and the copy.

Another criticism is the failure to show the reader a photograph of either Steinbeck or Capa. The journal contains the continual references to "I," "Capa," and "we," but the photos never show either of the authors.

The historical importance of the photographs cannot be overlooked, as they did serve their primary purpose: to show the world what Russia and the Russian people looked like and how they lived after World War II. Perhaps with the passage of time the photos will continue to grow in importance, with their value eventually exceeding that of the written text.

The remarkable thing was Capa's ability to take his cameras to Russia and then travel and photograph as widely and freely as he did. Not only was it amazing that the political system gave him so much freedom of movement; what was equally amazing was Capa's ability to photograph the people so candidly. Even in a completely free society,

when cameras are pointed at people, suspicions and questions are always raised.   Even when suspicions do not stop
a photographer from working, they at least impede his progress.   Despite the times, the restrictions, and the suspicions, Robert Capa did make a fine visual journal.

NOTES

1. John Steinbeck, A Russian Journal: With Pictures by
    Robert Capa (New York: Viking Press, 1948), p. 3.
    Hereafter references appear in the text preceded by
    RJ and the page number.

2. Richard O'Connor, John Steinbeck (New York: McGraw-
    Hill, 1970), p. 99.

3. John Steinbeck, Steinbeck: A Life in Letters, eds.
    Elaine Steinbeck and Robert Wallsten (New York:
    Viking, 1975), p. 139.   Hereafter references appear
    in the text prefaced by SLL and the page number.

4. Warren French, John Steinbeck (New York: Twayne,
    1961), p. 28.

5. ICP Library of Photographers, Robert Capa: 1913-1954
    (New York: Grossman Publishers, 1974).

6. Peter Lisca, "John Steinbeck: A Literary Biography,"
    in Steinbeck and His Critics: A Record of Twenty-
    Five Years, eds. E. W. Tedlock, Jr. and C. V.
    Wicker (Albuquerque: University of New Mexico
    Press, 1957), p. 18.

7. Peter Lisca, The Wide World of John Steinbeck (New
    Brunswick, New Jersey: Rutgers University Press,
    1958), p. 250.

8. I. Levidova, "The Post-War Books of John Steinbeck,"
    Soviet Review, 4 (Summer 1963), 9.

9. O'Connor, p. 100.

10. Joseph Fontenrose, John Steinbeck: An Introduction and
     Interpretation (New York: Barnes and Noble, 1963),
     p. 117.

11. John Gray, John Steinbeck (University of Minnesota
    Pamphlets of American Writers, No. 94) (Minneapolis:
    University of Minnesota Press, 1971), p. 31.

12. Richard Astro, "Travels with Steinbeck: The Laws of
    Thought and the Laws of Things," Steinbeck Quarterly,
    8 (Spring, 1975), 40. Hereafter references appear in
    the text by page number.

13. John F. Slater, "American Past and Soviet Present:
    The Double Consciousness of Steinbeck's A Russian
    Journal," Steinbeck Quarterly, 8 (Summer-Fall 1975),
    97. Hereafter references appear in the text by page
    number. (See p. 102, reference to Agee's precedent
    for photojournalism--Let Us Now Praise Famous Men.)

IV. APPARATUS FOR RESEARCH PAPERS

A. Ten Questions for Discussion

1. Does the text explain the photos, and vice-versa?
2. Why are there no photos of Capa, or Steinbeck, or both,
   either alone or with others?
3. Compare and contrast the role(s) of the American and
   Russian writer in the Journal.
4. Are there enough hard data in the work to make it more
   than a period piece?
5. Compare and contrast the American and Russian Dream--
   that is, discuss the applicable myths and their corres-
   ponding relations.
6. Characterize the style of A Russian Journal and relate
   it to the "new" journalism.
7. How traditional a journal is this? For example, see
   Steinbeck's reference to Sir John Mandeville (RJ, 7),
   and the essay by John F. Slater referred to in the
   Bibliography.
8. Explore the subjects of human rights, the press, and
   propaganda, using this journal as a point of departure.
9. Comment on the following quotation by Joseph Fontenrose,
   in John Steinbeck: An Introduction and Interpretation
   (New York: Barnes and Noble, 1963): "[Once, There
   Was a War and A Russian Journal] ... although pleasant
   reading, add nothing to Steinbeck's stature and are not
   significant, as was Sea of Cortez, for an understanding
   of his fiction" (117).
10. Characterize the principal narrator of A Russian Journal.

B.   Suggested Topics for Research Papers

1.   Do an analysis of the photos in relation to the text from the point of view of media.
2.   Why has so little been written about A Russian Journal? Trace its reputation in criticism on Steinbeck, and in his references to it in his letters.
3.   Investigate the possible existence of parallel works by Russians about America.
4.   Are there theories of either writing or of creative endeavors in A Russian Journal? If so, how traditional are they, and to what traditions do they relate?
5.   Is there a system or a subliminal structure in A Russian Journal besides the motif of travel by the calendar? Examine the structure of the work from this point of view.
6.   Examine secondary source material by English, French, and German visitors to Russia of the nineteenth century and relate these observations to A Russian Journal.
7.   Examine the journal from the point of view of the irony suggested by the allusion to Mandeville's work at its start.
8.   Do a linguistic study of the vocabulary and sentence structure in the work to reveal both intention and accomplishment.
9.   A Russian Journal is a work of non-fiction. Using the journal as the basis for examination, derive a pragmatic, working definition for this term--non-fiction--applicable to it, and to Travels with Charley, and America for Americans.
10. Discuss the variant poses of the author in the journal: i. e. , young adventurer in A Russian Journal, older and more worldly, if fragile figure in Travels with Charley.

C.   Selected Bibliography

Text:

1.   Steinbeck, John.   A Russian Journal: With Pictures by Robert Capa.   New York: Viking Press, 1948.

Letters:

1.   Steinbeck, John.   Steinbeck: A Life in Letters, eds. Elaine Steinbeck and Robert Wallsten.   New York: Viking, 1975.

2. ICP Library of Photographers. <u>Robert Capa:</u> 1913-1954.
    New York: Grossman Publishers, 1974.

    <u>Criticism:</u> (See bibliographical entry for <u>The Moon Is</u>
    <u>Down.</u>)

1. Astro, Richard. "Travels with Steinbeck: The Laws of
    Thought and the Laws of Things. " <u>Steinbeck Quarterly</u>
    8 (Spring, 1975), 33-44.
        Considers it lackluster, uninteresting in style, and a
    period piece.

2. Fontenrose, Joseph. <u>John Steinbeck: An Introduction</u>
    <u>and Interpretation.</u> New York: Barnes and Noble, 1963.
        Pleasant, but inconsequential, with no impact upon
    Steinbeck's role as a writer of fiction.

3. French, Warren. <u>John Steinbeck.</u> New York: Twayne,
    1961.
        Steinbeck's role as a writer of fiction, with summary
    praise for the journal.

4. Gray, John. <u>John Steinbeck</u> (University of Minnesota
    Pamphlets of American Writers, No. 94). Minneapolis:
    University of Minnesota Press, 1971.
        Considers it pedestrian journalism, if a defense of
    democratic government.

5. Levidova, I. "The Post-War Books of John Steinbeck"
    (Voprosy Literatury, 1962, # 8). <u>Soviet Review,</u> 4
    (Summer, 1963), 3-13.
        Admires the work, from the Russian viewpoint, for
    its objectivity, its regard for Russians, and its fidelity to
    its thesis.

6. Lisca, Peter. "John Steinbeck: A Literary Biography, "
    in <u>Steinbeck and His Critics: A Record of Twenty-Five</u>
    <u>Years,</u> eds. E. W. Tedlock, Jr. , and C. V. Wicker.
    Albuquerque: University of New Mexico Press, 1957.
        Calls it both interesting reporting and reading, and
    notes Steinbeck's dislike for suppression of individual rights.

7. _____ . <u>The Wide World of John Steinbeck.</u> New
    Brunswick, New Jersey: Rutgers University Press,
    1958.
        See entry above.

8. Morsberger, Robert E. "Steinbeck's Zapata: Rebel vs. Revolutionary," in Steinbeck: The Man and His Work, eds. Richard Astro and Tetsumaro Hayashi. Corvallis, Oregon: Oregon State University Press, 1971.
    It enunciates Steinbeck's dislike for dictatorial rule, and his regard for the little individuals who comprise a society.

9. O'Connor, Richard. John Steinbeck (American Writers Series). New York: McGraw-Hill, 1970.
    Considers it testimony of Steinbeck's fascination, curiosity, and regard for the Russian people.

10. Slater, John F. "American Past and Soviet Present: The Double Consciousness of Steinbeck's A Russian Journal," Steinbeck Quarterly, 8 (Summer-Fall 1975), 95-104.
    The most laudatory and specific essay on the Journal, marred by its convoluted style, and its tenuous and poorly expressed thesis.

11. Tuttleton, James W. "Steinbeck in Russia: The Rhetoric of Praise and Blame," Modern Fiction Studies, 11 (Spring, 1965), 79-89.
    Reviews Russian reaction to Steinbeck's work, and notes the clash of party line and practice evidenced by the turmoil at the literary dinner held for Steinbeck and Capa immediately before their departure from Moscow.

Chapter 8

STEINBECK'S SWEET THURSDAY (1954)

by Roy S. Simmonds

I. BACKGROUND

In early November 1951, Steinbeck completed the first draft of his major novel of the postwar period, East of Eden. The manuscript, almost a thousand pages long and containing over a quarter of a million words, was, according to Steinbeck, "Much the longest and surely the most difficult work I have ever done."[1] He anticipated that revising the manuscript would take until Christmas, and planned eventually to write a sequel which would carry on the history of the families of the Salinas Valley from 1918 to the present time. When he received the galleys of East of Eden in the May of the following year, he was in Europe with his wife, Elaine Steinbeck, on a foreign assignment for Collier's magazine. He had for some time been bemoaning the fact that he was going through "a fallow time," and that his pen had "gone rusty."[2]

While still in Europe, the Steinbecks met with the composer Frank Loesser and his wife, and out of this meeting was born the idea of turning Steinbeck's 1945 novel Cannery Row into a musical comedy. After the long emotional and physical strain of writing East of Eden, followed by the period of comparative creative infertility (during which, nevertheless, he managed to prepare an abortive film script based on the Ibsen play, "The Vikings at Helgoland," and write a number of articles for Collier's), such a project was clearly a literary departure which held obvious attractions for him. The theater had long fascinated him, and he had already written, with varying degrees of success, play versions of three of his novels, Of Mice and Men, The Moon Is Down, and Burning Bright.

Returning to America that fall, he started work on
the project and was soon happily proclaiming that he was
"coming to life again. "[3] He soon realized, however, that
there were difficulties in adapting Cannery Row for the stage,
and that consequently he would have to write "a whole new
story ... simply (setting it) against the old background. "[4]
If the concept of a sequel to East of Eden never came to
fruition, the book eventually published as Sweet Thursday
and which grew out of this musical comedy project is a true
sequel to Cannery Row, and thus remains the one and only
of Steinbeck's works in which he returns to the characters
as well as the locale of an earlier book.

According to Elaine Steinbeck and Robert Wallsten,
"The musical and the novel ... underwent several changes
of title.   Both were originally called Bear Flag.   Ultimately
the novel was published as Sweet Thursday (1954), and the
musical appeared on Broadway as Pipe Dream (1955). "[5]

On September 14, 1953, Steinbeck wrote his agent
and close friend, Miss Elizabeth R. Otis:

> There is a school of thought among writers
> which says that if you enjoy writing something it
> is automatically no good and should be thrown out.
> I can't agree with this.   Bear Flag may not be
> much good but for what it is, I think it is all
> right.   Also I think it makes a nice balance for
> the weight of Eden.   It is kind of light and gay
> and astringent.   It may even say some good things.
>   I'll be sad to finish Bear Flag.   I have really
> loved it.   I am reluctant to start into the last two
> chapters.   But I will.   I do hope you love this
> book, a little self-indulgent though it may be.   Try
> to like it. [6]

He added a PS to this letter, which read: "It's very late
now, I just finished Bear Flag.   It's crazy. "

In a letter dated November 2, 1953, to his longtime
friend Carlton A. Sheffield, he reported, "... a new book
is finished in first draft.   I am going to put it away for a
few months.   See whether it makes any difference in the rewrite.   It should.   I always want to rewrite them after it is
too late. "[7]

Sweet Thursday was published in America on June 10,

1954, and in England on October 21, 1954.   The book bore
the dedication: "For Elizabeth with love."

    The reviews were generally somewhat less than en-
thusiastic.   The anonymous reviewer in Time condemned it
as reading "like stuff that has been salvaged from the waste-
basket."[8]   According to Ward Moore in the Nation, Steinbeck
had ceased to be "the poor man's Hemingway" and had become a "slightly raffish Faith Baldwin."[9]   The British critic
Maurice Richardson, writing in the New Statesman and Nation,
declared it was "rather too whimsical and Hollywooden"[10] for
him.   The anonymous reviewer in the Times Literary Supple-
ment, on the other hand, wound up his review by admitting
that "Mr. Steinbeck's handling, deft and casual, gives the
book very often a quality of inspired idiocy, a genuine hare-
brained charm."[11]

    Scholarly opinion of Sweet Thursday has continued until
recently to be correspondingly unfavorable and at best luke-
warm.   Even Steinbeck's most sympathetic critics have found
little to recommend the book, and accordingly have been
either cautiously hostile or almost patronizingly indulgent,
viewing it essentially as sad evidence of the declining powers
of a great writer.   Peter Lisca has called it "an inferior
novel" and made reference to its "irresponsible sentimental-
ity."[12]   Warren French, in the original Twayne edition of
his study of Steinbeck, calls it "an insensitive book by a
disgruntled man" and accuses Steinbeck of an "attempt to
exploit crude public tastes."[13]   French is even more critical in the revised edition of his Twayne study: "Sweet Thursday proves a patchwork quilt of reworked materials that
pushes the eccentricities of its characters to the point that
they possess no recognizably universal traits."[14]   V. S.
Naipaul makes a similar point, though not in such specifically
forceful terms, saying that Steinbeck "parodied his charm;
he turned the Row into fairyland."[15]   Perhaps one of the
worst condemnations of Sweet Thursday is made by James
Woodress in his 1964 essay, "John Steinbeck: Hostage to
Fortune."   He simply dismisses the book with these almost
contemptuous words: "It contributes nothing to Steinbeck's
literary stature and need not be examined here.   Yet one is
obliged to note that the work was a great financial success."[16]
Howard Levant, writing ten years later, does not agree, however, suggesting that "Sweet Thursday is not quite a mere
surrender to popular taste or so pointlessly stereotyped as
to elude critical analysis."[17]

The first extended study of Sweet Thursday which
considered in depth and effectively promulgated the novel as
a work of art worthy of serious critical attention was the
paper which Robert DeMott read at the 1970 Steinbeck Conference held at Corvallis, Oregon, and which was subsequently published under the intriguing title "Steinbeck and the
Creative Process: First Manifesto to End the Bringdown
Against Sweet Thursday," in Steinbeck: The Man and His
Work, eds. Richard Astro and Tetsumaro Hayashi (Corvallis:
Oregon State University Press, 1971), pp. 157-78.   DeMott's
stimulating essay marked a watershed in critical opinion
generally toward Sweet Thursday and from that time it was
perhaps not possible, as so many had done in the past, to
dismiss the book so offhandedly as a piece of superficial
frivolity.   Indeed, two years later, whilst expressing certain
inevitable reservations concerning the novel's literary qualities as such, Richard Astro was to maintain that, from one
standpoint at least, Sweet Thursday was "one of the most
important works in [Steinbeck's] entire canon."[18]   In his
most perceptive study, John Steinbeck and Edward Ricketts:
The Shaping of a Novelist, published in 1973, Astro explores
the relationship between the writer and the marine biologist
who was Steinbeck's close friend, and who appears, thinly
disguised, in many of Steinbeck's works.   Astro suggests
that it was in Sweet Thursday that Steinbeck endeavored to
lay down finally the ghost of Ricketts, killed in an automobile
accident in 1948, and that, because he did evidently succeed
in this deliberate act of literary exorcism, his subsequent
work proved to be nothing more than "a series of relatively
inconsequential books which are best described as footnotes
to his career as a whole."[19]

Astro's book is a pioneer study and will undoubtedly
be an essential source work for Steinbeck scholars, students,
and critics for many years to come.   Although many may
argue in part or degree with Astro's thesis relative to Steinbeck's basic indebtedness to Ricketts for the philosophies and
life-view so brilliantly exemplified in the novels, that thesis
cannot be ignored.   The very fact that Sweet Thursday occu-
pies the place it does in the Steinbeck canon--the last of the
California novels, the last work in which the many-faceted
Doc appears, and the one and only work in which Steinbeck
returns to both an earlier locale and an earlier cast of
characters--makes it, for all its faults and artistic limitations, a work, as Astro has suggested, worthy of considerably more than the comparatively scant critical attention it
has received to date.   The indications are that the scholarly
climate may be changing.

II. PLOT SYNOPSIS

The war has been over for two years and Doc returns
to Cannery Row after serving out his time as a sergeant in
the Army. He discovers that much has changed since he has
been away. The once-thriving fishing and canning industries
have gone out of business as a result of irresponsible over-
fishing during the war years. Although Mack and Hazel and
Eddie and Whitey No. 1 still occupy the Palace Flophouse,
Gay has been killed during a London air raid and his place
taken by Whitey No. 2. Lee Chong has sold his grocery
store to a wily Mexican-American named Joseph and Mary
(known as the Patron), purchased a schooner with the pro-
ceeds and sailed off to the South Seas. The madam of the
Bear Flag, Dora Flood, died in her sleep, and an older
sister, Fauna, has taken over the establishment.

Doc feels restless and discontented. When he enlisted, he left the business of the Western Biological Labora-
tories in the care of his millionaire friend, Old Jingleballicks,
who had, in the event, simply abandoned the place. Doc sets
to work to get things going again, but his heart is not really
in it. He determines to embark on a research project into
"Symptoms in Some Cephalopods Approximating Apoplexy," but
although he begins with some enthusiasm, lethargy soon over-
takes him. Mack and the boys decide that he "needs a
dame."

A young female vagrant, Suzy, arrives in town, and
is taken on by Fauna at the Bear Flag. Doc finds himself
attracted to her, but hides his feelings. Mack and the boys,
still perturbed at the way Doc has changed, convene a meeting with Fauna to plan what they should do about him. Fauna,
an amateur astrologer, undertakes to prepare Doc's horo-
scope, but no one can remember the date of his birthday.
Mack tells the boys that what Doc needs is not so much just
a dame but a wife, and that they should set about choosing a
suitable partner for him.

Mack and the boys call a further meeting with Fauna
and the girls of the Bear Flag, a meeting at which Suzy is
not present. The matchmaking desires of Fauna are set
aflame. She is certain that Suzy is not suited to the life of
a hustler, and she attempts to throw Doc and Suzy together.
But Doc and Suzy display no surface compatability. Nevertheless, Fauna is not to be denied. She predicts that Suzy,
a Pisces, will marry a Cancer, and when Doc, telling Mack

the first date that comes into his head, says that his birthday is July 4, Fauna is more than ever convinced that Doc
and Suzy are made for each other, that the match is inevitable. She prevails upon Doc to ask Suzy out to dinner, and
spends a great deal of time instructing Suzy how to behave.
The dinner, all the elements of which have been carefully
planned by Fauna, is a great success, but, although he knows
now for sure that he has fallen in love with Suzy, Doc makes
no advances, which convinces Suzy that he does not need her.

        At more or less the same time, Mack realizes with
horror that the Patron must be the present owner of the
Palace Flophouse. Transfer of ownership would have been
part and parcel of the deal when the Patron bought the grocery from Lee Chong. Mack, however, suspects that the
Patron is blissfully unaware that he owns the Palace Flophouse, else why is it that he has not been pestering them
for rent? If he were to discover that he was the owner,
there was the very real and horrifying possibility that he
would evict the boys. Mack tricks the Patron into agreeing
to participate in and to help organize a raffle to raise funds
to purchase the microscope Doc needs to enable him to carry
out his research. There has, of course, to be a prize, and
Mack suggests that this should be the Palace Flophouse.
The Patron, much to Mack's delight, gives his wholehearted
support to the idea, particularly when Mack tells him that
the raffle will be rigged so that Doc will win. As Mack explains it, Doc will get his microscope and, by his acquiring
ownership of the Palace Flophouse, the boys will be assured
of a permanent home. He carefully neglects to add that the
only person who will lose out on the deal will be the Patron
himself.

        The drawing of the raffle provides the excuse for
throwing a party that coming Saturday night. Fauna sees it
as a wonderful opportunity to bring Doc and Suzy finally
together, and she begins planning accordingly. The party
will be a masquerade on the theme of Snow White and the
Seven Dwarfs. By unspoken agreement among the townspeople, Suzy alone would attend as Snow White.

        On the night of the party, the raffle is drawn, and
Doc's ticket wins as planned. But Mack discovers that his
little scheme has backfired when Doc, taking him aside,
tells him that Lee Chong had provided the funds to pay the
taxes on the Palace Flophouse for the coming ten years, and,
without telling anyone but Doc, had transferred ownership of

the Palace to Mack and the boys, so that they would always
have a place to live. He knew that if they were aware that
they owned it, they would soon have mortgaged it off. Mack
asks Doc not to reveal the truth to the other boys, but to
make out that Doc is continuing to "rent" the place to them.

Suzy enters the party dressed in a white wedding
gown, and Fauna shouts to Doc to come and get his girl.
When Suzy sees the look on Doc's face, she runs from the
room and informs Fauna, who runs after her, that she cannot marry Doc--she loves him. Suzy leaves the Bear Flag
and gets herself a job at a nearby restaurant. She takes up
residence in the abandoned boiler on the vacant lot, and
transforms it into a comfortable home. When Doc calls on
her with flowers and candy, certain even more in his own
mind now that he wants to marry her, she rejects him, saying that she wants someone who really needs her, and that
in her opinion, Doc does not need her.

Old Jingleballicks sends Doc a telegram informing
him that he has set up a Cephalopod Research Section at the
California Institute of Technology, and that Doc should consider himself in charge. Doc plans to go to La Jolla to
collect more specimens for his research. Such an expedition will additionally give him the opportunity of escaping
from what has rapidly become an unbearably embarrassing
situation. Hazel, however, on the one occasion that he
brings himself to take any overt, self-decided action, creeps
up on Doc while he is asleep and breaks his arm with an
indoor-ball bat. Suzy now realizes that Doc has a real need
for her--with his broken arm he can neither drive his car
nor collect specimens on his own--and they drive off together
to La Jolla, with the concerted blessings of the Row, into
what will obviously be a bright, fairytale future.

III. CRITICAL EXPLICATION

The banality of the principal plot of Sweet Thursday
(boy meets girl, boy and girl have a misunderstanding, boy
and girl are reconciled, marry, and live happily ever after)
betrays its musical comedy origins. The whole tone of the
book is, as it were, two removes from reality, its setting
and its characters filtered first through the process of the
author's creativity into the fictional ambience of Cannery Row,
then that fictional ambience itself filtered and transformed
into the veritable fairyland that is Sweet Thursday. The very

simplicity of its main plot and character motivation, imposed
upon it by the theatrical conventions of its particular genre,
serves to give the book an overall unity, symmetry, and
strength of structure within which Steinbeck can indulge himself by freely developing, or picking up and dropping at ran-
dom, the interweaving sub-plots, as well as introducing,
whenever the opportunity seems to present itself, various
authorial interpolations on those social issues which had
concerned him so greatly and for so long: the apparent
indifference of both people and government to the possibility
of future ecological disaster, together with the quickening,
widespread drift toward materialism and the lowering of moral
standards in most walks of life.

        In some respects, there is a case for arguing that the
basic superficiality of the book is such that Steinbeck's inter-
mittent serious moments, even when thinly disguised in the
general fun mood that the book essentially exudes, cannot be
contained comfortably within the substance of the work as a
whole.   His philosophizing, his preaching, and his occasional
vicious attacks on certain sections of society tend to stand
out like isolated tracts, unabsorbed into the narrative.

        But there is possibly another way of looking at it.
When he completed East of Eden, Steinbeck made and carved
a box to contain the manuscript, and this he presented to his
editor, Pascal Covici.   On the dedication page of the published book, the following words appear:

> ... here's your box.   Nearly everything I have is
> in it, and it is not full.   Pain and excitement are
> in it, and feeling good or bad and evil thoughts
> and good thoughts--the pleasure of design and the
> indescribable joy of creation....   And still the box
> is not full. 20

Perhaps Sweet Thursday is metaphorically a similar sort of
box, the main Doc-Suzy plot structure serving as the sides,
bottom, and lid to contain at least some of those things
Steinbeck was unable to put into East of Eden.

        In his first Twayne study, Warren French accuses
Sweet Thursday of being "a cantankerous book--a work that
does not satirize those who hurt and delude themselves, but
rather complains peevishly about those who annoy the author
personally. "21   It cannot be denied that here and there in
Sweet Thursday Steinbeck can be seen to be apparently paying

off old scores: an oblique reference to the writer and critic
Anthony West, who had reviewed East of Eden unfavorably in
the New Yorker; the satirizing, through the medium of the
character Joe Elegant, of the life-styles and the obscure
rococo literary styles of some of the younger and more
flamboyant writers of the day; the ridiculing of the behavior
of the citizens of Pacific Grove, among whom Steinbeck lived
during his early days as a writer. In his jibes against the
residents of this small coastal community, Steinbeck is
clearly letting his prejudices run riot. At the end of his
recounting of "The Great Roque War," for instance, he feels
obliged to add the following rider: "There are people who
will say that this whole account is a lie, but a thing isn't
necessarily a lie even if it didn't necessarily happen."22
Such an admission tends to confirm the point that Warren
French is making, although the counter-argument can be
advanced that exception cannot seriously be taken to an author
embellishing a fairy story with what he freely admits is
another fairy story. Generally speaking, however, Steinbeck's oblique and sometimes very petty attacks are few and
far between. By no means do they dominate the book.

      Patently more significant, although again they do not
dominate, are Steinbeck's airings of what he considers to be
the great social evils of his time. In the second paragraph
of the very first chapter of the book, he demonstrates his
concern over the manner in which unthinking society, on the
excuse of expediency, persists in ignoring the danger signs
of the ecological catastrophes surely to come unless the
necessary preventive and remedial measures are taken:

> The canneries themselves fought the war by getting
> the limit taken off fish and catching them all. It
> was done for patriotic reasons, but that didn't
> bring the fish back. As with the oysters in Alice,
> "They'd eaten every one." It was the same noble
> impulse that stripped the forests of the West and
> right now is pumping water out of California's
> earth faster than it can rain back in. When the
> desert comes, people will be sad.... (3)

      Later in the book, through the medium of Old Jingle-
ballicks, Steinbeck forecasts one of the progressions by which,
not by war or disease but by the inevitable accumulation of
scientific and medical knowledge, the ultimate catastrophe--
the end of the world itself--could be brought about:

Man, in saving himself, has destroyed himself.... Predators he has removed from the earth; heat and cold he has ruined aside; communicable disease he has practically eliminated. The old live on, the young do not die.... The population grows and the productivity of the earth decreases. In a foreseeable future we shall be smothered by our own numbers. Only birth control could save us, and that is one thing mankind is never going to practice.... It is a cosmic joke. Preoccupation with survival has set the stage for extinction. (167-68)

In such passages it is Steinbeck, the marine biologist, who is writing. The effect and the importance that his immense interest in and knowledge of the science of marine biology has had on his fictional writings is a subject which is engaging the growing attention of Steinbeck scholars and critics. His role as a social commentator--in such widely different books as In Dubious Battle, The Grapes of Wrath, The Wayward Bus, and The Winter of Our Discontent--has long been recognized. It is a role he adopts yet again in Sweet Thursday. The ever-increasing materialism of modern society, the undoubted decline in moral standards, and the spread of artificially inspired neuroses and psychosomatic disorders not only sadden him but also move him to anger. He sees these undesirable manifestations of the human psyche as veritable cancers eating away at the vitality of the nation. It is his belief that the old moral standards and codes of behavior, tried and found to be true over the years, are, more often than not, the only good ones. As he argues, the words put once more into the mouth of Old Jingleballicks, the Establishment itself is not by any means without guilt:

If a man has money he doesn't ask, "Can I afford this?" but "Can I deduct it?" Two men fight over a luncheon check when both of them are going to deduct it anyway--a whole nation conditioned to dishonesty by its laws, because honesty is penalized. (184)

It could be that this can be written off as the cynical view of the hard-headed businessman trying to excuse his own attitude to such matters, and thus justify his own dubious code of behavior; but even Mack, expounding his quaint cracker-barrel philosophies of life, can often himself hit the nail on the head with equivalent cynicism:

> You take a dame and she's married to a guy that's
> making twenty-five bucks a week. You can't kill
> her with a meat ax. She's got kids and does the
> washing--may get a little tired but that's the worst
> that can happen to her. But let the guy get raised
> to seventy-five bucks a week and she begins to get
> colds and take vitamins.... Guy gets up to a
> hundred a week and this same dame reads Time
> magazine and she's got the newest disease before
> she even finished the page.... They got stuff
> called allergy now. Used to call it hay fever--
> made you sneeze. Guy that figured out allergy
> should of got a patent. A allergy is, you get sick
> when there's something you don't want to do. I've
> knew dames that was allergic to dishwater. Mar-
> ried guy starts making dough--he's got a patient
> on his hands. (100-01)

It cannot be denied, however, that there is a certain
disturbing ambivalence about Steinbeck's attitudes toward
society. Mack and the boys are ostensibly presented for
our admiration, and are almost extolled as a small group of
human beings who have discovered the secret of the perfect
way of life. Yet one cannot overlook the fact that they are
simply bums, living off their wits, and quite ready, willing,
and able to take anyone for an easy buck, not least Doc,
who is supposedly the sun around whom they all revolve.
But Steinbeck subtly directs the reader into suspending judgment and accepting the specious tenet that Mack and the boys
are basically harmless and infinitely lovable wastrels, with
such disarming observations as: "Their association with
larceny, fraud, loitering, illegal congregation, and conspiracy on all levels was not only accepted, but to a certain
extent had become a matter of pride to the inhabitants of
Cannery Row" (13). He even seems to be requiring our
grudging admiration of Joseph and Mary, in comparison with
whom Mack and the boys "were lamblike children of probity
and virtue" (13). The Patron has his own uncompromising
and cynical view of human nature which has served him extremely well in the past:

> He knew that the only person you can trust is an
> absolutely selfish person. He always runs true to
> form. You know everything he'll do. But you
> take somebody with an underlying kindness, and
> he might fool you. The only satisfactory sucker
> is the one who is entirely selfish. (50)

Early in the book, when Steinbeck gives us the ad-
mittedly amusing, but nevertheless appalling, story of Joseph
and Mary's life of crime, we are told that the Patron "rejected the theory of private ownership of removable property
almost from birth" (13-14). Later in the book, it suddenly
occurring to them that the Patron must unknowingly own the
Palace Flophouse and that their tenancy might therefore be--
to put it mildly--somewhat insecure, Mack and the boys begin to appreciate the "injustice in the theory of private ownership of real estate" (88), and consider ways and means by
which they can effectively deprive the unsuspecting (as they
believe) Patron of his property. Thus the mores of the
lovable bums are identified with those of the petty criminal.
The identification becomes even more positive, the full
circle completed, when at the end of the book it is suggested
that the Patron himself may be developing into the same sort
of sentimental and adorable scoundrel as the rest of them.
The implied metamorphosis is, of course, yet another convention of the musical comedy genre or of the fairytale.
Accordingly, Steinbeck can, for the most part, evade the
criticisms leveled against the blatant ambivalence he displays in Sweet Thursday simply because he makes no pre-
tense that the book itself mirrors reality.

In a 1953 letter to the friend he portrays in Cannery
Row and Sweet Thursday as the character Mack, Steinbeck
wrote:

> I've just finished another book about the Row. It
> is a continuation concerned not with what did hap-
> pen but with what might have happened. The one
> can be as true as the other. I think it is a funny
> book, and sad too because it is what might have
> happened to Ed and didn't. I don't seem able to
> get over his death. But this will be the last piece
> about him. 23

Many critics have been troubled by the character of
Doc that Steinbeck presents in Sweet Thursday, so unlike the
fictional Ed Ricketts figure who had appeared in different
guises, but with a recognizable consistency of characterization, in such earlier works as In Dubious Battle (Doc Burton), "The Snake" (young Dr. Phillips), The Moon Is Down
(Doctor Winter), and Cannery Row (Doc). Steinbeck had
already sentimentalized the fictional Ricketts figure almost
out of existence in the novel Burning Bright, published in
1950, two years after Ricketts' death, and he had ostensibly

said all that he had to say about Ricketts the man in his
tribute "About Ed Ricketts," which he published in 1951 as
the prologue to The Log from the Sea of Cortez. Even in
that non-fictional essay, he still felt bound to warn his
readers that the demarcation line dividing truth from fiction
is often indefinable:

> It is going to be difficult to write down the things
> about Ed Ricketts that must be written, hard to
> separate entities. And anyone who knew him would
> find it difficult. Maybe some of the events are
> imagined. And perhaps some very small happen-
> ings have grown out of all proportion in the mind. [24]

When he came to write Sweet Thursday, however,
Steinbeck was not dealing with quasi-reality, but with wholly-
imagined situations in which the real-life Ricketts could
never have participated. What, we may ask, was Steinbeck
referring to in that 1953 letter to "Mack" when he wrote of
the sadness inherent in the book "because it is what might
have happened to Ed and didn't"? Possibly he was referring
to the fact in the novel Doc is given the opportunity, through
Old Jingleballicks' tax-deductible endowment, to become head
of a section at the California Institute of Technology, with a
handsome salary to go with the post and presumably unlimited funds to carry out the research it is his true destiny to
accomplish. The real-life Ricketts was not so fortunate.
According to Astro, he was unable even to obtain a Guggen-
heim grant to further his research on the fauna of Vancouver
Island and the Queen Charlottes and to write, as a result of
his findings, "a comprehensive study of the marine inverte-
brates of the northernmost coast of North America to be
called 'The Outer Shores.'"[25] Alternatively, it could be, as
Astro has claimed,[26] that Steinbeck is predicting in Sweet
Thursday the manner in which Ricketts would ultimately have
become a victim of society had he lived, a sort of anachron-
ism, his philosophies and his life-style completely out of step
with contemporary values and modes of behavior.

There is, of course, no way of knowing if Steinbeck's
predictions would have proved correct. What, however, is
much more apparent is that in the Doc of Sweet Thursday
Steinbeck was attributing to the fictional Ricketts his own
increasing sense of loss of a whole way of life and an alienation from the California scene he so loved. After more
than ten years of residence on the East Coast, he was extremely conscious of the fact that since he had left California,

evolution had inevitably been taking place, and that despite
his visits he had not changed with it.   He knew too that
some of the things he had written about in his books had
greatly upset certain sections of the California communities.
Writing in March 1953 to an old classmate, Steinbeck was
forced to admit, "I do not think they approve of me very
highly.   It occurs to me that probably the most heart-breaking
title in the world is Tom Wolfe's 'You Can't Go Home
Again'--it's literally true.   They want no part of me except
in a pine box. "27

     It is therefore not altogether fanciful to regard the
Doc of <u>Sweet Thursday</u> as a partial portrait of the author
himself, describing not how Ricketts, the biologist, actually
felt when he returned to the Row after the war, but rather
how Steinbeck, the writer, would probably have felt had he
returned to the Central California Coast to live after Ricketts'
death.   As Robert DeMott has put it, "he integrated and
projected his own struggle with the demon of creativity into
Doc who metamorphosed into scientist-as-artist and vice
versa. "28

     There is much in the book to give validity to such a
reading of <u>Sweet Thursday</u>.   As has already been noted,
consequent to the completion of the long haul of work on
<u>East of Eden</u> and prior to being stimulated into embarking
on the musical comedy/novel project, Steinbeck suffered a
writing "block" which, from all accounts, lasted several
months.   In describing Doc's efforts to begin writing his
paper on octopi, Steinbeck is here undoubtedly describing
his own abortive creative agonies of a comparatively short
time before:

       He sat in front of the yellow pad again and drew
       lace around all the letters of the title, tore off the
       page, and threw it away.   Five pencil points were
       broken now.   He sharpened them and lined them up
       with their brothers. . . .   It's always hard to start
       to concentrate.   The mind darts like a chicken,
       trying to escape thinking even though thinking is
       the most rewarding function of man.   (43-44)

And later:

       He picked up a pencil and wrote. . . .   His pencil
       point broke.   He took another, and it broke with
       a jerk, making a little tear in the paper.   He read

what he had written; dull, desiccated, he thought.
(44-45)

Doc's stubborn feeling of discontent runs parallel to
a perhaps even more persistent sense of loneliness. He is
aware of "a tone within himself, or several tones, as though
he heard music distantly" (24). These "tones" or "voices"
manifest themselves on three distinct levels of consciousness.
The top voice, which is his thinking mind, evaluates with
scientific precision and objectivity his observations. The
middle voice questions the direction of his life-drive and his
sense of values.

> And the third voice, which came from his marrow,
> would sing, "Lonesome! Lonesome! What good
> is it? Who benefits? Thought is the evasion of
> feeling. You're only walling up the leaking lone-
> liness." (25)

Sweet Thursday is indeed an impressive study of
human loneliness and of the individual's craving and absolute
need for love, whether it be love in its ultimate personal
and physical sense, or, in the broadest universal sense, the
love which manifests itself in the concern and respect that
one human being can show toward his fellow man. In addition to Doc, many of the other principal characters in the
book exist in a state of loneliness of one sort or another.
Hazel, for instance, is for most of the book transformed
into a man apart by Fauna's prediction that he will become
President of the United States. His normal, if comparative,
serenity is shattered by his awareness of the terrifying
responsibility that has been placed on his unwilling shoulders.
Joseph and Mary is estranged from the close-knit community
of the Row by his past life of crime, his deviousness, and
his uncompromising materialistic and cynical view of life.
Joe Elegant, "a pale young man with bangs" (81), is sexually
isolated, hired eunuch-like as cook in Fauna's establishment.
An intellectual anchorite nobody really understands, he
spends most of his free time in writing a preposterous
novel entitled The Pi Root of Oedipus. He is further author-
ially isolated by Steinbeck's undisguished dislike for his emotional and artistic type. Old Jingleballicks, the supreme
materialist, is clearly unloved because he himself has no
love to give: his money denies him any sort of genuine and
meaningful relationship. Suzy, the tough but good-hearted
vagrant, is the stranger who, while (unlike Joseph and Mary,
Joe Elegant, and Old Jingleballicks) being accepted unreserv-

edly by the denizens of the Row, is nevertheless out of place among the other girls of the Bear Flag. As Fauna, who hired her, says, "She got no future as a floozy.... She's a character. That ain't no good in a house.... This kid Suzy's lousy with new roses. She ain't a good hustler because of that streak of lady" (131-32).

Doc endeavors to assuage his loneliness and discontent by immersing himself in work, but he is fooling nobody, least of all himself. His middle voice sings to him, "Are you better than Mack that you should use the secret priestly words of science to cover the fact that you have nothing to say?" In response to which, his lower voice grieves, "Lonesome! Lonesome! Let me up into the light and warmth. Lonesome!" (45). It takes the seer, whom Doc meets on the sea shore, to put into words and rationalize in Doc's own mind the nub of his problem. In the final moments of their conversation, the book's central theme is stated:

> "I've tried to think," said Doc. "I want to take everything I've seen and thought and learned and reduce them and relate them and refine them until I have something of meaning, something of use. And I can't seem to do it."
> "Maybe you aren't ready. And maybe you need help."
> "What kind of help?"
> "There are some things a man can't do alone. I wouldn't think of trying anything so big without--" He stopped....
> "Without what?" Doc asked.
> "Without love," said the seer. (73)

Doc's self-confessed frustrated efforts to crystallize his scientific thinking into meaningful expression are again uncomfortably reminiscent of Steinbeck's own creative problems immediately prior to the composition of Sweet Thursday. Sustained by the love and companionship afforded by a happy marriage, Steinbeck was, of course, able to reach his own solution by embarking on a wave of renewed creativity. He predictably resolves Doc's loneliness and discontent by arranging a similarly happy marriage for him. Suzy herself consequently finds at last her assured place in the world, loved for what she is, wanted as she desires to be. Love, then, is the answer. Love is the panacea. Love is the universal truth. Even if it all seems a little too pat, we can be in no doubt concerning Steinbeck's sincerity. The

Ricketts and Steinbeck identities embodied in the character
of Doc merge even closer, so that inevitably, as Robert
DeMott suggests, they become interchangeable.

While the implications of the authorial treatment of
Doc and the critical and expository nature of some of the
topics raised throughout the book cannot be ignored, it is as
well to remind ourselves that Sweet Thursday was written
principally as a form of "relaxation"--if one can use such a
word in connection with any aspect of artistic creation--
after the rigors of writing East of Eden. There is the very
real danger of attempting to read into the book far greater
depth than it possesses or can sustain. Being essentially a
"fun" book, it is possible to read it at this level with un-
diminished enjoyment and satisfaction, without having any
knowledge of the underlying implications of its plot or its
general emotional background. And this, of course, is pre-
cisely the level on which the general reader will accept it
as a work of art, albeit a minor work of art.

Certainly, it is an immensely funny book, although
here Steinbeck is the exponent of the more knockabout style
of humor. The controlled, gentle humor which prevailed in
Tortilla Flat (1935) has been replaced nineteen years later
by what is often an almost embarrassing facetiousness,
lapsing occasionally here and there into an unrestrained
guffawing. Steinbeck can be guilty of such quips as, "I've
wore my brains down to the knuckles, trying to do something
nice for you" (137). But at other times, to be fair, his
touch is sure, his flair for that quiet category of humor
with its throwaway lines losing none of its attractions.

Here are Mack and Fauna discussing the possibility
of throwing a party at the Palace Flophouse in Doc's honor:

> "Don't think that there ain't been parties before
> at the Palace, and fights," he said. "Why, when
> the news come that Gay had went to his reward we
> give a memorial shindig that they don't hardly do
> no better at the Salinas Rodeo. Gay would have
> been proud of it--if he could of got in."
> Fauna said, "There's talk around that three
> mourners went to join Gay before nightfall next
> day."
> "Well, you got to expect a certain amount of
> accidents," said Mack modestly. (172)

There is the Patron's puzzled disbelief when faced
with the fact of Doc's inherent honesty:

> As he got to know him, Joseph and Mary regarded
> Doc with something akin to love--for love feeds on
> the unknown and unknowable. Doc's honesty was
> exotic to Joseph and Mary. He found it strange.
> It attracted him in spite of the fact that he could
> not understand it. He felt that there was some-
> thing he had missed, though he could not figure
> what it was. (32)

When Doc introduces the Patron to the game of chess and
proves to him that it is a game in which it is impossible to
cheat, the Patron's mind, quite unable to accept the concept
of a situation in which cheating cannot be made ultimately to
pay, turns to the thought that perhaps Doc has worked out a
perfect racket for himself:

> In the back of his mind an idea stirred. Suppose
> you took honesty and made a racket of it--it might
> be the toughest of all to break. It was so new to
> him that his mind recoiled from it, but still it
> wouldn't let him alone. His eyes narrowed. "May-
> be he's worked out a system," he said to himself.
> (33-34)

Sweet Thursday contains at least one superb comic
character, and like all great comic characters--Chaplin's
little tramp, for instance--an aura of pathos, even of tragedy, surrounds him. We can laugh, and yet on reflection
feel guilty because we realize that there has been a vein of
subconscious cruelty in our laughter. Hazel in Sweet Thursday is a continuing portrait from Cannery Row. In the
earlier book, we learned how he came about his unusual
name, how his mother "became confused about his sex when
he was born,"[29] naming him after a reputedly moneyed
great aunt before she realized she had given birth to a boy,
and then became "used to the name and never bothered to
change it."[30]

Hazel is mentally retarded, unable apparently even to
count the toes on his feet, vulnerable to all the jokes,
trickeries, and cruelties that his fellow-men, were they so
inclined, could subject him to: it is doubtful if he would
even be aware that they were making a fool of him. There
is, however, an understanding among the inhabitants of the

Row that nobody shall take advantage of Hazel. It is only
an outsider who would presume to ignore the tacit rules--
someone like Joe Elegant, who maliciously designs and
makes the outrageous Prince Charming costume that Hazel
wears to the riotous masquerade party, thus using Hazel as
an instrument "to get his revenge on mankind" (192).

There is no intrinsic harm in Hazel himself, and yet
some of the solutions sparked off or dreamed up in his simple mind are positively harmful themselves. When Mack and
the boys discuss ways and means by which they can wrest
ownership of the Palace Flophouse from the Patron, Hazel's
immediate reaction, echoing an earlier flippant comment by
Mack is, "We could kill him" (88). He worships Doc.
"Hazel thought Mack was the world's greatest human, while
Doc he didn't consider human at all. Sometimes he said
his prayers to Doc" (212). When he feels that Mack is not
doing enough to help Doc, and his words of entreaty seem to
be falling on deaf ears, he has to resort to violence to make
his point: he hits Mack over the back of the head with a
barrel stave, "so hard that (Mack's) pants split" (216).
Again, in his imposed role of future President of the United
States, he knows it is incumbent upon him to bring Doc and
Suzy together. He suggests to Doc that he should court
Suzy with flowers and candy, but when this ploy proves
abortive, Hazel is once more driven to extreme measures:
he breaks Doc's arm with an indoor-ball bat. Fortunately,
before he gets "another noble idea" and possibly "kill(s)
somebody, " Fauna discovers that due to a fly speck on her
astrological chart she has been mistaken in her prediction
concerning Hazel's future greatness. "Who you think they'll
get instead of me?" the relieved Hazel asks. "Nobody
knows, " Fauna tells him. "Well, he better be good, " is
Hazel's threatening comment (267).

It is possibly significant that despite all the careful
conniving and planning of Mack and Fauna, some of it
curiously inept, it is the mentally retarded Hazel who
achieves the ultimately successful matchmaking, and Old
Jingleballicks who blesses the union with the offer of financial security. The simpleton and the materialist become
the instruments by which the fairytale is satisfactorily brought
to its time-honored happy conclusion.

Thus--like the final "yes" of James Joyce's Ulysses--
Sweet Thursday ends on a note of affirmation. Steinbeck
preaches universal love, but like most idealists he tends to

over-state, over-simplify, and over-sentimentalize his case.
The affirmation that he presents in this book is conditioned
and marred by an underlying irony and ambivalence.   Love
alone is evidently not good enough.   It has to be buttressed
by the material surety of Doc's permanent and remunerative
post in the Cephalopod Research Section at the California
Institute of Technology.   Although there is a certain ambigu-
ity about whether or not Doc will accept the post, if convention is followed he undoubtedly will.   We can perhaps be for-
given for speculating as to just how long it will take for the
fair Suzy to become "a patient," like the wife of Mack's one-
hundred-bucks-a-week married guy.

One's ultimate valuation of Sweet Thursday must inevitably depend on one's own reaction to it.   The general
reader, who does not need or wish to seek out the book's
deeper implications and meanings, will find it excellent
entertainment value, and immensely rewarding on this level.
But if we do not seek pure entertainment alone, what is it
that Sweet Thursday can offer us?   It is possible, as some
scholars have done, to excuse the ambivalence and lack of
depth in this book, as with the majority of Steinbeck's post-
war works, by interpreting it in terms of the fabular form.
In the long run, however, the literary conventions must be
observed, and the contents of Sweet Thursday, within the
boundaries of its rigid main plot structure, remind us rather
unhappily of the contents of Hazel's mind: "Everything was
thrown together like fishing tackle in the bottom of a row-
boat, hooks and sinkers and line and lures and gaffs all
snarled up."31

The importance of Sweet Thursday in the Steinbeck
canon lies not so much in its literary merit (which is argu-
able), nor in its thematic design (which is dissipated), nor
even in its philosophical content (which is confused), but
simply for being the sort of book it is and for what, on the
esoteric plane, it tells us about its author.

NOTES

1.   John Steinbeck, Steinbeck: A Life in Letters, eds.
      Elaine Steinbeck and Robert Wallsten (New York:
      Viking Press, 1975), p. 431.

2.   Ibid. , pp. 443-44.

3. Ibid., p. 462.

4. Ibid.

5. Ibid., p. 472.

6. Ibid., pp. 472-73.

7. Ibid., pp. 473-74.

8. Anon., "Back to the Riffraff," Time, 63 (June 14, 1954),
    60.

9. Ward Moore, "Cannery Row Revisited: Steinbeck and
    the Sardine," Nation, 179 (October 16, 1954), 327.

10. Maurice Richardson, "New Novels," New Statesman and
    Nation, 48 (November 6, 1954), 590.

11. Anon., "John Steinbeck: Sweet Thursday," Times Lit-
    erary Supplement (November 26, 1954), 753.

12. Peter Lisca, The Wide World of John Steinbeck (New
    Brunswick: Rutgers University Press, 1958), p. 284.

13. Warren French, John Steinbeck (New York: Twayne
    Publishers, 1961), p. 160.

14. Warren French, John Steinbeck (Boston: Twayne Pub-
    lishers, 1975), p. 157.

15. V. S. Naipaul, The Overcrowded Barracoon and Other
    Articles (London: Andre Deutsch, 1972), p. 163.

16. James Woodress, "John Steinbeck: Hostage to Fortune,"
    South Atlantic Quarterly, 63 (Summer, 1964), 395.

17. Howard Levant, The Novels of John Steinbeck: A Crit-
    ical Study (Columbia: University of Missouri Press,
    1974), p. 261.

18. Richard Astro, John Steinbeck and Edward F. Ricketts:
    The Shaping of a Novelist (Minneapolis: University
    of Minnesota Press, 1973), p. 193.

19. Ibid., p. 206.

20. John Steinbeck, East of Eden (New York: Viking Press, 1952).

21. French. p. 158.

22. John Steinbeck, Sweet Thursday (New York: Viking Press, 1954), p. 57. All subsequent references to this work are indicated by page numbers in parentheses following quotes.

23. Steinbeck: A Life in Letters, p. 474.

24. John Steinbeck, The Log from the Sea of Cortez (New York: Viking Press, 1951), p. x.

25. Astro, p. 20.

26. Ibid., pp. 180-81.

27. Steinbeck: A Life in Letters, p. 467.

28. Robert DeMott, "Steinbeck and the Creative Process: First Manifesto to End the Bringdown Against Sweet Thursday," in Steinbeck: The Man and His Work, eds. Richard Astro and Tetsumaro Hayashi (Corvallis: Oregon State University Press, 1971), p. 161.

29. John Steinbeck, Cannery Row (New York: Viking Press, 1945), p. 32.

30. Ibid.

31. Ibid., p. 34.

IV.   APPARATUS FOR RESEARCH PAPERS

A.   Ten Questions for Discussion

1.   The double spoiling of Doc's starfish embryo slides in Chapters 17 and 18 are repetitions of an incident which occurs in the early short story, "The Snake." In what way does Steinbeck's treatment of the incident in the short story differ from the treatment he gives the episodes in Sweet Thursday? How do the incidents themselves advance the narrative and emotional structure of the two works in which they appear?

2. In what specific ways does Steinbeck demonstrate the unity of the Row?
3. To what degree, and with what success, does Steinbeck follow the suggestions offered by Mack in the Prologue as to the manner in which the book should be written?
4. How does Steinbeck utilize the so-called "inter-chapters" (i. e., Chapters 3, 8, and 38) to advance the narrative continuity of the book?
5. Sweet Thursday was the last of Steinbeck's novels in which, through the medium of Mack and the boys, he introduced the concept of the Arthurian Round Table. Does Steinbeck make this concept at all explicit, and, if he does, in what way or ways?
6. Consider the narrative time sequence in Sweet Thursday. Does this give an overall shape to the book in addition to the principal boy-meets-girl plot-line?
7. "Cannery Row is a microcosm of the human condition." Is this true? If not, in what way is it a misleading statement?
8. In what ways, voluntarily or involuntarily, does Joe Elegant play a part in bringing Doc and Suzy together?
9. What is the importance of the minor character Joe Blaikey? What precise role does he play in the book's main plot?
10. Is it true to say that the efforts of Mack and the boys to help Doc are generally ineffectual, and, if anything, prove on balance to be more detrimental than beneficial to Doc's well-being?

B.   Suggested Topics for Research Papers

1. Discuss the quality of humor in Sweet Thursday, and the manner in which it is employed to provide insights into character.
2. Discuss the language and dialogue of Sweet Thursday, and consider to what extent Steinbeck has succeeded in satisfying Mack's requirement of figuring out "what the guy's thinking by what he says" (pp. vii-viii).
3. Examine the concept of good and evil in Sweet Thursday, and the extent to which the distinction between the two extremes is blurred by Steinbeck's sentimentalizing of his characters.
4. Discuss the proposition that, despite the frequent examples of the deliberate inversion of normal concepts of morality, Sweet Thursday is an extremely moral work.
5. Examine the incidence and the relative importance of

animal imagery in Sweet Thursday in establishing both
mood and characterization.

6. Consider the treatment of the new arrivals (Fauna,
    Joseph and Mary, Joe Elegant, and Suzy) to the Row,
    and the reasons for their acceptance or rejection by the
    residents.

7. Discuss the extent to which Steinbeck's comments on the
    social and ecological issues of the day (i. e. in 1954) are
    still valid today; the extent to which situations have
    evolved, for better or for worse; the extent to which
    Steinbeck's warnings can be seen to have come true or
    to be coming true; the extent to which, by reasons of
    these incidental preoccupations, Sweet Thursday could be
    said to have dated.

8. Examine the evolution of the Ricketts' character in
    Steinbeck's novels from In Dubious Battle to Sweet Thurs-
    day, and compare these fictional portraits with the os-
    tensibly true portrait in "About Ed Ricketts. "

9. Compare Hazel with the many other mentally retarded
    characters who appear so frequently in Steinbeck's
    novels and stories. In particular, examine for what
    reasons and in what manner the day-to-day childlike
    innocence of these unfortunates erupts into violence.

10. Consider how Steinbeck's writings have turned Cannery
    Row into a tourist attraction and the extent to which, by
    thus inevitably changing the environment, the ambience
    that Steinbeck so lovingly described has in the process
    been ironically destroyed, perhaps forever.

C.   Selected Bibliography

1. Astro, Richard. John Steinbeck and Edward F. Ricketts:
    The Shaping of a Novelist. Minneapolis: University of
    Minnesota Press, 1973, pp. 193-206.
        Places Sweet Thursday in its true context in the
    Steinbeck-Ricketts relationship. The whole book is essential
    reading for a comprehensive understanding of the influence
    Ricketts had on Steinbeck's literary career.

2. _____ . "Steinbeck's Bittersweet Thursday. "   Stein-
    beck Quarterly, 4 (Spring, 1971), 36-48.
        Posits the thesis that by the time he came to write
    Sweet Thursday Steinbeck had, through his controversial
    characterization of Doc, "come to recognize the futility of
    an inherent and intrinsically charming way of life. "

3. DeMott, Robert. "Steinbeck and the Creative Process:
   First Manifesto to End the Bringdown Against Sweet
   Thursday," eds. Richard Astro and Tetsumaro Hayashi.
   Steinbeck: The Man and His Work, Corvallis: Oregon
   State University Press, 1971, pp. 157-78.
       Considers the theory that Sweet Thursday is a novel
   about the writing of a novel, and that as a study of creativity
   its insights far outweigh the banality of its plot.

4. Fontenrose, Joseph. John Steinbeck: An Introduction
   and Interpretation. New York: Holt, Rinehart and
   Winston, 1963, pp. 127-30.
       Suggests that the serious moral undertone in Sweet
   Thursday was a result of Steinbeck's deliberate attempt "to
   reject the teaching of Cannery Row and replace it with a
   newer gospel."

5. French, Warren. John Steinbeck. New York: Twayne
   Publishers, 1961, pp. 156-60.
       Advances an unfavorable assessment of Sweet Thurs-
   day by one of the most illustrious of Steinbeck scholars.

6. _____. John Steinbeck. Boston: Twayne Publishers,
   1975, pp. 154-57.
       Views Sweet Thursday as evidence of Steinbeck's
   "long-running attack on middle-class respectability."

7. Hedgpeth, Joel W. "Philosophy on Cannery Row," in
   Astro and Hayashi, pp. 89-129.
       Provides a memoir of Edward F. Ricketts, and a
   preliminary study of his work and his relationship with
   Steinbeck.

8. Levant, Howard. The Novels of John Steinbeck: A
   Critical Study. Columbia: University of Missouri Press,
   1974, pp. 259-72.
       Considers the element of self-parody in Sweet Thurs-
   day, while finding the work itself highly polished and beautifully structured.

9. Lisca, Peter. The Wide World of John Steinbeck. New
   Brunswick: Rutgers University Press, 1958, pp. 276-84.
       Suggests that in Sweet Thursday can be seen Stein-
   beck's continuing capitulation to his own materials.

10. Marks, Lester Jay. Thematic Design in the Novels of
    John Steinbeck, The Hague: Mouton and Co., 1969,

pp. 132-34.
    Refers briefly to Sweet Thursday in terms of a
"mediocre comic diversion."

11. Metzger, Charles R. "Steinbeck's Version of the Pastor-
    al," Modern Fiction Studies, 6 (Summer, 1960), 115-24.
    Posits a fascinating interpretation of Sweet Thursday
which examines the novel in the light of William Empson's
Some Versions of the Pastoral.

12. Moore, Ward. "Cannery Row Revisited: Steinbeck and
    the Sardine," Nation, 179 (October 16, 1954), 325-27.
    Contrasts Steinbeck's fictional representation of Can-
nery Row with the actual locale.

13. Morsberger, Robert. "Steinbeck's Happy Hookers,"
    Steinbeck Quarterly, 9 (Summer-Fall, 1976), 101-15.
    Discusses Sweet Thursday as being at heart "a naive
and contrived picture of prostitution."

14. Watt, F. W. Steinbeck. Edinburgh and London: Oliver
    and Boyd, 1962, pp. 99-101.
    Notes the lack of vitality in both the characters and
Steinbeck's prose in Sweet Thursday compared with the
earlier Cannery Row.

15. Weber, Tom. All the Heroes Are Dead: The Ecology
    of Steinbeck's Cannery Row. San Francisco: Ramparts
    Press, 1974.
    Combines evocative photographs with poetic commen-
tary to provide an illuminating background to Steinbeck's
novels.

Chapter 9

STEINBECK'S TRAVELS WITH CHARLEY IN SEARCH OF AMERICA (1962)

by Roy S. Simmonds

I. BACKGROUND

In November 1959, Steinbeck returned to America after having spent the greater part of that year in England, researching Arthurian legend and, in the solitude of a tiny cottage near the Somerset town of Bruton, writing his modern version of Malory's Morte D'Arthur. From New York, on November 5, he wrote Adlai Stevenson: "Back from Camelot, and, reading the papers not at all sure it was wise. Two first impressions. First a creeping, all-pervading nerve-gas of immorality which starts in the nursery and does not stop before it reaches the highest offices, both corporate and governmental. Two, a nervous restlessness, a hunger, a thirst, a yearning for something unknown-- perhaps morality. Then there's the violence, cruelty and hypocrisy symptomatic of a people which has too much, and last the surly ill-temper which only shows up in humans when they are frightened." He ended the letter: "Someone has to reinspect our system and that soon.... On all levels it is rigged, Adlai. Maybe nothing can be done about it, but I am stupid enough and naively hopeful enough to want to try. How about you?"[1]

The letter and Adlai Stevenson's introductory comments were published in the December 22, 1959 issue of the Long Island newspaper Newsday under the heading ADLAI STEVENSON AND JOHN STEINBECK DISCUSS THE PAST AND THE PRESENT. Steinbeck, however, having raised the issue, had little opportunity to do anything about it immediately, for on the Sunday following Thanksgiving he suffered what was ostensibly a "mild stroke" and was hospitalized for seven to ten days. In his own mind, he saw the illness not

165

so much a failure of the physical body as a manifestation of
his sense of intense frustration--specific frustration at becoming bogged down in the Arthur book and being unable to
finish it, and the more general, but none the less potent,
frustration he experienced in observing the wayward path he
considered the nation was inevitably taking.

When the November 5 letter to Adlai Stevenson was
reprinted in the March 13, 1960 issue of the Toledo Blade,
the editor of that newspaper invited his readers to reply to
Steinbeck's criticisms, and offered a prize of twenty-five
dollars for the best letter.   The prize-winner opened his
letter with the rhetorical question: "Are you the same John
Steinbeck who wrote so eloquently and morbidly in the '30s
of the migrant workers in The Grapes of Wrath?"   He went
on to note that that book was a plea for better conditions,
and that despite fighting two wars since those days the
country enjoyed a more widely-spread higher standard of
living than at any time in its history.   "Now," the reader
continued, "you are still in throes of woe over our society.
Then we had too little, now it is too much.   To you, Mr.
Steinbeck, and other contemporaries of yours, if you are
genuinely disturbed, why not write more novels of strength
and character in which the heroes do not succumb to the
evils you depict?   Let the writers bring back morality in
their novels and stories which are found in bookstands,
movies, and TV channels.   I wonder in what circles you
travel that you seem aware of only the pleasure-hungry,
restless, ill-tempered humans you refer to.   Isn't it true
that we see reflected in others that which is most true of
ourselves?   Look within yourself before pronouncing a diag-
nosis of our country from an ivory tower in Camelot.
'Physician, heal thyself.'"[2]

By the time that letter appeared in the Toledo Blade,
Steinbeck was already "in the middle of" a new novel, The
Winter of Our Discontent,[3] which explored in great depth
the new morality he so deplored, imposing upon the ending
the morality which he and presumably the prizewinning
Toledo Blade reader upheld.   As if he had also predicted
that reader's recommendations, Steinbeck was setting in
motion plans to travel around America.   "I just want to look
and listen," he wrote to Mr. and Mrs. Frank Loesser on
May 25, 1960.   "What I'll get I need badly--a re-knowledge
of my own country, of its speeches, its views, its attitudes,
and its changes.   It's long overdue--very long.   New York
is not America.   I am very excited about doing this.   It
will be a kind of a rebirth."[4]

He completed The Winter of Our Discontent in July-
August 1960, and planned to set off on "Operation Windmills,"
as he jokingly called the project, directly after Labor Day.
His plans, however, were delayed by Hurricane Donna, and
it was not until September 23 that he embarked with the
poodle Charley in his custom-built pickup truck with a camper
top.

One gets the impression from the letters he wrote his
wife along the way (which have since been published in Steinbeck: A Life in Letters) that, despite his real initial enthusiasm for the trip and the retrospective enthusiasm he
conjures up in the book, Travels with Charley, his heart was
not altogether in the project.

He was back home on the east coast in time to attend
President Kennedy's inauguration, and after a short vacation
in Barbados with his wife, he was soon off again to San
Diego to join the Mohole Expedition as its official historian.
These various activities interrupted work on Travels with
Charley, which he had begun shortly after his return to New
York in late 1960, and it was not until June of 1961 that he
was able to resume work on the book. He reported that he
was having some trouble in "getting back the rhythm and
flow" of the work, [5] but the book was presumably completed
by September 1961 when Steinbeck, accompanied by his wife
and his two sons, set off on a round-the-world trip. Their
itinerary took them to London, Bruton, Dublin, Nice, and
Milan. It was here that Steinbeck suffered a further slight
stroke or cardiac failure. He was obliged to rest up for a
few weeks, and for the next few months to proceed at a more
leisurely pace through Italy: Florence, Rome, and Capri.
During this period, he attended to the galley proofs of Travels with Charley, forced against his will to modify the language in the New Orleans section of the book. By April, he
was apparently fit enough to continue the world trip, and the
family traveled on to Greece. But by the end of May, Steinbeck was hankering to return home: everywhere had for him
a "sameness." [6] They returned to the United States. Travels with Charley was published in July 1962, and in the
October of that year Steinbeck heard that he had been awarded
the Nobel Prize for Literature.

Steinbeck attended the ceremony in Stockholm. The
Permanent Secretary of the Swedish Academy, Anders Osterling, made reference to Travels with Charley in his presentation address: "We see here what a very experienced ob-

server and raisonneur he is.   In a series of admirable ex-
plorations into local color, he rediscovers his country and
its people.   In its informal way this book is also a forceful
criticism of society. "7   The Swedish Academy's citation
read: "For his realistic as well as imaginative writings,
distinguished by a sympathetic humor and a keen social perception. "

        Dogged by indifferent health and the inhibitions that
he felt the Nobel Prize had imposed upon him as a writer,
Steinbeck was to produce only one further book, the expository America and Americans (1966), before his death in New
York on December 20, 1968.

II.   SYNOPSIS

        Steinbeck's journey "In Search of America" began
from his home in Sag Harbor, Long Island.   After being
delayed by the hurricane Donna, he eventually set forth in
his three-quarter-ton custom-built pickup truck, which he
had named Rocinante after Don Quixote's horse.   He took
along, principally for companionship but ostensibly as provider of a certain element of protection, the "old French
gentleman poodle known as Charley. "   His route initially
took him through Connecticut, Massachusetts, Vermont, and
New Hampshire, through the spectacular fall arboreal beauty
of New England, into Maine, where he made a brief detour
to Deer Isle, arranged for him by his friend and literary
agent, Elizabeth Otis.

        Driving up into northern Maine, near the Canadian
border, he passed a happy evening entertaining in his
cramped quarters a family of French-Canadian migrant
workers, then drove back across northern New Hampshire,
Vermont, and New York State, with the intention of visiting
Niagara Falls, making a shallow excursion into Canada, and
crossing the border again at Detroit.   This plan did not,
however, materialize.   Charley, who had been so successfully instrumental in breaking the ice when Steinbeck met up
with the Canuck migrant workers, proved a stumbling block
as far as the U.S. customs authorities were concerned.
After crossing the no man's land between the two customs
barriers, the Canadian officials warned him that although he
would be allowed to enter Canada with Charley, he would
not be allowed back into the U.S. by the American customs,
unless he could produce a rabies vaccination certificate for

the dog. He therefore had no other choice but to turn back
without crossing the border into Canada, but this did not save
him from being questioned at some length by suspicious U. S.
customs officials before he was cleared and allowed to proceed on his way back into his own country. It was the first
really jarring note in what had been until then a pleasant
voyage of rediscovery.

He took highway US 90 through Pennsylvania and
Michigan, and then drove into Illinois. Here, in Chicago,
he broke his journey. His wife flew out from New York to
join him, and he spent a few days with her in the comfort
of the Ambassador East Hotel.

Resuming his journey, he passed through Wisconsin,
lost himself among the milling traffic in the twin cities of
St. Paul and Minneapolis, crossed Minnesota, and thence on
to North Dakota and Montana, the state which he asserts was
his "favorite" and his "love. "

He crossed Idaho and the Great Divide, recalling with
a sense of deep respect and humility the pioneers who had
made the crossing on foot over a century and a half before.
It was at this stage of the journey that Charley began to
display unhappy symptoms of bladder trouble, and, pressing
on quickly to Spokane, Steinbeck took his companion to the
local veterinary doctor, who provided temporary, albeit un-
sympathetic, treatment.

With the state of Washington behind them, Rocinante
bore the two travelers into the impressive redwood country
in southern Oregon. Charley, much to Steinbeck's chagrin,
was unimpressed.

The return to his native California was, for Steinbeck,
something of an emotional disaster. The reunion with his
two sisters, as he tells it, was not the overwhelmingly happy
family affair he had undoubtedly anticipated, deteriorating as
it did in bouts of political argument, and ending on a somewhat sour note. When he went in search of his old compan-
ions, he discovered that they had either died or changed--or
that he had changed--during the time he had been away, and
that the relationships he had cherished in memory existed no
longer.

Fleeing from this "homecoming" debacle, he crossed
the Mojave Desert, passed through Arizona and New Mexico

into Texas, where, after leaving Charley for treatment with
a more sympathetic veterinarian in Amarillo, he was again
joined by his wife, a Texan herself by birth, at the ranch of a
friend, where for three or four days they indulged themselves
in a "Thanksgiving orgy" of eating, drinking, and hunting.

Collecting Charley, now cured, from the veterinarian,
Steinbeck made his way to New Orleans, where he observed
the notorious Cheerleaders screaming their daily quota of
obscenities outside the school where two small Negro children
had been enrolled. He had felt compelled to witness for
himself this manifestation of racial hatred, unwilling perhaps
to accept that such things were taking place in his homeland
and were not simply improbable, staged performances for
the benefit of television cameras and newspaper reporters.
What he saw and heard so sickened him that he apparently
made his way back to New York by what seems to have been
comparatively the shortest route possible.

III.   CRITICAL EXPLICATION

Travels with Charley is more than merely a travel
book per se.   It is, as much as anything else, the very
readable account of a writer's dual odyssey: first, his
attempt to rediscover the country of his birth after years
of residence in New York and travel abroad; and second,
and perhaps more importantly--certainly more importantly
for Steinbeck himself--a personal quest to find his own
identity and roots in the vastness of his homeland.   Intent
on unraveling just what it was that made America and its
people tick, on isolating the disparate factors that had drawn
together over the years and had, so he feared, launched the
country along a road which could lead only to sure disaster,
then publishing his findings in the hope that he might be able
to point the way to national salvation, he underestimated the
extent of his own personal involvement in the project and
was finally forced to flee back to the sanctuary of wife and
home on the East Coast.   It cannot be gainsaid that, just
as the circular journey that Steinbeck made around the outer
regions of the United States ended in personal failure, the
book that grew from this journey also ended, as so many of
his postwar works did, in artistic failure.   Having said that,
I must immediately and unequivocably admit that he had given
us in Travels with Charley not only a rich, consistently
amusing and thought-provoking work, but surely one of the
most delightful books in his impressive and varied canon.

In Travels with Charley, Steinbeck can be compared to a cross between a latter-day Sir Galahad setting out in search of the Holy Grail and an intermittently eccentric and occasionally irascible Knight of La Mancha tilting at windmills. Steinbeck was, however, unsuccessful in seeking out his own personal version of the Grail. His desire to reestablish roots and identity in his birthplace was elusively denied him. As he had all along suspected, "Tom Wolfe was right. You can't go home again because home has ceased to exist except in the mothballs of memory."[8] If any confirmation was needed after the elegiac and sentimental unreality of Sweet Thursday that Steinbeck had lost touch with life on the California Central Coast, such confirmation was explicit in the account he gives of his true-life return in Travels with Charley.

There can be no denying that Steinbeck felt at the back of his mind that in setting out on this exploratory trip he was fulfilling some sort of destiny. It is not without significance, of course, that one of his favorite books was Cervantes' masterpiece. By naming his truck Rocinante, Steinbeck was consciously identifying himself with Don Quixote, who

> thought it fit and proper, both in order to increase his renown and to serve the state, to turn knight errant and travel through the world with horse and armour in search of adventures, following in every way the practice of the knights errant he had read of, redressing all manner of wrongs, and exposing himself to chances and dangers, by the overcoming of which he might win eternal honour and renown.[9]

Steinbeck, however, for all the physical aspects of his journey, clearly regarded his own aims in purely literary terms. It was certainly not his purpose or intention to expose himself to chance and danger. The good he would do as knight errant, the righting of wrongs, would be accomplished after his return from his travels by duly committing his findings and, where possible, his solutions to paper.

He found much to disturb him. In a letter written in July 1961 to his editor and friend, Pascal Covici, Steinbeck reported progress on the writing of the book, and had this to say about the state of the nation as he saw it during the course of his journeying:

> In all my travels I saw very little real poverty, I
> mean the grinding terrifying poorness of the
> Thirties.   That at least was real and tangible.
> No, it was a sickness, a kind of wasting disease.
> There were wishes but no wants.   And underneath
> it all the building energy like gasses in a corpse.
> When that explodes, I tremble to think what will
> be the result.   Over and over I thought we lack
> the pressures that make men strong and the anguish
> that makes men great.   The pressures are debts,
> the desires are for more material toys and the
> anguish is boredom.   Through time, the nation has
> become a discontented land.   I've sought for an
> out on this--saying it is my aging eyes seeing it,
> my waning energy feeling it, my warped vision that
> is distorting it, but it is only partly true.   The
> thing I have described is really there.   I did not
> create it.   It's very well for me to write jokes
> and anecdotes but the haunting decay is there
> under it. [10]

His principal preoccupations with the social and moral
climate of the nation, as well as his concern over ecological
matters, are fully demonstrated in the pages of this book.
Through the people he meets, he attempts to judge the mood
of the country.   He discusses politics with a New England
farmer, who seems to exemplify the widespread sense of uncertainty felt by ordinary decent men and women in that
election year of 1960.   They both agree that there is an
unhealthy apathy among the population as a whole toward
matters political.   He tries to joke with the listless waitress
in the restaurant near Bangor, but she has become a pathetic
victim to the emptiness of her life style.   He finds a certain
affinity with the strolling actor, content in having discovered
his true role in life, who shows Steinbeck the treasured letter he received from Sir John Gielgud.   He advises the son
of a motel proprietor who hankers to be a ladies' hairdresser
in New York and who fumes with discontent because he is
trapped in the wilds of Idaho, denied his ambition by the
derisive opposition of a contemptuous father.   He rejoices
in the simple goodness of the evil-looking Oregon service
station owner who, reacting to an emergency situation on a
wet Sunday with everywhere closed up, puts himself to an
immense amount of trouble telephoning around and persuading
other people to help in finding a set of heavy-duty tires for
Rocinante.   If the evil-looking service station man regenerates
Steinbeck's faith in man, the parking-lot attendant and the taxi

driver he meets in New Orleans and the hitch-hiker he subsequently picks up en route to Jackson surely do not. Their
bigoted approach to the racial question and their delighted
approval of the Cheerleaders rouses Steinbeck's anger, an
anger which is also to a considerable degree a reaction to
fear. He professes his faith in the ultimate future. "(T)he
end is not in question," he avers; then voices his doubts in
relation to the period of transitions: "It's the means--the
dreadful uncertainty of the means" (242).

He is impressed, if not entirely surprised, by the
sense of restlessness he finds among the American people.
Everywhere, he tells us, in every state he visits, he sees
"a burning desire to go, to move, to get under way, any
place, away from any Here" (10). Visiting those contemporary true transients, the people who live in mobile homes,
he questions the disadvantages of their obvious lack of roots,
lack of permanence. "Who's got permanence?" he is asked.
"Factory closes down, you move on. Good times and things
opening up, you move on where it's better. You got roots,
you sit and starve. You take the pioneers in the history
books. They were movers. Take up land, sell it, move
on" (91-92). Steinbeck concludes that as far as the American people are concerned this restlessness is and always
has been endemic, noting that "every one of us, except the
Negroes forced here as slaves, are descended from the restless ones, the wayward ones who were not content to stay at
home" (93). He notes approvingly the signs of the future
general drift of people from the cities back to the countryside, but for the most part he sees the people of America
standing at the crossroads, uncertain which path to take.

He rails against the hygienic packaging in so many
areas of contemporary life:

> It is life at a peak of some kind of civilization.
> The restaurant accommodations, great scallops of
> counters with simulated leather stools, are as
> spotless as and not unlike the lavatories. Every-
> thing that can be captured and held down is sealed
> in clear plastic. The food is oven-fresh, spotless
> and tasteless; untouched by human hands. I re-
> membered with an ache certain dishes in France
> and Italy touched by innumerable human hands.
> (82-83)

It is not until he reaches Idaho that he comes across

a lunch room whose signs are unashamedly "old and auto-
graphed by the flies of many past summers." Steinbeck
adds with approval: "There would be no cellophane on the
food here" (152).

He contrasts the overly hygienic treatment of food
with the criminally unthinking despoliation of the countryside
surrounding the cities. "American cities," he accuses,
"are like badger holes, ringed with trash--all of them--
surrounded by piles of wrecked and rusting automobiles, and
almost smothered with rubbish" (25), rubbish incidentally
provided by the excessive and for the most part useless
packaging we have been conditioned to regard as essential
to our contemporary way of life. He ponders upon the problem:

> ... I do wonder whether there will come a time
> when we can no longer afford our wastefulness--
> chemical wastes in the rivers, metal wastes every-
> where, and atomic wastes buried deep in the earth
> or sunk in the sea. When an Indian village became
> too deep in its own filth, the inhabitants moved.
> And we have no place to which to move. (25)

But, despite his pessimism, ironic cheerfulness breaks
through. Contemplating the proliferation of antique shops
scattered throughout the length and breadth of New England,
he suggests that if these shops can provide a good living
from the sale of the "authentic and attested trash from an
earlier time" (40), there might be some commercial merit
in gathering up the discarded junk from the trash heaps of
today and mothballing it for our descendants to sell to the
gullible customers of the future. "Lord, the possibilities
are endless! Things we have to pay to have hauled away
could bring fortunes" (41).

Echoing the prophecies of Doc's friend, Old Jingleballicks in the novel Sweet Thursday (1954), Steinbeck views
the rapidly increasing population with some alarm:

> Even those people who joy in numbers and are
> impressed with bigness are beginning to worry,
> gradually becoming aware that there must be a
> saturation point and the progress may be a pro-
> gression toward strangulation. And no solution
> has been found. You can't forbid people to be
> born--at least not yet. (174)

Or, as he puts it in another way:

> If the most versatile of living forms, the human,
> now fights for survival as it always has, it can
> eliminate not only itself but all other life. (192)

The author's indomitable humor, however, keeps
percolating through the underlying mood of critical pessimism
which persists throughout the book, and is an essential ingredient of the emotional tone of the work. For, as well
as being a very personal portrait of America, Travels with
Charley is a unique self-portrait of one of the least autobiographical of major twentieth-century American writers.
Steinbeck has a delicious sense of quiet humor, which, although not without its occasional barbs, becomes an integral
part of the work, giving it, even in its deepest philosophical
moments, a refreshing lightness of touch and a truly be-
guiling flavor.

The portrait Steinbeck draws of himself in the pages
of this book does not attempt to disguise the warts, and consequently he comes over to the reader as a very warm and
very human personality, fallible like the rest of us, subject
to the same sort of pressures, emotions, needs, and fears
we all experience from time to time, possessing a certain
wisdom, but also not without prejudice and idiosyncrasy.

As far as the journey itself is concerned, he professes
a desire to retain anonymity, wishing simply to be allowed
to move freely around the country, observing, and avoiding
completely the sort of distractions that recognition might
engender. Happily for this professed desire, the name
Rocinante painted on the side of the truck--surely an incon-
gruous gesture by someone avowedly eschewing the lime-
light--elicits no comment or inquiries from any of the people
he encounters on his travels.

Steinbeck is properly cognizant of the concern expressed by his family and friends "that a stranger's purpose
in moving about the country might cause inquiry or even
suspicion" (7). He possibly recalled the reaction his fictional Doc of Cannery Row (1945) attracted when traveling on
foot through Indiana, Kentucky, North Carolina, Georgia, and
Florida:

> And everywhere people asked him why he was
> walking through the country. Because he loved

true things he tried to explain. He said he was
nervous and besides he wanted to see the country,
smell the ground and look at grass and birds and
trees, to savor the country, and there was no
other way to do it save on foot. And people didn't
like him for telling the truth. They scowled, or
shook and tapped their heads, they laughed as
though they knew it was a lie and they appreciated
a liar. And some, afraid for their daughters or
their pigs, told him to move on, to get going, just
not to stop near their place if he knew what was
good for him. 11

To placate the people he met, Doc found himself obliged to
desist from telling the truth. Instead, he told people he was
making the walk for a bet.

Everyone liked him then and believed him. They
asked him in to dinner and gave him a bed and they
put lunches up for him and wished him good luck
and thought he was a hell of a fine fellow. 12

Whether or not he remembered Doc's problems and
his solution to them, Steinbeck takes appropriate precautions:

... I racked a shotgun, two rifles, and a couple
of fishing rods in my truck, for it is my experience
that if a man is going hunting or fishing his purpose is understood and even applauded. (7)

Steinbeck is also cognizant of the fears of his family
and friends concerning the dangers inherent in his traveling
alone, fears from which he admits he was not himself entirely immune. For this reason, more to engender a sense
of false security apparently than anything else, he takes the
poodle Charley along with him.

Charley, of course, is very much a character in his
own right. His real name, so we are told, is Charles le
Chien. He was born near Paris and is more ready to obey
commands in French than in English. Together with Steinbeck, his presence dominates the first five-sixths of the
book. He is more than simply a traveling companion, for
he acts as a sounding board for Steinbeck's philosophical
musings along the way, as "ambassador" in making contacts
with strangers, as conscience, as occasional deus ex machina,
and as a frequent provider of solace.

Certain vignettes remain in the mind long after the
reader has turned the last page of the book: Charley's
abortive encounter with the "stout and bedizened Pomeran-
ian" and her equally stout and bedizened mistress; Charley's
tail bound in red Kleenex as tentative defence against the
mistaken sightings of over-enthusiastic hunters in Maine;
Charley's outburst of maniacal rage on seeing the bear in
Yellowstone Park.

Although at times Steinbeck seems to endow him with
quasi-human characteristics, Charley is first and foremost
a dog, with all the usual canine preoccupations. He has,
however, the unique facility for pronouncing the consonant
"F," and whenever he wishes "to salute a bush or tree," as
Steinbeck euphemistically puts it, he utters the sound "Ftt,"
which is his way of asking his master to stop the truck and
let him out to go about his "ceremony."

> He doesn't have to think about it to do it well. It
> is my experience that in some areas Charley is
> more intelligent than I am, but in others he is
> abysmally ignorant. He can't read, can't drive a
> car, and has no grasp of mathematics. But in his
> own field of endeavor, which he was now practic-
> ing, the slow, imperial smelling over and anointing
> of an area, he has no peer. Of course his hori-
> zons are limited, but how wide are mine? (23-24)

Such speculation can inspire a sense of humility in
Steinbeck toward his own talent in his chosen art. Pulling
up on a quiet country road in northern Michigan, the author
ruminates that "Charley could with his delicate exploring nose
read his own particular literature on bushes and tree trunks
and leave his message there, perhaps as important in endless time as these pen scratches I put down on perishable
paper" (97-98).

Approaching the giant redwood country of southern
Oregon, Steinbeck observes that Charley "was rapidly becoming a tree expert of enormous background," but wonders
if the experience of encountering the immensity of the redwood might translate him "mystically to another plane of
existence, to another dimension," indeed "might even drive
him mad" (168). The giant redwood, to Steinbeck's way of
thinking, would surely prove to be Charley's Grail. In one
of the most amusing passages in the book, Steinbeck relates
how the perverse Charley is singularly unimpressed on even-

tually being confronted with "the serene grandfather of
Titans" Steinbeck has carefully selected for him, preferring
instead a weed, a sapling, and a hazelnut bush. It is only
by the most circumspect of trickery that Charley is ultimately persuaded to leave his visiting card against the redwood
bark.

Charley's role in the journey is somewhat muted from
Idaho onward, after the first symptons of prostatitis make
themselves evident. Just as Charley's lack of a rabies vaccination certificate prevents Steinbeck from crossing the border into Canada, so the state of Charley's health at this
stage of the journey inevitably conditions to some extent
Steinbeck's subsequent movements. When his own adminis-
trations prove ineffective, Steinbeck rushes Charley to a
veterinary in Spokane, who provides some pills but little
else. By the time they reach Texas, Charley is again in
need of urgent, expert attention, and Steinbeck leaves him
in the care of another veterinary in Amarillo. Whereas
Steinbeck had noted "the look of veiled contempt" Charley
had had for the Spokane doctor, he is encouraged to see the
"instant rapport" between Charley and this new doctor, and
how "content and confident" Charley seems to be in this
man's capable hands. When Steinbeck collects him four
days later, Charley "looked half his age and felt wonderful,
and to prove it he ran and jumped and rolled and laughed
and gave little yips of pure joy" (221). This happy picture
is almost our last sight of Charley, for apart from being
mistaken for a "nigger" by a New Orleans parking lot attendant, he plays hardly any part at all in Steinbeck's account of the remainder of the journey.

Structurally, the book leaves a great deal to be desired, and this structural flaw is the principal reason for
the feeling of disappointment and dissatisfaction that the
reader experiences when he reaches the final page. As John
Ditsky has observed:

> One-half of the book is taken up with travel from
> Long Island to Chicago, where a planned break
> occurs; yet only a quarter of the national perime-
> ter has been traveled. Rushing down to the Pacific,
> Steinbeck has consumed fully two-thirds of his
> eventual total writing space; and by the time he
> turns his Rocinante eastward once again (185-86),
> he has remaining only sixty pages out of two hun-
> dred forty-six with which to cover the country!

Small wonder if the reader senses that his author has lost interest in his project. Moreover, that reader is, in great part, left denied much access to the fleeing Steinbeck's thoughts. [13]

It is not the lack of a basic correlation between linear proportion and narrative pattern alone which the perceptive reader finds unsatisfactory, and even disturbing. The book possesses two climactic sequences: the abortive "homecoming" to Monterey, and the frightening account of the Cheerleaders in New Orleans. Considered from the structural aspect again, they are positioned too closely together in the final quarter of the book, so that they contrive to work against each other and thereby lose some of their individual emotional impact.

Although the avowed objective of Steinbeck's journey was "to try to rediscover this monster land" (5), the second unstated objective, the personal quest to rediscover his own identity in the land of his birth, was the one which eventually dominated his mind. By his own admission, he failed in his first objective. "It would be pleasant," he writes, "to be able to say of my travels with Charley, 'I went out to find the truth about my country and I found it'" (185). The evidence points rather to the fact that Steinbeck returned from his travels in a more confused state of mind than when he had set out, and this confusion led him, rightly or wrongly, to the ultimate revelation that he no longer had any roots anywhere. Two years later, shortly after receiving the Nobel Prize for Literature, in a letter dated January 14, 1963, to his friend Carlton A. Sheffield, he referred to the time in the late 1940s when

> I really tried to go back to Pacific Grove to live after my breakup with my second wife. I stayed nearly a year or maybe more than a year. But it wasn't any good. I didn't belong there. I guess it was there or maybe not very long afterwards that I discovered what I should have known long before, that I don't belong anywhere. [14]

He should have known, too, that the return to Monterey in 1960 would only confirm what he had already discovered years before, and in the book Steinbeck prepares the reader for the debacle that is to come. While still in the Middle West, he asks the cook of a roadside restaurant the way to Sauk Center, because he wants to see the birthplace of Sin-

clair Lewis.   When at last he reaches the town, however,
he drives straight through without stopping.

> I had read <u>Main Street</u> when I was in high school,
> and I remember the violent hatred it aroused in the
> countryside of his nativity.
> Did he go back?
> Just went through now and again.   The only good
> writer was a dead writer.   Then he couldn't sur-
> prise anyone any more, couldn't hurt anyone any
> more.
> ... I've heard he died alone.   And now he's
> good for the town.   Brings in some tourists.   He's
> a good writer now.   (120)

The bitter passage seems in retrospect painfully
prophetic.   What Sinclair Lewis had experienced, what
Thomas Wolfe had experienced, so Steinbeck himself was to
experience, and like Lewis and Wolfe was to gain full acceptance and recognition in "the countryside of his nativity"
only after his death.

Seattle provides another omen of things to come.   "I
remembered Seattle as a town sitting on hills beside a match-
less harborage," Steinbeck recalls, and then observes: "This
Seattle had no relation to the one I remembered....   This
Seattle was not something changed that I once knew.   It was
a new thing.   Set down there not knowing it was Seattle, I
could not have told where I was" (162).

From the moment he arrives in Monterey, nothing is
as he has anticipated it would be.   The changes he sees
about him, the strangers who walk the streets, alienate him
from the place of his birth, "its outward appearance confus[ing]
and anger[ing]" him (182).   What should have been a happy
homecoming with his sisters swiftly deteriorates instead into
a series of prolonged, violent political arguments, leaving
them all "panting and spent with rage" (177), and causing
Steinbeck to wonder whether as a family they were perhaps
unique or whether such arguments were privately in progress
all over the country.   Possibly he and the New England
farmer had been wrong in their assumptions after all, and
it was "only publicly that the nation was tongue-tied" (178).

It is, however, not until he visits Johnny Garcia's bar
that it is forcibly brought to him just how abortive his homecoming has been.   The warmth of Johnny's welcome and his

urging of Steinbeck to come back to Monterey to live is
ironically the catalyst which finally brings Steinbeck to accept what he has been so reluctant to accept as the unpalat-
able truth for so many years. He tells Johnny:

> "... Let us not fool ourselves. What we knew is
> dead, and maybe the greatest part of what we were
> is dead. What's out there is new and perhaps
> good, but it's nothing we know."
> Johnny held his temples between his cupped
> hands and his eyes were bloodshot.
> "Where are the great ones? Tell me, where's
> Willie Trip?"
> "Dead," Johnny said hollowly.
> "Where is Pilon, Johnny, Pom Pom, Miz
> Gragg, Stevie Field?"
> "Dead, dead, dead," he echoed.
> "Ed Ricketts, Whiteys Number One and Two,
> where's Sonny Boy, Ankle Varney, Jesus Maria
> Corcoran, Joe Portagee, Shorty Lee, Flora Wood,
> and that girl who kept spiders in her hat?"
> "Dead--all dead," Johnny moaned.
> "It's like we was in a bucket of ghosts," said
> Johnny.
> "No. They're not true ghosts. We're the
> ghosts." (180-81)

There is no alternative left to Steinbeck but that he
should leave as quickly as possible. He makes one final
pilgrimage to Fremont's Peak, where he had spent so many
happy hours as a boy, and there gazes down once again on
the whole spread of the Salinas Valley, "the whole of my
childhood and youth" (183). And there, high on the peak,
remembering the safe, unchangeable past, the pain of present alienation is partly ameliorated as his "memory myth
repaired itself" (183).

The "homecoming" is thus the true emotional climax
of Travels with Charley, as well as being the book's true
narrative climax. Steinbeck's travels and search ended in
Monterey, and more specifically in Johnny Garcia's bar.
His departure from Monterey "was flight" (183). Camping
some days later on the Continental Divide, he sits in the
truck and

> faced what I had concealed from myself. I was
> driving myself, pounding out the miles because I

> was no longer hearing or seeing.... Why had I
> thought I could learn anything about the land? For
> the last hundreds of miles I had avoided people.
> (196)

Later that same evening, walking with Charley up the
trail in the little canyon in which he had parked the truck
for the night, Steinbeck comes upon a tiny talismanic object.15

> So dark was the night that it was prickled with
> fiery dots.   My light brought an answering flash
> up the steep rocky bank.   I climbed up, slipping
> and floundering, lost the echoed light and found it
> again, a good little new-split stone with a piece
> of mica in it--not a fortune but a good thing to
> have.   I put it in my pocket and we went to bed.
> (198)

It was to be the nearest approach to the Holy Grail that
Steinbeck was to discover in his wanderings, and here, at
the end of Part Three of the book, on this muted ironic note,
he should, from the aesthetic point of view, have brought
Travels with Charley to a close.

But, instead, in Part Four, he continues on for
another forty-six pages, which are mainly devoted to describing a Thanksgiving visit with his wife to a rich friend's
ranch in Texas, and the activities of the New Orleans
Cheerleaders.

The New Orleans experience is a traumatic one for
Steinbeck.   His initial motivation for visiting the city is
pure human curiosity.   Before he arrives in New Orleans,
he regards the activities of the Cheerleaders, as presented
by the media, as something akin to a circus act or a freak
show.   He is thus only half-prepared for the truth he wit-
nesses: the tiny black girl child walking the gauntlet through
the shrieking crowd; the theatrical posturings and gestures of
the Cheerleaders; the foul language which he now realizes has
always been carefully deleted from the media reportings, and
the white father and child who attract even more venom than
the black child herself.   Reading Steinbeck's description of
what he saw and heard that day, one has the impression that
even all those months after the event he had difficulty in
expressing himself adequately on paper.   It appears that his
original account was watered down by an over-cautious editor,
but, for all that, even in this emasculated version, the hor-

ror and the utter disgust he felt comes through undiluted on
the printed page:

> I've seen this kind bellow for blood at a prize
> fight, have orgasms when a man is gored in the
> bull ring, stare with vicarious lust at a highway
> accident, stand patiently in line for the privilege
> of watching any pain or any agony. But where were
> the others ... the ones whose arms would ache to
> gather up the small, scared black mite? (229)

By the mere fact of being a spectator at these modern
Roman Games and of being inescapably aware of his total inability to do anything to stop it happening, he feels tainted
with "weary, hopeless nausea" (230). For the second time
within the space of a couple of weeks or so, he finds himself forced to flee in confusion from a situation which has
emotionally overwhelmed him.

In the following days, he meets four people who each
serve to illustrate an approach, an attitude, toward the
vexed racial question. The conversations he has with these
people, however, seem as if they have been simply contrived
by Steinbeck to provide the opportunity of discussing the subject with an appropriate degree of desired objectivity after
all the emotion that has gone before. As descriptions of
factual encounters, they simply do not hold conviction for
the reader.

By this time, Steinbeck's journey and his book have
completely disintegrated. In three pages, he travels from
Montgomery, Alabama, back to New York, and thankfully declares that he is at last "home again."

The writer of fiction has an undoubted advantage over
the author of a work of non-fiction in that he possesses an
omnipotent power over his narrative and his cast of characters. Working from within himself, he can mold events and
people at will to produce the exact reaction he wishes to
arouse in the mind of his reader. The writer of non-fiction,
on the other hand, cannot possibly have the same wide-
ranging freedom of choice: the shape of the narrative is
already imposed on the work by external actuality, and the
characters he introduces have a life of their own which is
completely divorced from the will of the author. For all
that, the writer of non-fiction can select his material, casting out the irrelevant and retaining only that which is perti-

nent to his thesis, choosing which characters he will introduce into his narrative and which he will not, sharpening or
omitting detail without discarding basic veracity. To recognize the reasons why Steinbeck wrote of the events he describes in Part Four, and then did not even attempt to shape
the work into measured conclusion, is to recognize both his
integrity as a man in not shrinking from telling the odious
truth as he saw it, and his destructive impatience as an
artist to have the book finished and done with when he had
so obviously lost interest in it.

    To speculate in directions other than those already
discussed as to the factors which culminated in the double
failure of journey and book can be both interesting and, one
hopes, illuminating.   In the novel In Dubious Battle (1936),
the character Doc Burton, who (like Doc in Cannery Row and
Sweet Thursday) is a fictional representation of Steinbeck's
close friend Ed Ricketts, expresses a desire to achieve the
holistic experience: "I want to see the whole picture--as
nearly as I can. I don't want to put on the blinders of 'good'
and 'bad, ' and limit my vision.... Don't you see? I want
to be able to look at the whole thing. "16   Early on in his
travels, in that almost idyllic interlude when he entertains
the family of Canadian migrant workers in the cabin of
Rocinante, Steinbeck experiences, over a shared bottle of
cognac, the manifestation of those holistic theories he had
so often propounded in his novels:

> ... there came into Rocinante a triumphant human
> magic that can bless a house, or a truck for that
> matter--nine people gathered in complete silence
> and the nine parts making a whole as surely as my
> arms and legs are part of me, separate and in-
> separable. (63)

    There is a strange irony in the fact that probably the
only other occasion when Steinbeck comes near to a sense of
complete communion with the land and with all living things
is not in his hometown or amid the lush greenery of his
native California, nor in the bosom of his family or in the
company of his cherished Monterey friends, but in the moon
landscape ambience of the Mojave Desert, and with a pair of
unsuspecting coyotes. His desire to encompass the whole
American experience is, he discovers, too vast an under-
taking to be attempted in so short a time, and he is finally
and sadly obliged to admit, "I had seen so little of the
whole" (237).

Toward the beginning of Travels with Charley, Steinbeck draws a parallel between the act of starting out on his
journey and the act of commencing work on a new novel:

> When I face the desolate impossibility of writing
> five hundred pages a sick sense of failure falls on
> me and I know I can never do it. This happens
> every time. Then gradually I write one page and
> then another. One day's work is all I can permit
> myself to contemplate and I eliminate the possibil-
> ity of ever finishing. (23)

He also confesses that as a result of thirty years of
writing he has found that "I cannot write hot on an event.
It has to ferment. I must do what a friend calls 'mule it
over' for a time before it goes down" (11). He seems to
be putting this forward in the form of a vague apologia, for
it is certain that he did suspect very strongly that he had
not allowed sufficient fermentation time to elapse before
embarking on the book. It is not without significance, for
instance, that many of the more vivid and memorable passages in the book are those which deal with Steinbeck's
childhood and early manhood.

In the previously quoted letter of July 1961 to Covici,
Steinbeck wrote: "And the little book of ambulatory memoirs
staggers along, takes a spurt and lags. It's a formless,
shapeless, aimless thing and it is even pointless.... Some-
where there must be design if I can only find it."[17] Had he
allowed the process of fermentation, of subconscious assimi-
lation, to go on a little longer before he set pen to paper,
would Travels with Charley have been a better book? Would
he have discovered the design he was seeking? We shall
never know, and speculation of this nature is thus extremely
invidious. It would, however, probably have been a different book. The sense of spontaneity and possibly a great
deal of the humor which pervades so much of the first five-
sixths of his text might very well have been lost. As a
book, it might have become more self-conscious and serious
in tone, like the last book he published in his lifetime, the
expository America and Americans (1966), in which he again
endeavored to accomplish the impossible by capturing the
whole essence of the land and its people.

Charley survived the travels by only a little over
two years, succumbing toward the end of April 1963 to "what
would probably be called cirrhosis in a human."[18] Steinbeck

himself died in December 1968. They will both live long in
the pages of this flawed but entertaining, rich and rewarding
record of the journey they took together in the fall and early
winter of the year 1960.

NOTES

1. John Steinbeck, Steinbeck: A Life in Letters, eds.
   Elaine Steinbeck and Robert Wallsten (New York:
   Viking Press, 1975), pp. 651-53.

2. "Reader's Reply," Toledo Blade, March 27, 1960, VI, 1.

3. Steinbeck: A Life in Letters, p. 663.

4. Ibid., p. 667.

5. Ibid., p. 699.

6. Ibid., p. 742.

7. Anders Osterling, "Presentation Address," in Nobel
   Prize Library: William Faulkner, Eugene O'Neill,
   John Steinbeck (New York: Alexis Gregory, n. d.),
   p. 203.

8. John Steinbeck, Travels with Charley (New York:
   Viking Press, 1962), p. 183. All subsequent references to this work are indicated by page numbers in
   parentheses following quotes.

9. Miguel de Cervantes Saavedra, The Adventures of Don
   Quixote, tr. J. M. Cohen (Harmondsworth: Penguin
   Books, 1950), p. 33.

10. Steinbeck: A Life in Letters, pp. 702-03.

11. John Steinbeck, Cannery Row (New York: Viking Press,
    1945), p. 108.

12. Ibid.

13. John Ditsky, "Steinbeck's Travels with Charley: The
    Quest that Failed," Steinbeck Quarterly, 8 (Spring
    1975), 47.

14. Steinbeck: A Life in Letters, pp. 762-63.

15. See Todd M. Lieber's excellent and perceptive study of
the significance of talismanic symbols in Steinbeck's
fiction, in his "Talismanic Patterns in the Novels of
John Steinbeck," American Literature, 44 (May 1972),
262-75.

16. John Steinbeck, In Dubious Battle (New York: Covici
Friede, 1936), p. 149.

17. Steinbeck: A Life in Letters, p. 702.

18. Ibid., p. 771.

IV. APPARATUS FOR RESEARCH PAPERS

A.   Questions for Discussion

1. In what ways can Steinbeck be said to be fortunate or
unfortunate in the people he encounters, and what specifically does he learn from them about himself as well as
about America as a whole?
2. What explanation can you suggest to account for the
mysteriously deserted motel near Lancaster, New Hampshire?
3. In what ways does Charley serve to give unity to Steinbeck's narrative?
4. Charley's confrontation with the bear in Yellowstone Park
prompts Steinbeck to wonder "why we think the thoughts
and emotions of animals are simple?" In what respects,
if at all, can Charley himself be said to be a complex
character?
5. How thoroughly does Steinbeck's narrative encompass
ethnic groups in America?   Are there any important
ethnic groups he does not comment upon?
6. To what extent is it possible from a reading of the text
to suggest that here and there Steinbeck may be employ-
ing a degree of novelist's license to add color and interest to what might otherwise have seemed a rather prosaic
situation?
7. In what manner does Steinbeck introduce the Arthurian
theme into his narrative?   Do these references to the
age-old myths and legends have any relevance to his descriptions of modern America?
8. How successful do you think Steinbeck is in this book in
conveying the mood of the American people in the year
1960?

9. What specific aspects of the American scene does
    Steinbeck cover inadequately or even totally ignore?
10. Steinbeck notes that the people of America seem to him
    to be apathetic toward the 1960 Presidential election.
    Is it true to say that, as a generalization, people have
    become more politically aware during the intervening
    years, and, if they have, what factors account for this
    change?

B. Suggested Topics for Research Papers

1. Consider and discuss these two observations by Stein-
    beck:
    "In literary criticism the critic has no choice but to
    make over the victim of his attention into something
    the size and shape of himself" (69);
    and
    "If I found matter to criticize and deplore (in the
    American people), they were tendencies equally pres-
    ent in myself" (185).
2. Discuss the extent to which Travels with Charley can be
    regarded as a rounded "portrait of the artist."
3. From a comparative study of Travels with Charley and
    America and Americans consider the extent to which the
    latter book confirms, modifies, or rejects the views about
    his country and its people that Steinbeck has expressed
    in the earlier book.
4. Compare the style of Travels with Charley with Stein-
    beck's style in his first novel, Cup of Gold, and in the
    war novel The Moon Is Down, and discuss in what ways
    over the years the style has evolved.
5. Discuss Steinbeck's philosophy of life as expressed in
    the chapter describing his journey through the Mojave
    Desert, and the manner in which this philosophy is
    posited in his fictional works.
6. Consider Steinbeck's reactions to the various people he
    meets and discuss what those reactions tell us about
    Steinbeck himself; whether, for instance, they confirm
    or conflict with the declaratory statements he makes
    about himself.
7. Discuss Steinbeck's exposition of the Negro question in
    the penultimate chapter of the book and the extent to
    which it delves into or glosses over the essential issues.
8. List the literary allusions mentioned by Steinbeck. Dis-
    cuss his reasons for introducing them and the manner
    in which they give depth to his narrative and/or exposi-
    tion.

9. Discuss the extent to which Steinbeck's emotions are torn
between (a) his deeply-ingrained love for his country of
birth, and (b) his disgust at the way civilization has
despoiled the land and the people.
10. Compare the portrait of Charley with other canine literary portraits: e. g. Virginia Woolf's Flush, Gertrude
Stein's Basket I and Basket II in The Autobiography of
Alice B. Toklas and Wars I Have Seen, and MacKinlay
Kantor's Lobo.

C. Selected Bibliography

1. Astro, Richard. John Steinbeck and Edward F. Ricketts:
The Shaping of a Novelist. Minneapolis: University of
Minnesota Press, 1973, pp. 217-24.
    Discusses Travels with Charley in terms of a scientif-
ic study, with particular reference to Ricketts' influence on
Steinbeck's thinking.

2. _____ . "Travels with Steinbeck: The Laws of
Thought and the Laws of Things," Steinbeck Quarterly,
8 (Spring 1975), 35-44.
    Discusses Travels with Charley in the light of Stein-
beck's other travel books and makes the point that "Travels
with Charley is the only one of Steinbeck's travel volumes
which is not a collaboration."

3. Ditsky, John. "Steinbeck's Travels with Charley: The
Quest that Failed," Steinbeck Quarterly, 8 (Spring 1975),
45-50.
    Although recognizing the failure of the book as a
record of the failure of the journey itself, Ditsky suggests
that Travels with Charley is successful "as a record of what
seems to have gone on in Steinbeck's spirit as he drove."

4. Fontenrose, Joseph. John Steinbeck: An Introduction
and Interpretation. New York: Holt, Rinehart and
Winston, 1963, pp. 137-38.
    Briefly discusses Travels with Charley as an expres-
sion of Steinbeck's organismic theory, which has the effect
of giving some unity to a chaotically organized book.

5. Marovitz, Sanford E. "The Expository Prose of John
Steinbeck (Part II)," Steinbeck Quarterly, 7 (Summer-
Fall 1974), 88-102.
    Briefly discusses Travels with Charley in the context
of Steinbeck's non-fictional works as a whole.

6. _____ . "John Steinbeck and Adlai Stevenson: The
Shattered Image of America, " in Steinbeck's Literary
Dimension: A Guide to Comparative Studies, ed.
Tetsumaro Hayashi. Metuchen, N. J. : Scarecrow Press,
1973, pp. 116-29.
   An important study tracing how Stevenson's appeal for
Steinbeck as a politician blossomed into a close friendship
and how the aspirations of both the political man and the
literary man for their country ended in disillusionment.

Chapter 10

STEINBECK'S VIVA ZAPATA!
(Screenplay, 1952; published 1975)

by Robert E. Morsberger

I. BACKGROUND

John Steinbeck has had more success with motion
pictures than any other serious American writer. Thirteen
movies and four television films have been based upon his
work or written directly for the screen by Steinbeck himself.
Most have been both critical and commercial successes, and
several have become classics. They have received a total
of 25 Academy Award nominations, including three for Steinbeck himself as the best screenwriter of the year. Most of
his novels were adapted to the screen by others, but Steinbeck collaborated on the adaptation of The Pearl and wrote
alone The Forgotten Village, The Red Pony, and Viva Zapata!
As The Forgotten Village is a semi-documentary for which
Steinbeck wrote a narrative rather than dialogue, and The
Red Pony is an adaptation of four of his stories, Viva Zapata!
remains his only completely original screenplay with dramatic dialogue.

Elia Kazan, who directed the film, claims that the
proposal for a motion picture on Zapata came from him.
He and Steinbeck were friends and neighbors, so when he
began to develop the project, he asked Steinbeck "if he'd be
interested in working on it with me. He said he'd been
thinking about Z for years."[1] About 20 years, in fact, for
Steinbeck first became interested in the subject around 1930
from conversations with Reina Dunn, the daughter of a Hearst
journalist named H. H. Dunn who later wrote a book about
Zapata entitled The Crimson Jester, Zapata of Mexico.[2]
Published in 1934, Dunn's book is a sensationalist narrative
that repeats uncritically the tabloid tales of anti-Zapata news-
papers like the far from impartial Imparcial, which labeled

191

him "the modern Atilla" and described his followers not as
rebels against oppression but as anarchistic banditos indulg-
ing in an orgy of arson, plunder, and debauchery. Though
Steinbeck read Dunn's work, he discounted its lurid coloring
and did his own research to find the real Zapata.

This got underway in earnest when he went to Mexico
in 1940 to write the script for The Forgotten Village. In
collaboration with director Herbert Kline and cinematographer
Alexander Hackensmid (now Hammid), who had filmed several
anti-Fascist documentaries, Steinbeck planned to make a
film about the efforts of Mexican Fascists to overthrow the
liberal government of President Cardenas. Steinbeck actually
wrote a rough screen treatment on the subject, but when he
joined the production crew on location in Mexico, he became
intrigued with material Kline had discovered about resistance
among the Indian villagers to the efforts of rural doctors to
eradicate disease and superstition, and wrote a new script
documenting this conflict. His research and presence during
the filming on location gave Steinbeck a personal knowledge
of the peasant farmers who were the backbone of Zapata's
following; and despite his attack on the forgotten village's
superstitious fear of scientific medicine, he developed a
respect for the villagers' culture and character. The attempt by wealthy landowners to sabotage the production and
prevent the peasants from being paid fair wages gave Steinbeck experience with the reactionary forces that Zapata
worked to overthrow. The director, Herbert Kline, remembers that during the filming of The Forgotten Village he and
Steinbeck visited Chalco, a village in the heart of Zapata's
territory during the revolution. By coincidence the village
was celebrating in commemoration of Zapata; and in a local
pulqueria, some of the old-timers "spoke of the legend of
Zapata still being alive in the mountains nearby, riding his
horse ... and looking after the peons he came from and
loved. " Kline believes that the experience in Chalco gave
Steinbeck a vivid sense of life among the Zapatistas and
provided him with atmosphere for Viva Zapata! [3]

Steinbeck went on location again in Mexico during the
filming of The Pearl, for which he wrote the screenplay in
collaboration with Emilio Fernandez and Jack Wagner.
Directed by Fernandez, it was produced in Mexico with
Mexican performers acting in English. When RKO released
it in 1948, it was the first Mexican movie to have general
distribution in the United States. Though critics complained
that the players and costumes were too glamorous for Mexi-

can peasant life, the story's sympathy with the poor and its
harsh attack on their exploitation by the arrogantly and un-
justly wealthy relate it to Viva Zapata!

It was at this time that Steinbeck began his concentrated research on Emiliano Zapata and the Mexican revolution. Rejecting Dunn's distortions in The Crimson Jester,
Steinbeck relied on Zapata the Unconquerable (1941), a fictional biography by Edgcumb Pinchon, which was the most
recent book in English on Zapata until John Womack, Jr.'s
definitive biography appeared in 1969. Despite the fictional
elements, Pinchon did spend a year of research in Mexico,
and Womack judges his work as "a good popular biography."[4]
But Steinbeck used Pinchon only for the broad historical
outline; he omitted most of Pinchon's material and borrowed
only a few scenes (the opening audience with Diaz, Pablo's
return from Texas, the procession accompanying Zapata when
he is taken prisoner, the audience with Madero, and a dialogue between Villa and Zapata), all of which he trimmed
down and made more dramatic. The material that he added
is more significant, especially the role of Zapata's brother
Eufemio (whom Pinchon scarcely mentions), Zapata's courtship and marriage to a lady of quality, the execution of
Pablo, the death of Eufemio, Fernando's entire role, Zapata's
relinquishing power, and most of the film's political philosophy.

Steinbeck supplemented Pinchon with his own research
in Mexico, where he interviewed surviving Zapatistas and
other veterans of the revolution and got a first-hand sense
of people and places. This personal involvement contributes
to Viva Zapata!'s authenticity and helps make it a compelling
drama, by contrast to the melodramatic, sentimental, or
textbookish 1930's and 1940's film biographies of Disraeli,
the Duke of Wellington, the House of Rothschild, Parnell,
Henry Morton Stanley, Alexander Graham Bell, Chopin, and
various statesmen, inventors, artists, and composers.

II. PLOT SYNOPSIS

The Mexican revolution lasted for over ten years and
was too complex for any film to recreate it in detail, even
in a production as long as Lawrence of Arabia. Steinbeck
did not try; instead he wrote a screenplay organized like
Shakespeare's history plays, episodic in structure, with a
few skirmishes to represent an entire war, yet made tightly
coherent through character and theme.

The film begins with a deputation of peasants com-
plaining to the dictator Porfirio Diaz that "they" [the large
landowners] have taken the village land. The delegates
claim ownership from antiquity, before the Spanish conquest
and reinforced by papers from both the Spanish monarchy and
the Mexican republic. Responding with patriarchal attempts
at pacification, Diaz advises them to find the boundary stones
and check their grants and titles; the courts will settle things
in due time. At this point Zapata becomes the spokesman
for the group and points out the impossibility of checking
boundaries that are fenced and guarded by armed men. The
farmers need corn now, he says, and cannot rely on the
courts. He therefore requests authorization to cross the
fences in order to verify the boundaries. When Diaz protests that he can give no such authorization, but can only
advise, Zapata replies ironically that they will take his
advice. Diaz demands the spokesman's name and then circles it on the list of delegates. Zapata has been proscribed.

We next see a group of villagers approach a fenced
field in Morelos. Zapata orders his brother Eufemio to cut
the wire, and the men enter to find the boundary stones.
Suddenly, a troop of mounted rurales charge into the group,
and a machine gun opens fire on the farmers. Zapata,
mounted on a white horse, lassoes the machine gun. The
rurales are diverted into attempting to capture him, and in
the confusion both he and the remaining villagers escape.
Zapata has not planned to be a leader of an insurrection,
but his impulsive reaction against tyranny has made him a
marked man.

As he hides in the hills with a few followers, Fernando
Aguirre comes as an emissary to recruit Zapata and his band
under Francisco Madero, leader of the opposition to Diaz.
Learning that Madero is in Texas, Zapata sends a friend and
follower named Pablo to look in Madero's face and report
what he sees; Zapata is skeptical of rhetoric and wants to
evaluate the man before joining him.

During Pablo's absence, a wealthy patron, Don Nacio,
obtains a pardon for Zapata and rehires him as an appraiser
of horses. Zapata then pays court to the aristocratic Josefa
Espejo. She rebuffs his initial advances, but clearly finds
him attractive. If he can become respectable, he should
have a promising future. But again, he finds it impossible
to stand aside during episodes of oppression. The first occurs when Don Nacio's manager begins beating a starving

stable boy he finds stealing the horses' food. At the risk
of his job and his pardon, Zapata intervenes and knocks the
bully down. Don Nacio asks, "Are you responsible for
everybody? You can't be the conscience of the whole world,"
but Zapata protests, "He was hungry."[5] Yet he wants to
protect his private life, and so he apologizes. No sooner
has he done so than Pablo and Fernando appear with Madero's
offer of a command. Echoing Don Nacio, Zapata insists that
he does not want to be a leader or the conscience of the
world: "I don't want to be the conscience of anybody."[6]

But events again conspire to force him into action.
Coming across rurales dragging a farmer named Innocente
by a noose, because he had crawled through a fence one
night to plant a patch of corn, Zapata orders them to free
the prisoner. Instead, they spur their horses to a gallop and
drag the man to his death. Zapata cuts the rope, but not in
time. Again, his impetuous outrage against oppression makes
him an outlaw. As he departs from the Espejos' after another
attempt to court Josefa, rurales seize him and take him
away, like Innocente, with a noose around his neck. This
time the people thrust leadership upon him. Groups of villagers and farmers accompany him in a procession that
swells to such massive size that it stops the column of
captors and forces the captain to free Zapata. The people
bring him his white horse and thus symbolically make him
their leader. Now he acts decisively, ordering his brother
to cut the telegraph wires despite the captain's warning,
"This is rebellion!"[7]

The die is now cast for open warfare, and Diaz is
quickly defeated. Zapata is thankful that "The fighting is
over" and celebrates by marrying Josefa, but Fernando is
unable to enjoy the victory and insists that "There will have
to be a lot more blood shed."[8] Thus far the revolution has
been a spontaneous uprising of the people, but from here on
it is betrayed repeatedly by professionals seeking not reform
but totalitarian power for themselves.

Madero, the new president, is presented as a well-
meaning man who is duped into delaying land reform. Led
by Huerta, a group of right-wing officers starts a counter-
revolution, sending the army against Zapata and the farmers
of Morelos and murdering Madero. Zapata outmaneuvers
Huerta's surprise attack and resumes guerilla warfare against
the new tyrant. During the course of it, his forces are am-
bushed, and Fernando fixes the blame on Pablo, who had met

with Madero after Huerta betrayed the revolution. Pablo insists that Madero was not Huerta's ally but his victim, and that he was a good man who wanted to build and plant rather than destroy. He raises the question of whether the end justifies the means, whether violence and hatred will lead to peace or only perpetuate themselves. But Fernando, the ruthless ideologue, demands Pablo's death, and Zapata himself has to shoot his friend, though he acknowledges his message and insists that "The killing must stop!"[9]

Fernando, however, insists that purges are necessary, that the principle of successful rule is, "There can be no opposition."[10] Though he and Zapata are moving increasingly apart, Fernando joins Villa in proposing Zapata for president after Huerta is defeated and driven into exile. Zapata declines the office, but does take command in Mexico City, where he finds that power can corrupt even him. When a delegation from Morelos calls to ask him for justice against his brother Eufemio, who has been seizing their lands and women, Zapata at first temporizes and then, reenacting the first audience with Diaz, circles the name of the group's spokesman. Suddenly realizing with horror that he is following in Diaz' footsteps, he tears up the paper, seizes his rifle and sombrero, and joins the delegation, saying, "I'm going home. There are some things I forgot."[11]

Thematically, this is the film's climax, for as soon as he relinquishes power, Zapata is a doomed man, marked for betrayal and assassination. Fernando warns him, "I promise you you won't live long. . . . Thousands of men have died to give you power, and you're throwing it away." Zapata replies, "I'm taking it back where it belongs; to thousands of men."[12] All too often, revolutions have simply transferred power from one tyranny to another, and according to Elia Kazan, what particularly intrigued Steinbeck was "Z's giving up power when he had it, the fact that he found it corrupting and he went back to Morelos."[13]

There, he begins a program of rebuilding and planting while fighting against the new military opposition under Carranza and Obregon, meanwhile teaching the people that there are no infallible strong men to lead them; "There are only men like yourselves. . . . There's no leader but yourselves."[14]

Still fearing Zapata's leadership, the opposition plans his murder. Fernando is the Judas who arranged the plot, which he baits with a large cache of arms and ammunition

that a supposed defector arranges to turn over to Zapata.
Despite his wife's warning that it may be a trap, Zapata
goes to the rendezvous and is shot from ambush. His white
horse, however, escapes into the mountains and becomes a
symbol for the people of Zapata's deathless spirit. The
peasants who take his body for burial claim that the corpse
is not Zapata's, that he can't be killed, but is hiding in the
mountains. "But if we ever need him again--he'll be back. "15

III. CRITICAL EXPLICATION

     All motion pictures are a collaboration; but some
critics, dedicated to the auteur theory of filmmaking, insist
that a film is the sole creation of the director, who stamps
it with his own individual style. Such critics thus see Viva
Zapata! as a personal statement of director Elia Kazan, despite the fact that Steinbeck did the research and wrote the
screenplay. The film was made at the time that Kazan was
testifying before the House Un-American Activities Commit-
tee (HUAC) about his former Communist connections, and
some Leftist critics thought he had sold out to the Right wing
and that in order to justify his position, he made Viva Zapata!, with its emphasis on the revolution's being betrayed
and Zapata murdered by the scheming of ruthless ideologues.
Kazan did say that he and Steinbeck "were both reaching for
some way to express our feelings of being Left and progres-
sive, but at the same time anti-Stalinist. "16   But Kazan told
Michel Ciment that he was disgusted both with Communism
and McCarthyism; that he remained liberal, but had become
thoroughly disillusioned with the Communist Party, that he
found its thought-control disgusting, had come to despise its
cultural commissars, and was in revolt against having been
automated by Stalinist terrorism. Accordingly, he was attracted to the fact that Zapata "represented a Left position
that was anti-authoritarian, and the fact that in some way he
was related to my life story, at point in my life.... "17

     Like In Dubious Battle, Viva Zapata! had something
to offend everybody. The militant Right disapproved of revolution per se and considered Zapata a dangerous radical;
the liberals thought Kazan was collaborating with HUAC and
putting down revolution; and the Communists "condemned it
because they said I'd taken a revolutionary hero and made a
wavering intellectual of him, " said Kazan. 18 The Communist
Daily Worker attacked the film not as being Rightist but as
Trotskyist. There are, of course, no Communists in the

film and no mention of Communism, though Fernando resembles Communist terrorists and the ruthless inquisitor of
Koestler's Darkness at Noon. In addition, Kazan claims
"that the communists of Mexico were beginning to think of
Zapata as useful, a figure they could glamorize in anti-
gringo, pro-Mexican nationalist struggles. They thought,
especially since he was dead and it was long ago, he could
become a useful idol or god to call on. They didn't like our
film because it showed him as being unclear."[19] Its stress
upon Zapata's renunciation of power certainly spoiled him as
a symbol for totalitarian propaganda. Kazan says that both
he and Steinbeck "were interested in his [Zapata's] tragic
dilemma; after you get power, after you make a revolution,
what do you do with the power and what kind of a structure
do you build?"[20]

     Steinbeck and Kazan were friends and neighbors when
they collaborated on Viva Zapata!, but the controversy over
HUAC is irrelevant to Steinbeck's contribution. In fact, the
issues of the film concerned him as far back as his first
novel, Cup of Gold (1929), in which the buccaneer leader
Henry Morgan challenges the tyranny of Spain but finds his
own power corrupting. Steinbeck was never a Communist,
never testified before HUAC, and had nothing to do with it;
he had weathered attacks by the far Right following the publication of The Grapes of Wrath, at the time when 10-year-
old Shirley Temple was being denounced by the Dies Com-
mittee as a Red for contributing to the Loyalist cause in
Spain.

     Viva Zapata! is significant in Steinbeck's canon for
summing up themes he had been concerned with since the
mid-1930s. Their Blood Is Strong and The Grapes of Wrath
present the need for land reform. In Dubious Battle (1936)
deals with a strike by migrant fruit pickers in California;
Steinbeck is sympathetic towards their cause, but is deeply
critical of the Communist leaders who manipulate the workers for their own ends. To Mac, the Communist organizer,
individuals are expendable for the cause; he cannot afford to
like people, and judges an ineffectual colleague's being murdered as the best thing he ever did, for the victim can now
be used as propaganda against the strike-breakers. He risks
his followers' lives and actually hopes some will be killed;
preferring slogans to people and abstractions to individuals,
Mac cares nothing about the strikers and is willing to ruin
them all to bring about ultimate revolution. Jim, his apos-
tle, begins by sympathizing with the strikers, but ends up an

even more inhuman fanatic than Mac. In their willingness to
adopt any means, including torture and killing, to bring about
a proletarian utopia, Mac and Jim foreshadow Fernando, the
ruthless Machiavellian villain of Viva Zapata!

By contrast, Zapata never seeks personal power,
shuns leadership until it is inevitable, and relinquishes it
when it becomes too heavy a burden. He is like Tom Joad,
who only wants to stay out of trouble but finds that he cannot stand passively by in the face of oppression, and who
eventually accepts Casy's message that one must give himself for the service of others. Zapata is never a dialectual
revolutionary, only a farmer driven to the breaking point by
despotism. So long as he gets land reform and freedom for
his followers, he is relatively indifferent to politics. Zapata
agrees with Pablo, who says, "Our cause was land--not a
thought, but corn-planted earth to feed the families. And
Liberty--not a word, but a man sitting safely in front of his
house in the evening. And Peace, not a dream--but a time
of rest and kindness. " And just as Doc Burton tells Jim in
In Dubious Battle that "you can only build a violent thing
with violence,"21 so Pablo asks, "Can peace come from so
much killing? Can kindness finally come from so much violence? And can a man whose thoughts are born in anger and
hatred, can such a man lead to peace? And govern in
peace?"22

Steinbeck, however, does not condemn the Mexican
revolution any more than he does the apple pickers of In
Dubious Battle or the desperate migrants of The Grapes of
Wrath. He is definitely on the side of reform; and though
Zapata is killed, he is not defeated, for his memory continues to inspire the peasants fighting the latest version of
oppression. Kazan comments: "We were very conscious
that it could be taken to be saying that the revolution was
futile. But we tried very definitely to avoid that by saying,
at the end, 'The people still think of him, he's still
alive.... '"23 The true revolution, according to Steinbeck,
must take place in the hearts of the people, to whom Zapata
repeatedly insists that "There's no leader but yourselves"
and that "A strong people does not need a strong man. "
Thus, like the Joads, the Zapatistas can go on. As Mayor
Orden tells the Nazi invaders in The Moon Is Down, "authority is in the town" rather than in any official; "we have as
many heads as we have people, and in a time of need leaders pop up among us like mushrooms. "24 In A Russian
Journal, published after his visit to Russia shortly before

he wrote Viva Zapata!, Steinbeck repeatedly denounced the
deification of the strong man. To the Russians, he and his
traveling companion Robert Capa "tried to explain our fear
of dictatorship, our fear of leaders with too much power,
so that our government is designed to keep anyone from
getting too much power, or having got it, from keeping
it."25

        In my introduction to the published text of Viva
Zapata! I develop this argument at length, pointing out close
parallels between Viva Zapata! and Steinbeck's work in general and Camus' studies of rebellion that make a fundamental distinction between the rebel and the revolutionary, the
former being a free spirit resisting oppression of any sort,
whereas the latter establishes a new tyranny in the name of
liberty, and terror in the name of brotherhood. According
to Camus, "the great event of the twentieth century was the
forsaking of the values of freedom by the revolutionary movement," which contended "that we needed justice first and
that we could come to freedom later on, as if slaves could
ever hope to achieve justice."26 By this terminology, Zapata is the rebel and Fernando the revolutionary who betrays the original aims of the revolution, just as Lenin and
Stalin perverted the first democratic revolution in Russia
and as other dictators and demagogues have done elsewhere.
There is no need to repeat my argument at length. Kazan
notes that a decade after the Stalinists denounced Viva Zapata!, "the New Left ... the non-communist Left, the Left
I've always felt an allegiance towards ... loved Viva Zapata! ... The change in what the Left is reversed the attitude towards the picture."27 Despite several Academy
Award nominations, the film was not a box office success
when first released, but it has proved to be far more durable than bigger moneymakers and is frequently revived both
in art theatres and on television. Kazan observes that "In
Turkey or Greece, where they have that problem of land,
they scream their approval...."28

        Viva Zapata! was the first film that Kazan made
without using a professional screenwriter. He told Cimet,
"I began to go to authors like Steinbeck, Budd Schulberg [On
the Waterfront, A Face in the Crowd], Inge [Splendor in the
Grass]--who were not screenwriters.... What I needed
most was someone who saw in Zapata what I saw in Zapata."29
When Steinbeck returned after months of research in Mexico,
he had a massive amount of material, enough for several
books. "You could tell a hundred different stories with that

material," said Kazan. As he and Steinbeck studied it, it
fell into three acts: Zapata's being drawn into rebellion
against repression and organizing his followers to overthrow
Diaz; Zapata's gaining power, being bewildered by it, and
finding it corrupting; and his renunciation of power so that
he became vulnerable, a man marked for murder. "So we
organized John's material we wanted to use, where it would
fit in and how it would work."30

    Such a focus provides dramatic tension and a series
of climaxes. To achieve them, Steinbeck practiced the art
of omission, making his work cinematic rather than expository. We learn nothing about the background of Diaz and
his development from a youthful follower of the liberal
Juarez into an aged despot. (In the 1940 film Juarez, Diaz
is played by a romantic young John Garfield.) Instead of
explaining historical detail on political and economic conditions, Steinbeck dramatizes the conflicts in a few vivid epi-
sodes--the audience with Diaz, the fight in the field where
rurales fire on unarmed peasants, the bullying of the stable
manager, the murder of Innocente, and the arrest of Zapata.
The exposition is not documentary but dramatic, making us
involved more than informed. We learn nothing of Madero's
career, but are impressed by Pablo's trust in him; later we
see him as a well-meaning weakling and experience the
catharsis of his murder by Huerta. The military campaigns
are never mapped out; a few quick episodes of action represent an entire war. After Diaz is deposed, Huerta appears
from nowhere. He has only two brief scenes, but they fully
establish his treachery and cruelty. All we see of the campaign against him is the opening fight when Zapata ambushes
what was to have been Huerta's surprise attack, and the
episode in which Zapata kills Pablo for supposedly consorting
with the enemy. Immediately following it, we cut to the
victorious generals Villa and Zapata posing for their photograph, a scene that Kazan duplicated exactly from a photograph in Historia Gráfica de la Revolución in the Mexican
archives. Villa casually names Zapata president because he
can read, and we next see him in audience, at which time
we learn that there is a new military opposition led by Carranza and Obregon, about whom we are otherwise told nothing. Zapata ends the audience when he finds himself reenacting Diaz' despotism from the opening scene of the film;
he goes home, relinquishing power in the very next scene
after he has reluctantly accepted it. The remaining fifth of
the film dramatizes the death of Eufemio and Zapata's betrayal and murder.

A historian might object that Steinbeck's screenplay
vastly oversimplifies the actual events, which covered a ten-
year period from 1909 to 1919. The film gives no sense of
such a time span, nor do any of its characters age percept-
ibly. But it is possible to get at the essence of events better through drama than documentation, and Harvard professor
John Womack, Jr., Zapata's biographer, has called the film
"a distinguished achievement" which, despite inevitable distortions that result from condensing the revolution into a
taut tragedy, "quickly and vividly develops a portrayal of
Zapata, the villagers, and the nature of their relations and
movement that I find still subtle, powerful, and true."[31]

Steinbeck's technique is like that of Shakespeare's
history plays, that may sprawl over a great deal of time and
geography to telescope into a compelling drama a complexity
of events,

> Carry them here and there, jumping o'er times,
> Turning th' accomplishment of many years
> Into an hourglass. . . . [32]

Kazan was aware of the Shakespearean quality of Steinbeck's
script and commented that "Shakespeare is more contemporary than the plays that are being written today. He leaps
from here to there, he goes to climaxes, and the figures are
big-sized."[33]

Like Shakespeare, Steinbeck concentrated on characterization. Emiliano Zapata is a soft, slow-spoken man,
naturally thoughtful, patient, even cautious, whose impetuous
outbursts and episodes of action are a striking contrast
forced upon him by events, not of his own seeking. His
fiery, flamboyant brother is a dramatic foil to him. So is
Fernando, whose cold, calculating exterior masks a fanatical
revolutionary fervor. Brief portraits of peasants--Pablo, the
Soldadera, a boy to whom Zapata gives his horse and who is
later killed, a woman who offers Zapata a chicken, farmers
and delegates from Morelos--provide the context for the revolution and bring the Zapatistas to life. The presentation of
Madero and Huerta is condensed but memorably incisive.

Steinbeck discovered documentation of the marriage
between Zapata and Josefa Espejo that historians were unaware of. The relationship between them is not an obliga-
tory Hollywood love story, but serves to highlight Zapata's
character and to dignify the depth of his sacrifice. It is the

hope of marriage with a well-bred woman of respectable
family that makes Zapata at first reluctant to commit himself to revolution. She repeatedly tells him that she does
not want to become a widow or to end up as the wife of a
proscribed outlaw, patting tortillas and doing laundry in a
ditch like an Indian. Her father is at first scornful of
Zapata, but is obsequious to him after he has become a
victorious general. In its satire upon social caste, Zapata's
courtship provides some of the film's humor, especially in
the scene where he calls formally upon Josefa and they converse in dichos--traditional folk sayings, pithy proverbs that
are also used for verbal fencing. Steinbeck collected hundreds of these during his research in Mexico, and the dialogue in the courtship scene at the Espejos' consists almost
entirely of them. Steinbeck says that they were "well enough
known so that they could be instantly recognized by a Spanish-
speaking audience" and that "Solely with dichos, I hoped not
only to show the developing courtship but also to indicate the
characters of the two people. Such courtships were and are,
in many cases, carried on under the eyes and ears of members of the girls' families, who not only maintain the propri-
eties, but act as scorekeepers and critics of proper usage."³⁴

        One of the most touching moments in the film is
Zapata's wedding night, when he laments that he cannot read
and urges his wife to teach him. She begins with the opening of Genesis, and he repeats after her. While outside,
drunken crowds celebrate their nuptials, they are in bed like
innocent children with the book between them. Historically,
this in inaccurate, for Zapata was not illiterate before his
wedding, but it is dramatically effective in showing his vul-
nerability and Josefa's devotion to him. Kazan later objected
to this scene on the grounds that the performers and the
lighting were too glamorous, but that is the director's responsibility, not the author's. The episode is all the more
erotic for omitting explicit eroticism and offering emotional
intimacy instead. Later, Josefa's prophecy of her fate as
the wife of an outlaw does come true, and her pleading with
Zapata not to go to the final rendezvous with the treacherous
Guajardo both prepares us for his doom and intensifies its
poignancy.

        Though chronicling history, Steinbeck's screenplay
seems as much parable, poetry, and folklore. Perhaps this
is one reason for the film's staying power, for these elements have a more universal appeal than the precise and
complex details of events in Mexico between 1909 and 1919.

At one time Steinbeck attempted to have "corridos," a running commentary of traditional Mexican songs, "to be written
by a wandering poet named John Steinbeck to music by Alex
North" and performed by one of Zapata's men, or else "to
be accompanied by either guitar music solo or music from
our conception of a typical five-piece Mexican Country
band."[35] Unfortunately, this device interrupted the narrative
and was consequently dropped. But for background music,
Kazan got together a group of old-time Mexican musicians with
antiquated instruments and had them play classic Mexican
songs and songs of revolution, which he taped and which became the basis of Alex North's score. Instead of creating
the customary symphonic background music of the 1950s,
North had most of his music function as a natural part of
the action--as mariachi bands, military parades, serenades,
religious chants, songs and celebrations--all in indigenous
Mexican modes, to accentuate the ballad-like quality of the
film.

Steinbeck did not write his script with any particular
players in mind. Darryl F. Zanuck was strongly opposed to
the casting of Marlon Brando, who had appeared so far in
only two films; but Kazan, who had directed Brando in both
the stage and screen versions of A Streetcar Named Desire,
insisted upon him. Only 28 years old at the time, Brando
gave one of his most subtle and durable performances and
won an Academy Award nomination for the best actor of the
year. He lost to Gary Cooper in High Noon, but Zapata's
biographer John Womack, Jr. writes that "Brando captured
wonderfully" the character of Zapata, his "integrity, his
suspicion of all outsiders, his absolute sense of responsibility."[36] Anthony Quinn did win the Academy Award as best
supporting actor for his role as Eufemio, and Steinbeck himself was nominated in two categories, for best story and best
screenplay. Though those awards went to The Lavender Hill
Mob, Viva Zapata! is not only a distinguished piece of screen-
writing but possibly Steinbeck's best work since Cannery Row.
In any case, it is his ultimate statement on issues that had
long been central to his work and is therefore essential to
any study of the literature of John Steinbeck.

NOTES

1.   Elia Kazan, Letter to Robert E. Morsberger, March
     29, 1973.

2. Richard Astro, Letter to Robert E. Morsberger, September 29, 1971.

3. Herbert Kline, Letter to Robert E. Morsberger, June 5, 1973.

4. John Womack, Jr., Zapata and the Mexican Revolution (New York: Alfred A. Knopf, 1969), p. 422.

5. John Steinbeck, Viva Zapata! The Original Screenplay, ed. Robert E. Morsberger (New York: Viking, 1975), p. 29.

6. Ibid., p. 34.

7. Ibid., p. 47.

8. Ibid., p. 67.

9. Ibid., p. 91.

10. Ibid., p. 97.

11. Ibid., p. 100.

12. Ibid., p. 102.

13. Kazan to Morsberger, March 29, 1973.

14. Viva Zapata!, p. 104.

15. Ibid., p. 122.

16. Michel Ciment, Kazan on Kazan (New York: Viking, 1974), p. 88.

17. Ibid., p. 89.

18. Ibid., p. 94.

19. Ibid., p. 90.

20. Ibid., p. 88.

21. John Steinbeck, In Dubious Battle (New York: Viking Compass Books, 1963), p. 230.

22. Viva Zapata!, pp. 86-7.

23. Ciment, p. 93.

24. John Steinbeck, The Moon Is Down (New York: Viking, 1942), p. 175.

25. John Steinbeck, A Russian Journal (New York: Viking, 1948), p. 57.

26. Albert Camus, Resistance, Rebellion, and Death, tr. Justin O'Brien (New York: Alfred A. Knopf, 1961), pp. 90-91.

27. Ciment, p. 94.

28. Ibid., p. 98.

29. Ibid., p. 97.

30. Ibid., p. 90.

31. Womack, p. 420.

32. William Shakespeare, Henry V, Prologue: 29-31.

33. Ciment, p. 176.

34. John Steinbeck, "Dichos: The Way of Wisdom," Saturday Review, 40 (November 9, 1957), 13.

35. John Steinbeck, "Note to the Reader," Twentieth Century-Fox, July 31, 1950.

36. John Womack, Jr., Letter to Robert E. Morsberger, April 28, 1973.

IV.   APPARATUS FOR RESEARCH PAPERS

A.   Ten Questions for Discussion

1. In "Ethan Brand," Hawthorne defines the unpardonable sin as the development of one's intellect at the expense of his humanity, so that people become only the objects of his experiments.   How is Fernando guilty of this sin?

2. Discuss Steinbeck's views on land ownership and land re-

form in In Dubious Battle, The Grapes of Wrath, Their
Blood Is Strong, and Viva Zapata!
3. Compare Fernando to other terrorist and totalitarian
intellectuals in literature and history.
4. Some critics have objected to Steinbeck's characterization of Mexican-Americans. Discuss his presentation of
Mexicans in Viva Zapata!
5. Compare Steinbeck's picture of revolutionary Mexico
with that of post-revolutionary Russia in A Russian Journal.
6. Some Chicano critics say that Zapata should have been
played by a Mexican actor rather than by the Anglo
Marlon Brando. What do you think? (One actor who
would have been well cast was the late Pedro Armendariz,
who played Kino in The Pearl and who, with a moustache,
closely resembled Zapata.) Should all roles be played
by performers of the same racial, national, or ethnic
background as the characters? Discuss with specific
examples. Consider all the ethnic and national back-
grounds of roles played by Anthony Quinn (who is half
Mexican, half Irish), who has portrayed an Eskimo,
Greeks, Italians, a Portuguese, numerous Indians, Mexicans, Attila the Hun, Arabs, Israelis, a Frenchman,
Englishmen, a Russian pope, and numerous Americans.
When Quinn wanted to play the black Haiti general
Christophe, black militants objected. Is the objection
valid? What of blacks playing roles initially written for
whites?
7. Compare Viva Zapata! to other movies about revolutionary Mexico such as Viva Villa!, Villa Rides, The Fugi-
tive, and to films about revolutions and civil wars such
as Nicholas and Alexandra, Dr. Zhivago, Cromwell,
Birth of a Nation, A Tale of Two Cities, Gone with the
Wind, The Adventures of Robin Hood, and Lawrence of
Arabia.
8. Discuss Viva Zapata! as cinema, considering the performances, direction, cinematography, sets and costumes, and musical score.
9. Compare Steinbeck's treatment of civil war and ruthless
revolutionaries with Hemingway's in For Whom the Bell
Tolls.
10. Why do you think Viva Zapata! was not a box office success in 1952, but has been popular on television and in
art-house revivals?

B. Suggested Topics for Research Papers

1. Compare Viva Zapata! to Steinbeck's portraits of Mexico
    and Mexicans in The Forgotten Village and The Pearl.
2. Study Zapata in relationship to Steinbeck's other studies
    of leadership, for example In Dubious Battle, The Grapes
    of Wrath, "The Leader of the People," The Moon Is
    Down, Lifeboat, The Short Reign of Pippin IV.
3. Compare Viva Zapata! to other literary studies of rev-
    olutionary Mexico such as Katherine Anne Porter's
    "Flowering Judas" and Graham Greene's The Power and
    the Glory.
4. Read the screenplay for the movie Juarez (published in
    20 Best Film Plays, eds. John Gassner and Dudley
    Nichols. New York: Crown, 1943) and compare it to
    Viva Zapata! as a study of war to overthrow oppression
    in Mexico.
5. Compare Steinbeck's characterization of Mexicans in
    Viva Zapata! with that of the paisanos in Tortilla Flat.
6. Read a historical study of Zapata and the Mexican rev-
    olution and discuss the accuracy of Steinbeck's treatment.
    In what ways does he oversimplify events?

C. Selected Bibliography

1. Ciment, Michel. Kazan on Kazan. New York: Viking,
    1974.

2. French, Warren. John Steinbeck, 2nd ed. revised.
    Boston: Twayne, 1975.

3. Hartung, Philip T. "Review of Viva Zapata!" Common-
    weal, 55 (February 29, 1952), 517.

4. Hobson, Laura Z. "Trade Winds," Saturday Review, 35
    (March 1, 1952), 6.

5. Kazan, Elia. "Letters to the Editor," Saturday Review,
    35 (April 5, 1952), 22; (May 24, 1952), 25, 28.

6. McCarten, John. "Wool from the West," New Yorker,
    27 (February 16, 1952), 106.

7. McDonald, Gerald D. "Review of Viva Zapata!" Library
    Journal, 77 (February 15, 1952), 21.

8. Pinchon, Edgcumb. Zapata the Unconquerable. New
    York: Doubleday, Doran, 1941.

9. Steinbeck, Elaine and Robert Wallsten, eds. Steinbeck:
    A Life in Letters. New York: Viking, 1975.

10. Steinbeck, John. "Dichos: The Way of Wisdom,"
    Saturday Review, 40 (November 9, 1957), 13.

11. _____. Viva Zapata!, the Original Screenplay, ed.
    Robert E. Morsberger. New York: Viking, 1975.

12. Womack, John Jr. Zapata and the Mexican Revolution.
    New York: Alfred A. Knopf, 1969.

Chapter 11

STEINBECK'S THE WAYWARD BUS (1947)

by Robert E. Morsberger

I. BACKGROUND

The Wayward Bus is Steinbeck's first book after
World War II and his first full-length novel after The Grapes
of Wrath, eight years earlier. During those eight years,
he had written the narration for the semidocumentary film
The Forgotten Village, a minor and controversial wartime
novella The Moon Is Down, a treatment for Alfred Hitchcock's
movie Lifeboat, Cannery Row (which he described as something amusing to entertain the troops), the magazine version
of The Pearl, and the war reporting collected as Bombs
Away.

This is a respectable output, far more productive than
Hemingway or Faulkner during the same period, but none of
these works seemed a substantial successor to The Grapes
of Wrath. Readers and critics were waiting for the next big
book by Steinbeck, and expectation ran so high that advance
sales of The Wayward Bus, a Book-of-the-Month selection,
ran to 600,000 copies. Clearly Steinbeck had arrived; the
hand-to-mouth writer of the early 1930s, the novelist denounced by the right-wing in 1939 as a subversive radical,
was now a respectable "big money" author.

One gauntlet that American writers run is the fact
that our critics, both academic and commercial, persist in
looking for the newest "great American novelist" to canon-
ize. If a promising candidate fails them by falling below
expectations (like Hemingway with Across the River and Into
the Trees, James Gould Cozzens with By Love Possessed,
William Styron with Set This House on Fire and The Confes-
sions of Nat Turner, Kurt Vonnegut with Breakfast of Cham-
pions and Slapstick, John Updike with everything after The

210

Centaur), they turn upon him with disappointed rage, scorn,
or contempt, followed by neglect. To a degree this happened
to Steinbeck. During the war years, critics were willing to
wait, but they now expected a major performance. Steinbeck
seems to have been aware of this, for The Wayward Bus is
his longest and most ambitious work after The Grapes of
Wrath. Unfortunately, it was not what anybody expected,
not even subscribers to The Book-of-the-Month Club. Steinbeck's decline in critical favor began with The Wayward Bus,
and it remains the most neglected of his major works.

The dust jacket claims that The Wayward Bus "illustrates again the amazing versatility" of Steinbeck's "interests
and his genius. Steinbeck is a writer who is still developing, who still refuses to conform to any expected pattern,
who still brings to each book a fresh and new approach."
This boast sounds somewhat defensive, and indeed one res-
ervation critics had raised about Steinbeck was the unpre-
dictable variety of his work. Objecting to Steinbeck's being
awarded the Nobel Prize in 1962, Arthur Mizener asked if
the prize was justified by a moral vision of the 1930s.
Mizener and others seemed to think that Steinbeck dwindled
into insignificance once he stopped writing about the Depression. But Steinbeck was not content to live in the past or
imitate past triumphs, and now that both the Depression and
the war were over, he turned to new concerns. What he
offered in The Wayward Bus was a moral vision of the post-
war years.

Those years were a time of readjustment, both psychological and economic. The movies discovered psychiatry
and churned out a series of melodramas dealing with psychological maladjustment (Spellbound, The Seventh Veil, Cross-
fire, A Double Life, and Undercurrent). The bouyancy of
the post-war boom was deflated by the gray frustration of
the cold war and by witch-hunting at home. The idealism
of the war years was replaced by commercial greed. Once
again, the world was not made safe for democracy.

II.   PLOT SYNOPSIS

To deal with these matters, Steinbeck developed an
allegorical framework for his novel. The bus of the title is
a dilapidated vehicle that transfers passengers on a run that
Greyhound does not handle, on a cut-off between Rebel Corners and San Juan de la Cruz. Steinbeck assembles a rep-

resentative group of characters to make the trip, isolates
them, and lets the interaction among them reveal their underlying and authentic selves.   The driver is Juan Chicoy, "part
Mexican and part Irish, perhaps fifty years old, with clear
black eyes, a good head of hair, and a dark and handsome
face" (WB, 6).[1] His assistant is Ed Carson, nicknamed
Pimples because of an adolescent acne that aggravates his
intense sexual frustrations.   Besides driving the bus, Juan
owns a store-restaurant-garage and service station.   The
store and lunchroom part of the operation are run by his
wife Alice, a "wide-hipped and sag-chested" slattern who is
quarrelsome and drinks too much.   The latest in a series of
hired girls helping her is Norma, who is shy, dresses drab-
ly, does not know how to improve her appearance, but has
a crush on Clark Gable and fantasizes about being a movie
star.

        The passengers consist of Mr. and Mrs. Pritchard
and their daughter Mildred, Ernest Horton, Camille Oaks,
and Van Brunt.   Elliott Pritchard is a Babbitt-type businessman, ultra-conservative and conformist, who fears unpre-
dictable individualism and thinks mostly of profits.   His ex-
ceedingly proper wife Bernice seems sweet and gentle, but
uses these qualities, plus her frigidity and psychosomatic
headaches, to dominate her husband.   Mildred, a college
student studying Spanish, is sexually promiscuous.   The
Pritchards are bound for a vacation in Mexico, allegedly for
Mildred's sake, but neither she nor her father really wants
to go, though Mrs. Pritchard maneuvered them into thinking
they did.   Ernest Horton, a little man with a moustache, is
a veteran of the war, now employed as a traveling salesman
of gadgets for practical jokes.   Camille Oaks (not her real
name) is a stripper headed for Los Angeles.   Van Brunt, a
crotchety old man with a heart condition, warns them all
that heavy rains will wash out the bridge over the San Ysidro
River, but goes along out of perverse curiosity to see the
bridge.

        One reason for the disappointment in The Wayward
Bus may be the meagerness of its plot.   Steinbeck takes
eight chapters and 139 pages introducing and analyzing his
characters before the bus ride begins.   Pimples goes along
for the ride, and Norma joins the passengers after Alice
quarrels with her, pries into her things, and drives her
away.   After the bus departs, Alice drinks herself into a
stupor.   The ride itself does not amount to much; Juan
Chicoy drives to the river, finds the bridge in danger of

being washed away by flood water, takes an abandoned old
stage road instead, and deliberately mires the bus in the
mud as an excuse to abandon it, his wife, and his responsibilities, and takes off to Mexico. He gets as far as a barn,
where Mildred Pritchard catches up with him and seduces
him. While she is doing so, Mr. Pritchard offers Camille
a job in his firm, which she rejects, rightly informing him
that the offer is simply the prelude to a seduction attempt.
Jolted by this frank recognition of a motive he could not
consciously acknowledge, Pritchard reacts by raping his wife
in a cave where he has taken her for shelter. Norma, made
more attractive by Camille's redoing her hair and makeup,
arouses the lust of Pimples, whom she fights off when he
paws all over her. Van Brunt has a stroke that leaves him
at death's door. After making love to Mildred, Juan gives
up his notion of Mexico, digs the bus out, and takes the
passengers on to San Juan de la Cruz.

III.   CRITICAL EXPLICATION

        Most critical treatments of The Wayward Bus con-
centrate on the allegory: in traveling from Rebel Corners
to San Juan de la Cruz, the passengers are pilgrims pro-
gressing from sin to salvation. The driver's initials are
the same as Jesus Christ's, but the bus, formerly named
"el Gran Poder de Jesus," "the great power of Jesus," has
been renamed "Sweetheart." Along with a plastic kewpie
doll, a tiny boxing glove, and a baby's shoe hanging from
the windshield, Juan has as one of his penates an icon of
the Virgin of Guadalupe, to whom he occasionally prays
and to whom he makes the wager that if she bogs down the
bus, he will run off to Mexico. Along the route, they encounter a warning sign, "Repent."

        As allegory, these ingredients do not hold up. Aside
from the names, San Juan de la Cruz is no more a heavenly
destination than Rebel Corners is a hell. On the contrary,
Steinbeck describes Rebel Corners as an intensely beautiful
place; in the spring "there was no more lovely place in the
world." There, the Chicoys flourished, with "money in the
bank and a degree of security and happiness" (WB, 12).
Juan Chicoy, though intended to be admirable, is no Christ
figure, and his wager to the Virgin is not a prayer but an
evasion of responsibility. There is much recognition of sin,
but very little repentance, and no one is any closer to salvation at the end than at the beginning. Peter Lisca elabor-

ates on the allegory by dividing the characters into three
main groups: "the damned, those in purgatory, and the
saved or elect. " In Lisca's doomsday book, the damned
are Mr. and Mrs. Pritchard, Alice Chicoy, Louis (the first
bus driver), Norma, and Van Brunt; those in purgatory are
Mildred Pritchard and Pimples; the saved are Juan Chicoy,
Ernest Horton, and Camille Oaks. [2]   But this division is
dogmatic and superimposes on Steinbeck a teleology that is
at odds with what Lisca himself analyzes as Steinbeck's
"non-teleological" thinking.   Furthermore, Lisca himself is
inconsistent, for he promotes Norma from damnation to
purgatory.

If the book existed primarily for the allegory, it
would have to be rated a dismal failure.   Steinbeck's other
attempts at allegory and at philosophical abstraction (notably
in To a God Unknown, parts of The Grapes of Wrath, Lifeboat, The Pearl, and East of Eden) are too often pretentious,
ponderous, and puerile; he is not at his most effective when
generalizing but when dealing in realistic details with individualized characters and graphic situations.   Fortunately, the
novel does not really depend upon allegory.   It functions
primarily as a study of character, and on that level is one
of Steinbeck's most subtle and successful performances.   The
dust jacket is accurate when it notes that "The story of what
happens on the bus ride, though it grips the reader from
first page to last, is not of paramount importance.   What
matters is the sense it gives us of people and how they react to one another--bewildered, aimless, driven by ordinary
human impulses, restless and uneasy in our bewildered and
aimless times. "

Basically, the novel is about illusion and reality,
success and failure, frustration and fulfillment, and masculinity and femininity.   To a considerable extent these are
interrelated.   All of the characters and relationships are
defined primarily in terms of sexuality, and when the novel
first appeared, it was considered mildly shocking and scan-
dalous for its outspokenness on the subject.   By contemporary
standards, The Wayward Bus is quite restrained and deserves
no more than a GP rating; but in 1947, it seemed daring,
and several reviewers objected.   J. M. Lalley in the New
Yorker complained of "Steinbeck's priapic persuasion, " Bernard DeVoto found "a long-winded insistence on sexual
pruritus" that was "fearfully boring, " and Frank O'Malley
for the Catholic journal Commonweal protested that "Steinbeck's dreary, prurient pilgrimage has no real human or

universal significance. It is nothing more than an unusually
dismal bus ride--more dismal, depraved and meaningless
than any man elsewhere has ever taken"--a sweeping and
hyperbolic generalization.³ In fact the sex is all in the
minds of the characters; Steinbeck provides no graphic details of coupling. He gives only the dialogue leading up to
the sex between Juan and Mildred and then cuts off the scene
abruptly. The description of Pritchard's conjugal rape consists only of his wife's protesting that he is tearing her dress
and then crying "softly in fear and in horror." Steinbeck
spends little time stripping away clothes and instead concentrates on stripping away sexual stereotypes to reveal the
complexity beneath them. In its treatment of sex, the novel
was ahead of its time; and in the era of women's liberation,
with its rejection of rigid sex roles and its expanded awareness of individuality, The Wayward Bus should find a more
responsive audience.

The one person who is partially stereotyped is Juan
Chicoy, in some ways the book's least successful character.
With the initials J. C. , he is intended to be something of a
Christ figure; Steinbeck wrote to Peter Lisca that Juan was
to be "all the god the fathers you ever saw driving a six-
cylinder, broken down battered world through time and
space."⁴ But the analogy between the driver of a jalopy and
the creator of the world does not hold up, and the reader is
unlikely to conceive of the man behind the wheel of a bus,
whatever its condition, as a deity. Furthermore, though
Juan provides a touch of redemption for Pimples and for
Mildred and repeatedly forgives Alice for her transgressions,
his deserting the bus and passengers that he himself has
stranded and then returning to dig them out after making
love to Mildred fits no divine allegory. To argue that he is
alternately a providential and an uncaring, absentee god is
too contrived and strains credulity beyond the breaking point.

Seen in purely human terms, Juan is the macho male.
Steinbeck calls him "a fine, steady man" and "a magnificent
mechanic" (6-7). His wife is both madly in love with him
"and a little afraid of him too, because he was a man, and
there aren't very many of them, as Alice Chicoy had found
out. There aren't very many of them in the world, as
everyone finds out sooner or later" (6). His manhood seems
to consist primarily of competence and self-confidence. Except for his temporary uncertainty about his future during the
bus trip, Juan never seems to experience a moment's doubt
about himself, his work, or his relations to others. "His

movements were sure even when he was not doing anything
that required sureness" (15).   Though about fifty years old,
with a scarred cheek, large nose, and missing joint on the
third finger of his left hand, Juan looks young and vigorous,
has a fierce smile, a relaxed sense of humor, and conveys
a sensual grace and vitality.   His absolute assurance with
women seems to be what attracts Mildred Pritchard to him,
so that he doesn't even have to try to seduce her and she is
left to make all the overtures to him.   But Juan takes his
sexuality so much for granted that he has no need to engage
in seductions.   Though his wife is a frump, he is satisfied
with her, but is not averse to accepting extra-marital sex
when it is offered him.   For him, sex is not a problem, so
perhaps it is more accurate to say that he is beyond being
"macho."   Unlike other drivers, he does not like to hit rab-
bits, and being secure in his manhood, he washes up as a
matter of fact the dirty dishes his wife has left.   The idea
that this would threaten him is absurd.   Having complete
self-respect, he is ready to respect manhood or a groping
towards it on the part of others.   When Ed Carson requests
that Juan stop calling him Pimples, Juan wins his hero-
worship by accepting him as Kit.   With his own inner
strength, Juan exhibits great tolerance, patience, and sympathetic understanding towards others.   Unlike the others, he
has no need of illusions and no dreams of fame and fortune.
He is quite content to be himself.

It is his gentleness that terrifies Alice, who feels
that Juan should have hit her after she created a hysterical
scene with Norma and Ernest Horton.   It is Mildred Pritchard
who tempts Juan to cruelty.   Observing her voluptuous body,
he feels for a moment "an imp of hatred" stir towards her
blond hair and blue eyes, the hatred of the Chicano for the
conquering Nordic Americans.   "Juan felt the stirring like a
little heat lightning, and he felt a glow of pleasure, knowing
that he could take this girl and twist her and outrage her if
he wanted to.   He could disturb her and seduce her mentally,
and physically too, and then throw her away" (83-84).   Mildred, in turn, "thought there was a cruel, leering triumph
in his face ... " (86).   But she also thinks him "a man of
complete manness.   This was the kind of a man that a pure
woman would want to have because he wouldn't even want to
be part woman.   He wouldn't ever try to understand women
and that would be a relief.   He would just take what he
wanted from them" (222).   When she offers herself to him
in the barn, he refuses to help her.   His forcing her to
make all the advances is in itself a sort of brutality, so

that she protests, "You don't give me any pride.   You don't
give me any violence to fall back on later" (268).   But they
are both honest about sex and enjoy the episode on its own
terms.

Juan's antithesis is Elliott Pritchard, the business
executive.   In society's terms, Pritchard, an affluent and
influential man, is a success and Juan a shabby nobody, but
Pritchard is an embodiment of Steinbeck's statement in Cannery Row that "All of our so-called successful men are sick
men, with bad stomachs, and bad souls. ... "9   Wearing
square glasses, a gray suit, a lodge pin in his lapel, and a
gold watch and key chain across his vest, Pritchard "looked
like Truman and like the vice-presidents of companies and
like certified public accountants" (38).   Though president of
a medium-sized corporation, Pritchard utterly lacks Juan's
self-assurance.   Once recovered from a youthful radicalism
and experimental visit to a parlor house, Pritchard retreated
into the protective coloring of conservative conformity, reg-
ulated by identical business associates, his lodge, and his
church.

> Wherever he went he was not one man but a unit
> in a corporation, a unit in a club, in a lodge, in
> a church, in a political party.   His thoughts and
> ideas were never subjected to criticism since he
> was willingly associated only with people like him-
> self.   He read a newspaper written by and for his
> group.   The books that came into his house were
> chosen by a committee which deleted material that
> might irritate him.   He hated foreign countries and
> foreigners because it was difficult to find his
> counterpart in them.   (42)

He does not really want to go to Mexico, which he considers
a dangerously radical country, but has been manipulated by
his wife into thinking he wants to go for the sake of his
daughter's education.   His wife is frigid and uses a combination of psychosomatic headaches and sanctimonious gentility
to strangle Pritchard's libido in bed.   He finds release by
attending stag parties sponsored by his business or his lodge,
where he howls with laughter as naked girls dance on tables
and sit in gigantic glasses, from which he drinks the wine.
At such functions, he considers himself one of the boys, a
red-blooded virile American.

Steinbeck, however, is devastating on the hypocrisy

of stag orgies and their exploitation of women. Pritchard
"considered the young women who danced naked at stags depraved, but it would never have occurred to him that he who
watched and applauded and paid the girls was in any way
associated with depravity" (68).

One of the girls is Camille Oaks, whom Pritchard
vaguely remembers without recalling the occasion.   From
her perspective, the men in the audience are monstrous.
"There was something in their wet, bulging eyes and limp,
half-smiling mouths that frightened her.   She had a feeling
that if she looked directly at one he might leap on her.   To
her, her audiences were blobs of pink faces and hundreds of
white collars and neat four-in-hand ties.   The Two Fifty-
Three Thousands Clubs usually wore tuxedos" (129-30).
Clearly, Pritchard's diversions are degenerate rather than a
healthy expression of male sexuality.   As Camille finally
tells him, "I don't know what you get out of it and I don't
want to know.   But I know it isn't pretty" (287).   But
Pritchard is too incapable of self-criticism to be aware that
there is anything wrong, since all his associates do the same
thing.   He does, however, consider his wife's destructive
headaches a punishment that gave him "sins to be atoned for.
Mr. Pritchard needed sins.   There were none in his business
life, for the cruelties there were defined and pigeonholed as
necessity and responsibility to the stockholders.   And Mr.
Pritchard needed personal sins and personal atonement" (213).

Juan, by contrast, feels neither a need nor a sense
of sin.   He would agree with Emerson's statement in "Self-
Reliance," "I do not wish to expiate, but to live." He would
scorn the stag smokers as a perversion of virility and an
evasion of reality.   Juan does not deceive himself about sex,
but accepts it as a fact and feels no remorse after it.

Among Pritchard's hypocrisies is an unacknowledged
need to patronize and manipulate other people.   Fascinated
by Ernest Horton's grotesque gadgets for practical jokes and
vulgar novelties, Pritchard tries to draw him into a business
alliance.   Horton finds Pritchard's patronage tempting, but
implies that Pritchard is a conniving swindler practicing
high-class blackmail.   He proposes that in Los Angeles they
take some girls--perhaps Camille--to an apartment for a bit
of luscious relaxation.   Pritchard is offended, but later
makes an extremely circumlocutory attempt to proposition
Camille by offering her a job as a receptionist.   When she
tells him off with a blunt analysis of his real motives and a

scathing denunciation of the stag smoker where he first saw
her, he is shocked at the unfamiliar picture of himself. In
a mixture of horror and frustration, he responds by raping
his wife. Afterwards, he is sick with remorseful recognition. "What kind of thing am I?" he cried. "What makes
these terrible things in me?" (311). His illusions stripped
away, the American male is appalled at the revelation of
his real self.

A foil to both Juan and Pritchard is Louis, the driver
of the Greyhound that drops passengers at Rebel Corners.
In his self-sufficiency, Juan has no need to "make out";
Pritchard, in his self-deluding gentility, tries to hide from
himself his indirect efforts at seduction. But Louie is ob-
sessed with sex and is a crude "make-out artist." Like
others of his breed, he really despises women and considers
them only objects on which he can relieve his sexual frustration. "Nearly all his waking hours Louie thought about girls.
He liked to outrage them. He liked to have them fall in
love with him and then walk away. He called them pigs"
(99). When Camille rejects his crude advances, he is angry
with her and sneers at her as a "broad," a "pig," a "god-
damned hustler." Louie thinks he is tough and smart to
despise the women he desires, and the ticket taker is sufficiently impressed by his shallow swagger that he decides
to call women "pigs" too, and thus be a he-man like his
hero. This macho attitude rejects women as individuals and
blames them for male lust; it denies their humanity and
lumps them together as merely a piece of anatomy. Steinbeck condemns it as contemptible. Louie's aged counterpart
is Van Brunt, a dirty old man.

Pimples Carson, Juan's 17-year-old mechanic, is also
tormented by sex, but his is the frustrated yearning of an
acned adolescent. "Pimples was loaded with the concupis-
cent juices of adolescence" (223), but his preoccupation with
sex vacillates from direct expressions of lust to "deep and
tearful sentiment," or "a strong and musky religiosity."
Like Tom Hamilton in East of Eden and Uncle John Joad in
The Grapes of Wrath, "He had times of violent purity when
he howled at his own depravity" (17). His envy of Juan's
self-control is a "fawning adoration." Throughout the narrative, he lusts after Camille, but after she improves Norma's
appearance, he makes overtures to the latter, wins her
sympathy momentarily, and takes advantage of it to maul
her in a clumsy attempt at lovemaking that she indignantly
rejects. But there is hope for Pimples. He is a good

mechanic, he may outgrow his acne, and as Camille says,
"Oh, he's all right.   He's just a little goaty.   Most kids are
like that.   He'll probably get over it" (198).

The remaining male is Ernest Horton, a war veteran
employed by the Little Wonder Company as a traveling salesman of novelties and practical jokes such as a fake foot with
artificial crushed toes or a toy flush toilet that functions as
a shot glass.   He also dabbles in trivial inventions such as
lapel slip covers, to convert a dark suit into a tuxedo.
Horton cheerfully hawks these gadgets, but Pritchard's
Babbitt-like enthusiasm for them and for Horton's get-up-
and-go is far more vulgar.   The two men tangle, however,
over the post-war prospects of veterans.   Like the businessman in Lifeboat, Pritchard is a reactionary who wants business and government to protect the working man by crushing
unions, keeping down wages, and maximizing profits for
shareholders and executives.   Horton will have none of this;
like the migrants in The Grapes of Wrath, he knows that
businessmen's talk about service is like a bull's servicing a
cow; somebody is getting screwed.   Horton claims to be a
widower, but he had in fact been married and deserted his
wife two days later.   Though he talks about wanting a home
and family, "He loved moving around and seeing different
people.   He would run away from a home immediately" (150).
He likes women, however, and treats them with respect
while cheerfully and frankly trying to "make time" with them;
in consequence, Camille agrees to see him after they arrive
in Los Angeles.

Steinbeck's female readers might well observe that
none of these men is liberated.   Louie and Pritchard are
contemptible, Pimples is a frenzied adolescent, Van Brunt
is a dirty old man.   But Steinbeck has the perception to
portray them honestly.   However, the two men he presents
positively--Juan and Horton--are also flawed, Horton by ir-
responsibility and Juan by a sense of male superiority.

The Wayward Bus contains Steinbeck's most extended
and perceptive treatment of women.   With the possible exception of Mildred Pritchard, none of them is liberated either,
for they define themselves primarily in relationship to men.

Alice Chicoy is energetic and efficient in running the
restaurant, but her bad temper and her jealousy about Juan
make everyone dislike her.   She continually makes snide remarks about Pimples' acne and his eating habits (he spends

nearly all of his small salary on candy, cake, and pie) and,
unlike her husband, refuses to stop calling him Pimples when
he asks her. "I'll see how it goes," she tells him. Although madly in love with her husband, she has let herself
become slovenly, wide-hipped and sag-chested, as if out of
self-destructiveness. When drunk, she considers Juan "a
stinking greaser" (176), though in fact drunkenness gives her
an acid, bitter smell that he cannot stand. Until the bus
trip, Alice has no specific reason for jealousy; Juan has not
been unfaithful to her, but she fears that he might leave her
as he must have left other women. "How many she didn't
know because he'd never spoken of it, but a man of his at-
tractiveness must have left other women" (31). Here Alice
makes herself the victim of the myth that attractive men
cannot be monogamous. Perhaps her fear comes from her
first sexual experience with a callous character named Bud,
who hurt her and then left her. "You said you love me,"
she pleaded, to which he replied cynically, "Did I? ...
Listen, sister, you got laid, that's all. I didn't sign no
long-term contract" (176). Though Juan jokes that he married Alice "Because she can cook beans" (137), he tolerates
her erratic behavior and is reasonably satisfied with his
marriage. Mildred Pritchard realizes that "Juan and Alice
Chicoy regularly established a relationship which Mr. or
Mrs. Pritchard could not have conceived" (68). Thus Juan's
prayer to the Virgin of Guadalupe to give him a sign as to
whether he should desert his wife and his business seems
out of character, an aberration from his normal patience and
self-control. Alice's tantrum is nothing new; Juan is not
happy about it, but it hardly seems the final straw for him.
In one of her few moments of lucidity, Alice realizes that
Juan knows she loves him. "And you can't leave a thing
like that. It's a structure and it has an architecture, and
you can't leave it without tearing off a piece of yourself.
So if you want to remain whole you stay no matter how much
you may dislike staying. Juan was not a man who fooled
himself very much" (137).

       But Alice fools herself. Until Camille Oaks appears,
Alice has never seen a woman who looks like the calendar
and poster pin-ups that cover her lunchroom walls, pictures
of "bright, improbable girls with pumped-up breasts and no
hips ... so that a visitor of another species might judge
from the preoccupation of artist and audience that the seat
of procreation lay in the mammaries" (5). Steinbeck ridi-
cules these exaggerated images of male fantasy, knowing
that there is much more to women than their measurements,

but while Alice does not believe in them, she blinds herself
to her own deterioration. After the bus departs, she deliberately drinks herself into a series of fantasies and final
insensibility in a scene that is a literary tour-de-force.

Just as Elliott Pritchard is an antithesis to Juan
Chicoy, so Bernice Pritchard is the antithesis to Alice.
Whereas Alice is a slob, Bernice is all daintiness and false
delicacy, lavender and lace. Though fond of her husband,
she cannot respond to him sexually, being frigid from a
"nun's hood" as well as from psychological causes. "Women
of lusty appetites she spoke of as 'that kind of woman,' and
she was a little sorry for them as she was for dope fiends
and alcoholics" (63). She has a reputation for being sweet
and unselfish; her friends call her a saint. At first she
seems pleasantly harmless, but Steinbeck gradually strips
away her protective coloring to reveal her as a manipulating
monster of selfishness. She is a more elaborate portrait of
the kind of woman Steinbeck portrayed in Mary Teller, the
fastidious wife in "The White Quail" (The Long Valley), who
dominates her husband through her daintiness, using her
neurotic purity to make him feel gross and guilty, and pun-
ishing him with the misery of her psychosomatic headaches.
Like her admiring friends, her husband is deceived as to her
real nature; he likes her pretty hair, spotless clothes, efficient housekeeping, and considers her "shortcomings as a
woman the attributes of a lady...." His nerves, his bad
dreams, and the acrid pain that sometimes got into his upper
abdomen he put down to too much coffee and not enough
exercise" rather than frustration (65). But as Steinbeck
develops her character, her seeming assets are revealed as
weapons that she uses to subdue her husband to her will
without his being aware of it. He acts protectively, calls
her a "little girl" and himself a "big man." After he rapes
her in response to his rejection by Camille, she looks up
with ferocious eyes, tears her face with her nails, rubs dirt
into the blood, and treats him with the accusation of sancti-
fied silence, followed by perfect politeness and a sweet voice
that will smother him with reproach and make him wish he
rather than Van Brunt were dying. To herself, she says,
"I must think of no evil. Just because Elliott went down
under a brutishness is no reason for me to lose beauty and
toleration." With a flicker of triumph, she thinks, "I have
conquered anger, and I have conquered disgust. I can forgive
him, I know I can. But for his own sake it must not be too
soon--for his own good" (306). Neither of them can acknowledge her true nature, and they are left to simmer in her
extreme unction.

Their daughter Mildred sometimes hates her parents
and subconsciously wishes their death would set her free.
Mildred has an athletic body and a strong sex drive; she has
already had two "consummated affairs" and enjoyed them
without remorse, though she longs for a more permanent
relationship. Somewhat disguised by her heavy glasses, her
sensuality is less obvious than Camille's and more subtle.
Men do not make passes at her, but her sex life is more
satisfactory, though on primarily physical terms so far, for
she has nothing in common with Juan except animal magnetism. Twenty-one years old, she has thought "that the saps
and juices were all dried up at fifty ... a man or a woman
in love at fifty would have been an obscene spectacle to her"
(67). Here Steinbeck satirizes the intolerance and short-
sightedness of youth, for Juan, towards whom "her body
tingled with desire" and "itched with a pure sexual longing,"
is in fact fifty. Besides sex, Mildred has also dabbled in
radical politics more as a form of rebellion than a strong
commitment, but sufficiently to alarm her ultra-conservative
father, with his Cold War attitude that liberalism is a subversive conspiracy.

Camille Oaks gives the lie to the myth that a woman
who looks like a pin-up must be "that kind of woman."
Camille looks like a Hollywood starlet and cannot help radiating an intense sex appeal. "It was something about her,
and it wasn't makeup and it wasn't the way she walked, although that was part of it too. Whatever it was, it projected all around her" (103-04). But this quality is more a
curse than an asset. "Men fought each other viciously when
she was about. They fought like terriers, and she sometimes wished that women could like her, but they didn't.
And she was intelligent. She knew why, but there wasn't
anything she could do about it. What she really wanted was
a nice house in a nice town, two children, and a stairway
to stand on. She would be nicely dressed and people would
be coming in to dinner" (109). Unfortunately, she is typed
as a hooker. Men can't keep their hands off her, and women resent her. Actually, "Her sexual impulses were not
terribly strong nor very constant" (110), but men she finds
attractive cannot believe that a woman with such animal
appeal could remain faithful. Unable to hold an office job
because of the consternation her presence causes, she is
forced to exploit her sexuality and works as a stag stripper.

One might question whether this portrait is not over-
drawn and challenge Steinbeck's thesis that it is impossible

for such a woman to have a conventional career and a normal family life, but apparently Camille provokes the sort of
erotic response generated by Marilyn Monroe, Rita Hayworth,
Ava Gardner--Holywood's so-called sex goddesses--in their
prime.   Though saddened by the situation, Camille is a sur-
vivor and has learned how to cope.   Probing behind the
stereotype of the dumb blonde, Steinbeck portrays Camille
as sensitive, lonely, the victim of exploitation by men gov-
erned by their glands.

      Norma, the Chicoys' hired girl, is the most pathetic
female character.   Shy, drab, dressed in wash dresses
from the National Dollar Store, Norma nevertheless dreams
of being a movie star and has a crush on Clark Gable.
Throughout the book, Hollywood and movie stars serve as a
symbol of fantasy and romantic illusion at odds with the
reality of the characters' lives.   Steinbeck observes that
Hollywood is "where, eventually, all the adolescents in the
world will be congregated" (7).   Norma's nondescript appearance and naiveté are the antithesis of the movie world's
glamour and sophistication.   Clark Gable is not aware of
her existence and would not be enamored of her if he were.
Norma, however, prefers older men and sneers at the then
callow youth of Sinatra, Van Johnson, and Sonny Tufts.   The
young men she has known have tried to wrestle her clothes
off her, and she is certain that Gable would be more re-
spectful.   A female Walter Mitty, Norma compensates in an
intense dream life for the dull frustrations of the present.
When she discovers that Ernest Horton's wares include
photographs of movie stars that are three-dimensional, acid-
proof, moisture-proof, and guaranteed to last forever, she
talks him out of his sample picture of Gable, and learning
that he has a friend at M-G-M who sometimes lets him onto
the lots, asks him to deliver to Gable one of the long impas-
sioned letters she has written him.   Caught up in her fantasy, she claims to be Gable's cousin, a friend of Bette Davis,
Ingrid Bergman, and Joan Fontaine; she confides to Horton
that she is already an actress, a star even, taking some
time out to get experience studying people.   Ernest catches
on but sees behind the pathos to perceive in Norma "dignity
... courage, and a truly great flow of love" (56).   He therefore defends her when Alice accuses her of lying and then
charges him with fooling around with her in her bedroom.
It is this attack that drives Norma to leave and take the bus
to Los Angeles.

      When she encounters Camille, Norma latches on to

her like a drowning person grasping a life preserver. In
Camille, she perceives a glamorous woman of the world, a
big sister who can give her guidance and provide a model
for emulation. In her loneliness, Camille at first is glad
of the companionship, and she instructs Norma in how to
improve her appearance by subtle changes in her hairdo,
dress, and makeup. One reason for Alice's contempt of
her is that Norma has been starved for love. Now, taking
advantage of Camille's kindness, Norma makes a possessive
pest of herself, dreaming of their sharing an apartment together, becoming successes in Hollywood, and urging an increasingly reluctant Camille to commit herself. But despite
her romantic illusions, Norma has a core of practical
realism, and she tells herself, "If any of it comes through
it'll just be gravy. But I can't expect it, I can't let myself
expect it" (187).

The false and shallow glamour of Hollywood and of
pin-ups becomes for Steinbeck a symbol of the manipulation
of people by dream merchants, exploiting sex as a commodity.
In a book like The Image Maker, a collection of glamour
photographs from the studios, the men present an image of
virile assurance, while the women are filmed in absurdly
ecstatic, voluptuous, and mysterious poses and outlandish
attire to highlight their sultry or sensuous appeal. This is
not what love, let alone marriage, is about; such images reduce individual men and women into sex objects, while making the audience dissatisfied with their own lives. Even
Louis the Greyhound bus driver wishes he were Bob Hope or
Bing Crosby, and his contempt for the women he desires is
partly the result of his seeing them only in terms of movie
star sensuality. Norma tells Camille that she would "picture
like a certain movie star was--well, was my husband" (229).
Pimples confides to Mildred that he'd like to be "a mission-
ary like Spencer Tracy and go to China and cure them of
all those diseases ... Spencer Tracy just came along and he
cured them up and they loved him--and you know what he
done? He found his own soul" (160). After Juan abandons
the bus, Mr. Pritchard takes a pistol and imagines himself
as the hero of a frontier movie epic, bringing home "a great
slab of red meat" (280).

When Camille discusses matrimony with Pimples, he
says that if his wife weren't true, "I'll show her two can
play that game, like Cary Grant done in that movie" (281).
All of Alice's hired girls moon over movie magazines, and
in her boozy self-pity, Alice herself laments that she is

"Too far out in the country to go to the movies" (176).
Basically, Steinbeck protests that an uncritical addiction to
movies gives both men and women unrealistic ideals, melodramatic dreams, false concepts of love, of masculinity and
femininity, and a consequent dissatisfaction with their own
lives.

        As a case in point, a 1957 movie of The Wayward
Bus is the least satisfactory film adaptation of a work by
Steinbeck and provides a provocative contrast to the novel.
William Saroyan did a preliminary script that closely followed the book, but his scenario was rejected in favor of a
melodramatic one by Ivan Moffat that violated the novel in a
number of crucial ways.   Instead of dramatizing Steinbeck's
complexities of character, the film concentrated on the
spectacle of floods, landslides, and bridges being washed
away and provided a minor disaster epic.   Both the script
and the casting distort the original characters.   Steinbeck's
middle-aged Alice Chicoy is "wide-hipped and sag-chested,"
but in the film she is played by Joan Collins, a sexy pin-up
like the calendar and Coca-Cola girls in her lunchroom that
Alice finds unreal.   Instead of leaving Alice in a drunken
stupor, the film has her repent and meet her husband at the
end of the line.   Juan, played by Rick Jason, a twentyish
romantic lead, is equally miscast.   A fifty-year-old mixture
of Mexican and Irish ancestry, he would have been a perfect
role for Anthony Quinn.   The novel's Ernest Horton is a
small man with a "tight, hairy moustache," but in the film
he is played by tall Dan Dailey with a broad, clean-shaven
grin.   The most suitable casting was Jayne Mansfield, giving
her best performance as Camille Oaks, in an attempt on
this bumpy bus ride to repeat Marilyn Monroe's first respectable dramatic role the year before in Bus Stop.   But
she remains more the stereotyped dumb blonde than Steinbeck's intelligent and perceptive protagonist.   At the end of
the film, she agrees to marry Horton, when he promises
her a stove that plays "Tenderly" when the meat is done.

        When Philip T. Hartung wrote in his review of the
film for Commonweal that Steinbeck's novel "overloaded his
assembled group with problems and cliches,"[5] Paula Haigh
responded that he had neglected to note the differences between the film and the book and thus blamed Steinbeck for
the film's failings.   She insisted that a film critic should
first examine a movie's literary source before passing judgment on it for the faults of a different medium.

In its extensive analysis of sex, The Wayward Bus
was a new departure for Steinbeck. His earlier books dealt
mainly with footloose men who found casual sex mainly in
brothels. Tortilla Flat and Cannery Row presented a comic
version of the macho male gratifying himself with cheerfully
amoral wenches; their characters tend to be sexual stereotypes. Some of the short stories deal perceptively with
sexual conflicts, but The Wayward Bus is his first prolonged
attempt to study sexuality seriously and explore the complexity behind the stereotypes. The novel deals with lust more
than with love. Alice's love for Juan is a neurotic dependency that makes one-sided demands and does not respond
with any tenderness or consideration for him, and his attach-
ment to her seems primarily a habit that neither he nor
Steinbeck can account for. There is no love on either side
in his brief liaison with Mildred. What Steinbeck does a-
chieve is a scathing satire on sexual fantasies, as exemplified by Hollywood, pin-ups and stag smokers, and on the
exploitation of women by rutting or drooling males as no
more than sex objects. Insofar as they respond, like Camille
and Norma, by trying to make themselves look and act like
sexy stereotypes, the women collaborate with this state of
affairs, but Norma actually believes in it herself, while
Camille, though putting up with it because she lacks other
resources, despises it. On the other hand, Mrs. Pritchard's
squeamish and self-righteous gentility is equally despicable.
In offering as an alternative only a cheerful acceptance of
casual sex for the mutual fun of it, as in the episode between
Juan and Mildred or the implication of such an episode to
come later between Horton and Camille, Steinbeck gives too
limited a view. Sex of this sort amounts to little more than
animal magnetism, with Steinbeck's natural man and woman
"doing what comes naturally." There are other, more sensitive and substantial possibilities than this, or macho seductions, or marriage as only a trap. But at least The Wayward Bus challenges the cheap exploitation of sex and makes
us think about more honest and meaningful relationships between men and women.

NOTES

1. John Steinbeck, The Wayward Bus (New York: Viking
    Press, 1947), p. 6. All subsequent references to
    this novel are given in parentheses in the text.

2. Peter Lisca, The Wide World of John Steinbeck (New

Brunswick, N. J.: Rutgers University Press, 1958), pp. 233-39.

3. J. M. Lalley, "Review of The Wayward Bus," New Yorker, 23 (February 22, 1947), 94; Bernard DeVoto, "Review of The Wayward Bus," New York Herald Tribune Weekly Book Review, February 16, 1947, p. 1; Frank O'Malley, "Review of The Wayward Bus," Commonweal, 46 (April 25, 1947), 43.

4. Lisca, p. 232.

5. Phillip T. Hartung, "Review of The Wayward Bus," Commonweal, 66 (June 21, 1956), 66.

IV.   APPARATUS FOR RESEARCH PAPERS

A.   Ten Questions for Discussion

1. More than most Steinbeck novels, The Wayward Bus is a study of character. But some critics have complained that Steinbeck spends more time explaining the characters from the point of view of the omniscient author than he does presenting them in action and dialogue. Discuss the extent to which this is true. Is it necessarily a defect in the novel?
2. Analyze the relationship of the novel's women to its men and to each other.
3. Discuss The Wayward Bus as a comic novel.
4. In Sea of Cortez, Steinbeck wrote that "of the good we think always of wisdom, tolerance, kindliness, generosity, humility; and the qualities of cruelty, greed, self-interest, graspingness, and rapacity are universally considered undesirable. And yet in our structure of society, the so-called and considered good qualities are invariable concomitants of failure, while the bad ones are the cornerstones of success." To what extent, if any, is this true? Discuss The Wayward Bus in relation to this statement.
5. Compare Beatrice Pritchard to Mary Teller in "The White Quail" from Steinbeck's The Long Valley.
6. Compare the unfulfilled dreams of the characters in The Wayward Bus with those in Of Mice and Men.
7. The Wayward Bus contains many lyric descriptions of the land and of nature. How do these relate to and comment on the lives and actions of the human characters in the book?

8. A reviewer for Survey Graphic wrote in 1947 that The
    Wayward Bus contains "another load of sleazy characters
    who deserved oblivion rather than the accolade of a book
    club." Discuss.
9. Many critics mark The Wayward Bus as the beginning of
    a supposed decline in the quality of Steinbeck's fiction.
    Do you agree or not? Discuss.
10. Reviewing the novel in 1947, Edward Weeks praised The
    Wayward Bus for its "warm flow of vitality," its lovely
    landscape descriptions, its humor, but concludes, "one
    ends by wondering if American life is actually so empty,
    so devoid of meaning, so lonely for the Juans, the
    Pritchards, and the Camilles of today. God help us if
    it is." At the same time, Robert Halsband in the
    Chicago Sun Book Week praised the book because Stein-
    beck's "choice of characters and his emphasis on
    healthy, positive values may point to a revival of inter-
    est in the serious and significant themes of American
    life." Discuss the novel in terms of these contradictory
    comments.

B. Suggested Topics for Research Papers

1. Compare Juan Chicoy to Steinbeck's other "natural" men.
2. Read Sinclair Lewis's Babbitt and compare Babbitt to
    Elliott Pritchard and Ernest Horton.
3. Analyze Steinbeck as an allegorist.
4. Numerous films and works of fiction (e.g. "The Outcasts
    of Poker Flat," Grand Hotel, Stagecoach, Lost Horizon,
    Steinbeck's and Hitchcock's Lifeboat, The V.I.P.'s, The
    Poseidon Adventure, the various "Airport" films) isolate
    a group of people, usually through an emergency or a
    disaster, and then have them interact. What are the
    strengths and weaknesses of this dramatic device? Com-
    pare The Wayward Bus to some works in this genre.
5. Compare The Wayward Bus to Steinbeck's comments in
    America and Americans about male stereotyping of wo-
    men and about the purpose and goals of American life.
6. Steinbeck has been called the poet laureate of the jalopy.
    Discuss this aspect of his work in The Wayward Bus and
    other suitable volumes, such as The Grapes of Wrath
    and Cannery Row. What values beyond purely automotive
    ones does he find in being a competent mechanic?
7. Considering Elliott Pritchard and Ernest Horton, study
    and analyze Steinbeck's criticism of the business and
    agribusiness world in The Wayward Bus and selected

other works such as In Dubious Battle, The Grapes of
Wrath, Cannery Row, his script for Lifeboat [cf. Robert
E. Morsberger, "Adrift in Steinbeck's Lifeboat," Liter-
ature/Film Quarterly, 4 (Fall 1976) 325-38], Viva
Zapata!, and The Winter of Our Discontent.

C. Selected Bibliography

Following the initial reviews, The Wayward Bus has
not generated articles in the periodicals, but there are discussions of it in most of the books on Steinbeck.

1. Astro, Richard and Tetsumaro Hayashi, eds. Steinbeck:
    The Man and His Work. Corvallis: Oregon State Uni-
    versity Press, 1971.

2. Baker, Carlos. "Review of The Wayward Bus," New
    York Times Book Review, February 16, 1947, p. 1.

3. Clark, Eleanor. "Review of The Wayward Bus," Nation,
    164 (March 29, 1947), 370.

4. DeVoto, Bernard. "Review of The Wayward Bus," New
    York Herald Tribune Weekly Book Review, February 16,
    1947, p. 1.

5. Fontenrose, Joseph. John Steinbeck. New York: Holt,
    Rinehart and Winston, 1963.

6. French, Warren. John Steinbeck, 2nd ed. revised.
    Boston: Twayne, 1975.

7. Jones, Lawrence William. John Steinbeck as Fabulist,
    ed. Marston LaFrance (Steinbeck Monograph Series,
    No. 3). Muncie, Indiana: Steinbeck Society, Ball State
    University, 1973.

8. Lalley, J. M. "Review of The Wayward Bus," New
    Yorker, 23 (February 22, 1947), 94.

9. Levant, Howard. The Novels of John Steinbeck, A
    Critical Study. Columbia: University of Missouri Press,
    1974.

10. Lisca, Peter. The Wide World of John Steinbeck. New
    Brunswick, N. J.: Rutgers University Press, 1958.

11. Marks, Lester Jay. Thematic Design in the Novels of John Steinbeck. The Hague: Mouton, 1969.

12. Prescott, Orville. "Review of The Wayward Bus," Yale Review, 36 (Summer, 1947), 765.

13. Smith, Harrison. "Review of The Wayward Bus," Saturday Review of Literature, 30 (February 15, 1947), 14.

14. Watts, Richard. "Review of The Wayward Bus," New Republic, 116 (March 10, 1947), 37.

15. Weeks, Edward. "Review of The Wayward Bus," Atlantic Monthly, 179 (March, 1947), 126.

NOTES ON CONTRIBUTORS

CLANCY, CHARLES J. (Ph. D.)
Associate Professor of English and Director of the Graduate Program at Bradley University, Peoria, Illinois, Dr. Clancy is the author of two books, Lava, Hock and Soda-Water: Byron's Don Juan (1974) and A Selected Bibliography of English Romantic Drama (1976), and a monograph, A Review of Don Juan Criticism: 1900-1973 (1974). He is editing a six-volume series devoted to the drama of the English Romantic Period. He has also published articles on Byron, Steinbeck, and Yeats and received the Richard W. Burkhardt Prize for the Best Steinbeck Quarterly Article of the Year 1976.

COX, MARTHA HEASLEY (Ph. D.)
Professor of English and Director of the Steinbeck Research Center at San Jose State University, San Jose, California, Dr. Cox has published widely in American literature, including books on Nelson Algren and Maxwell Anderson. Among her numerous textbooks in literature and composition, A Reading Approach to College Writing is now in its 14th edition.

GARCIA, RELOY (Ph. D.)
Professor of English, Creighton University, Omaha, Nebraska, Dr. Garcia has been chairman of the Editorial Board of the Steinbeck Quarterly. Author and editor of several books and a monograph entitled Steinbeck and D. H. Lawrence: Fictive Voices and the Ethical Imperative (1972), he has published in such journals as D. H. Lawrence Review and Steinbeck Quarterly.

HAYASHI, TETSUMARO (Ph. D.), Editor
Professor of English at Ball State University, Dr. Hayashi is founder and President of the Steinbeck Society of America and Executive Director of the International Steinbeck Society. He is author/editor of 18 books and seven mono-

graphs on Elizabethan literature and American literature and author of over 60 articles and 12 short stories. Editor-in-chief of the Steinbeck Quarterly since 1968 and General Editor of the Steinbeck Monograph Series since 1970, he is a recipient of fellowships from the Folger Shakespeare Library, the American Philosophical Society and the American Council of Learned Societies, and teaches Shakespeare, Steinbeck, and Hemingway at Ball State University.

MORSBERGER, ROBERT E. (Ph. D.)
    Professor of English and Chairman of the Department of English and Modern Languages at the California State Polytechnic University, Pomona, California, Dr. Morsberger has published six books, including James Thurber and Commonsense Grammar and Style, and over fifty articles, a number of them on John Steinbeck. He also edited Steinbeck's screenplay, Viva Zapata! for the Viking Press in 1975.

PETERSON, RICHARD F. (Ph. D.)
    Associate Professor of English at Southern Illinois University, Carbondale, Illinois, Dr. Peterson has published a number of articles on modern British and American writers including Steinbeck, Faulkner, Joyce, and T. S. Eliot. His essays on Steinbeck have appeared in such books as Steinbeck's Literary Dimension (1973), A Study Guide to Steinbeck: A Handbook to His Major Works (1974), and A Study Guide to Steinbeck's "The Long Valley" (1976), which were all edited by Tetsumaro Hayashi. A member of the Editorial Board of the Steinbeck Quarterly and the Executive Board of the Steinbeck Society of America, he has edited a monograph with Tetsumaro Hayashi and Yasuo Hashiguchi, entitled John Steinbeck: East and West (1978).

SIEFKER, DONALD L. (M. A.), Indexer
    Assistant Professor of Library Service and Head of the Division of Information Sources at the Bracken Library, Ball State University, Muncie, Indiana, Mr. Siefker has been Managing Editor of the Steinbeck Quarterly and an indexer of the journal for many years. He is a co-compiler of The Special Steinbeck Collection of the Ball State University Library (1972) and has indexed several books on Steinbeck for Dr. Hayashi.

SIMMONDS, ROY S.
    A British civil servant in London, England, Mr. Simmonds has published a number of articles on Steinbeck and William March in such journals as Steinbeck Quarterly,

Mississippi Quarterly, Studies in American Fiction, Ball State University Forum, San Jose Studies, and Serif. He published a monograph, Steinbeck's Literary Achievement (1976).

INDEX

by Donald L. Siefker